ABSTRACT STUDIO

ISSUE No.
7
3.99 US

TERRY MOORE

RACHEL RISING

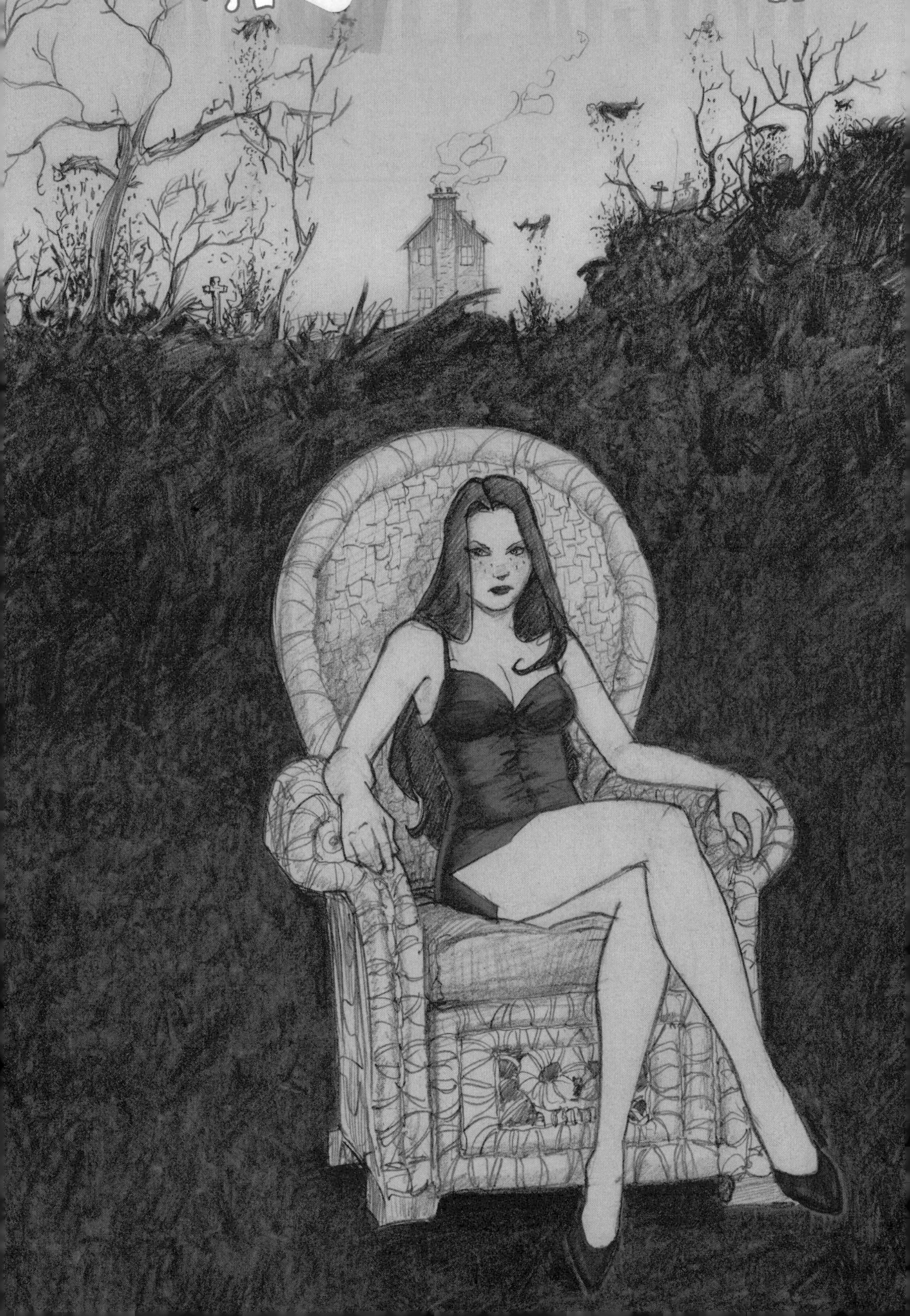

DEATH IS NOT A GAME THAT WILL
SOON BE OVER. DEATH IS A GAP YOU CAN'T SEE,
AND WHEN THE WIND BLOWS THROUGH IT,
IT MAKES NOT A SOUND.

—TOM STOPPARD

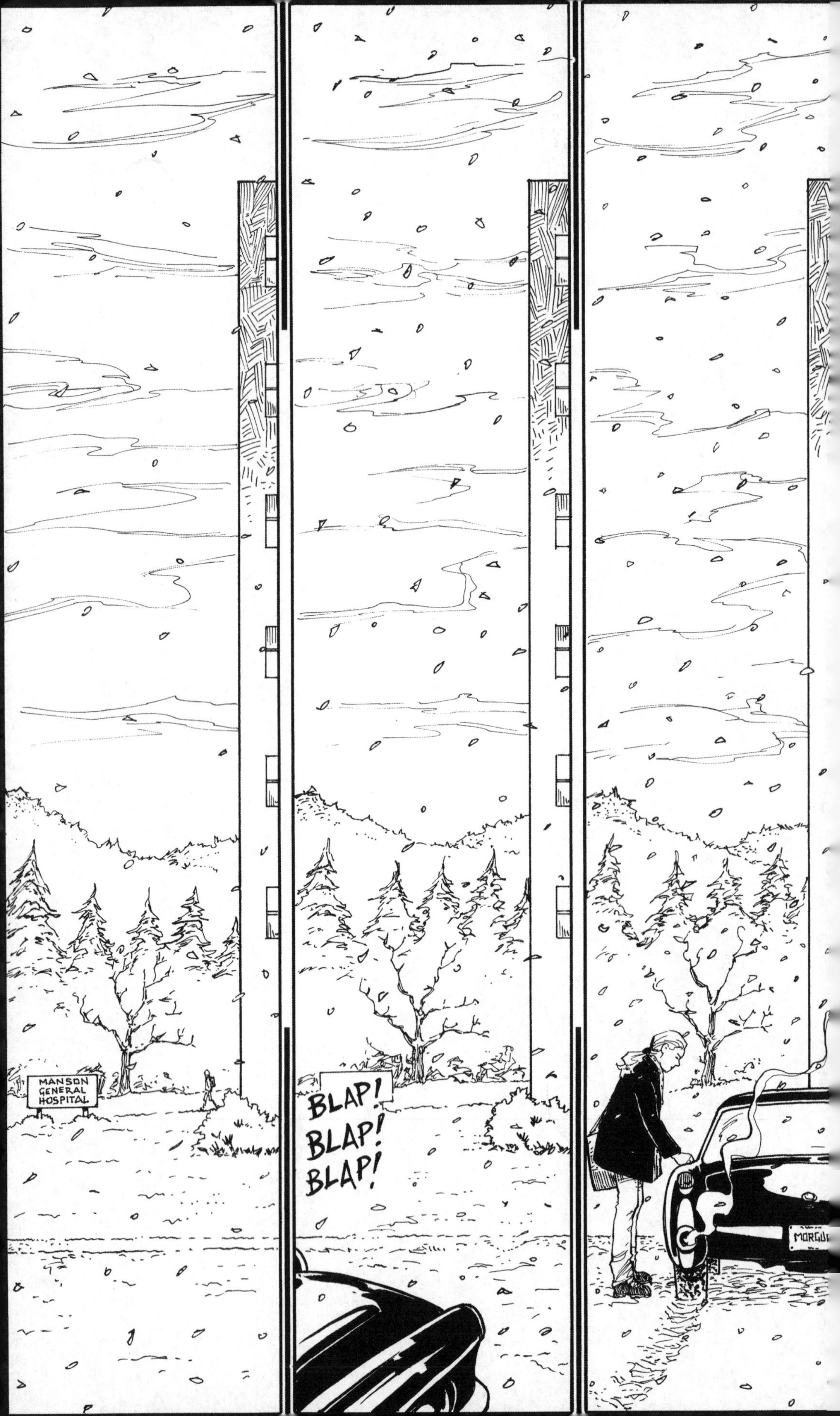
MANSON GENERAL HOSPITAL
BLAP! BLAP! BLAP!
MORGU

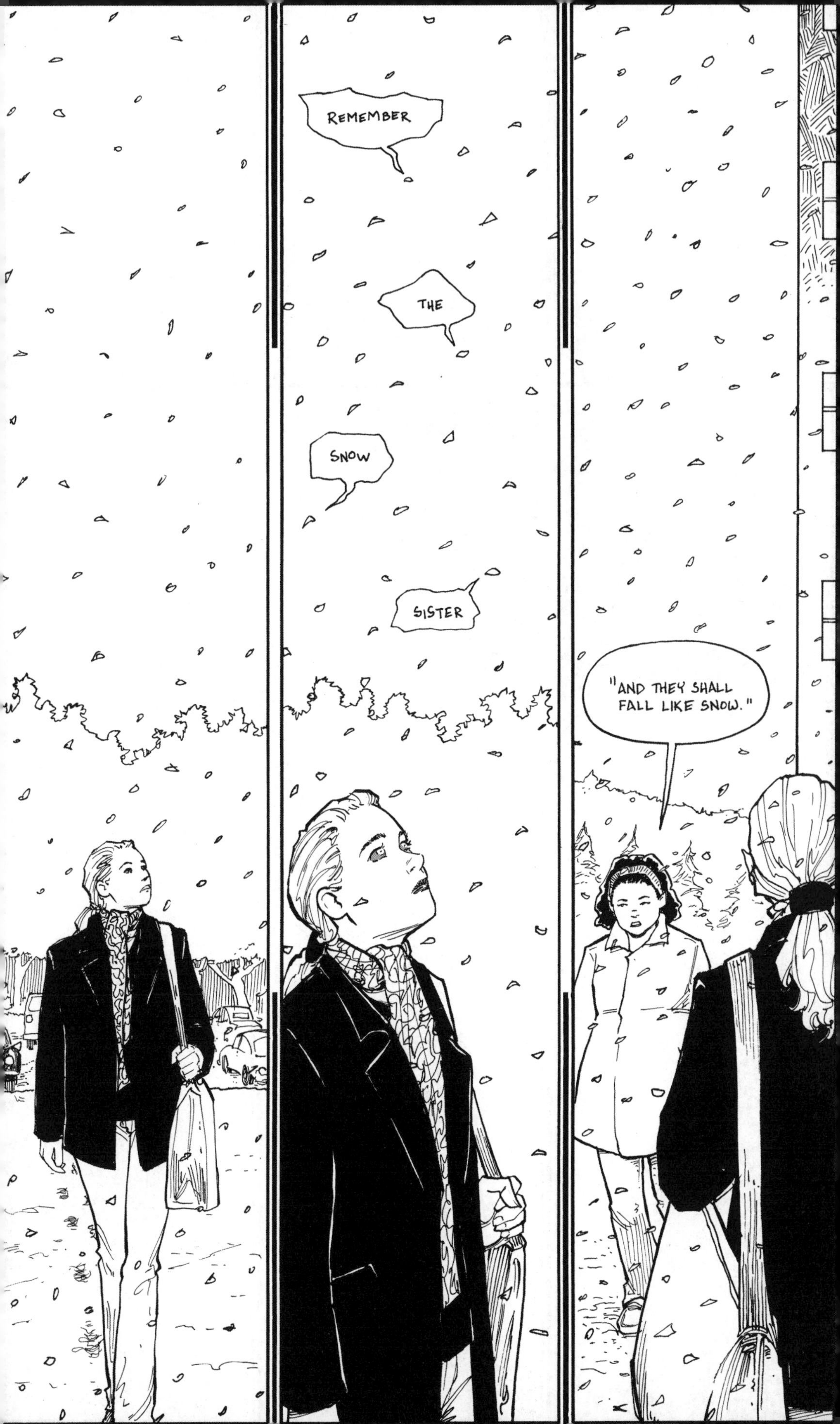
REMEMBER
THE
SNOW
SISTER
"AND THEY SHALL FALL LIKE SNOW."

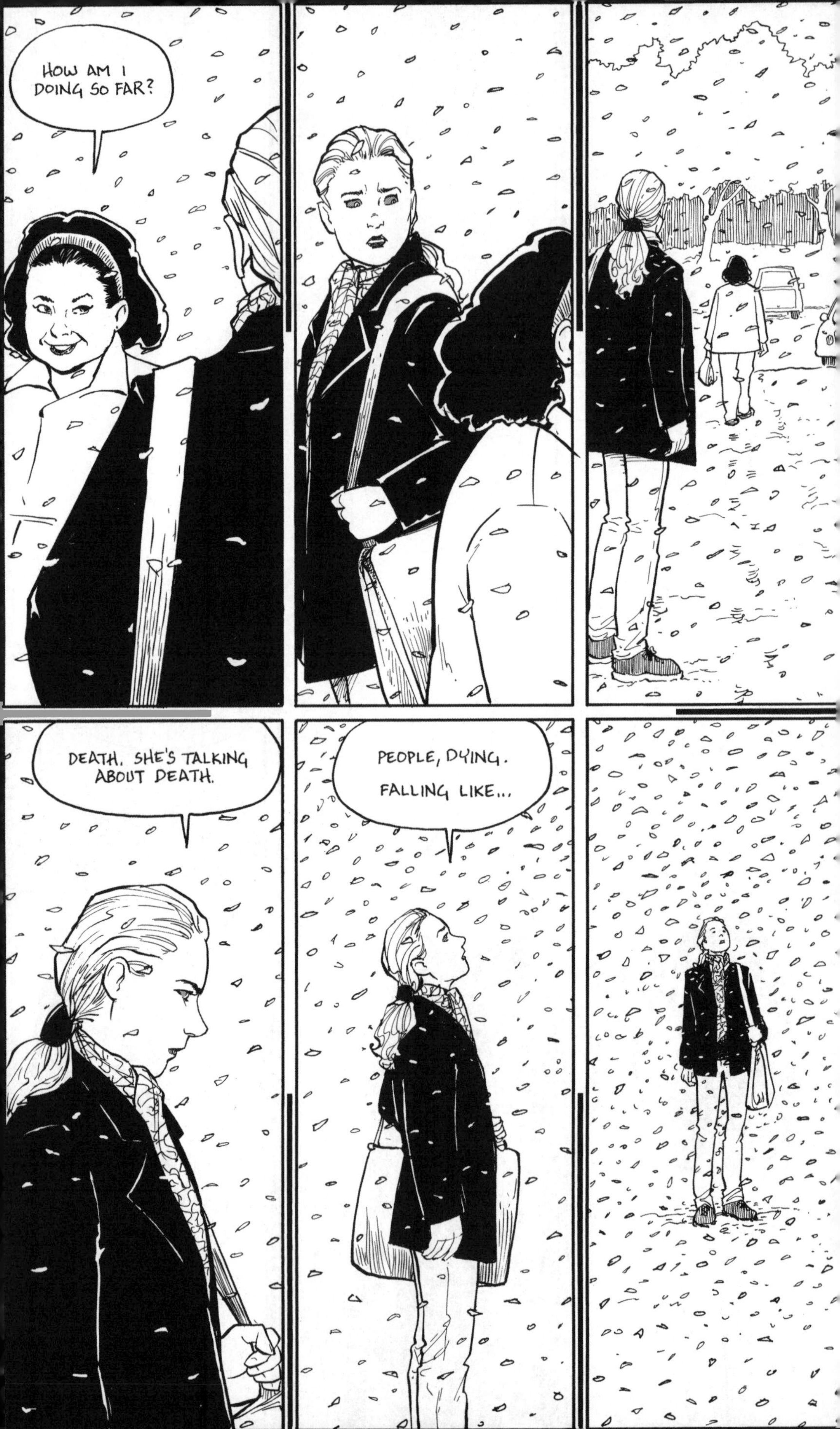
HOW AM I DOING SO FAR?
DEATH. SHE'S TALKING ABOUT DEATH.
PEOPLE, DYING. FALLING LIKE...

EXCUSE ME.

I'M LOOKING FOR JOHNNY WOODALL'S ROOM.

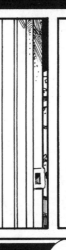

KNOCK! KNOCK!

HI. I'M SORRY TO BOTHER YOU. I'M DETECTIVE CORPELL, MANSON P.D.

IS THIS A BAD TIME?

YES.

BUT, THAT'S NOT YOUR FAULT.

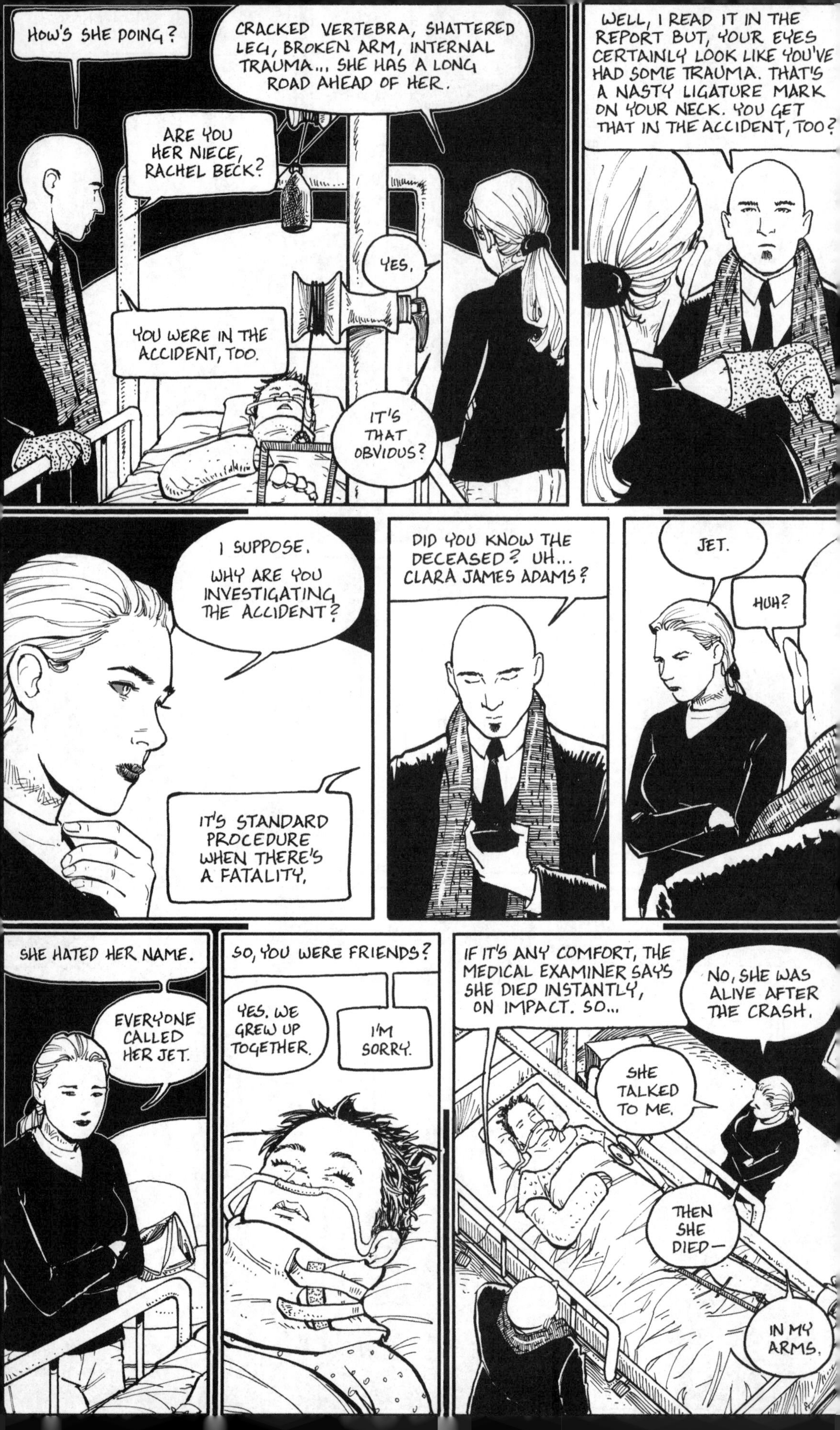
HOW'S SHE DOING?
CRACKED VERTEBRA, SHATTERED LEG, BROKEN ARM, INTERNAL TRAUMA... SHE HAS A LONG ROAD AHEAD OF HER.
ARE YOU HER NIECE, RACHEL BECK?
YES.
YOU WERE IN THE ACCIDENT, TOO.
IT'S THAT OBVIOUS?
WELL, I READ IT IN THE REPORT BUT, YOUR EYES CERTAINLY LOOK LIKE YOU'VE HAD SOME TRAUMA. THAT'S A NASTY LIGATURE MARK ON YOUR NECK. YOU GET THAT IN THE ACCIDENT, TOO?
I SUPPOSE.
WHY ARE YOU INVESTIGATING THE ACCIDENT?
IT'S STANDARD PROCEDURE WHEN THERE'S A FATALITY.
DID YOU KNOW THE DECEASED? UH... CLARA JAMES ADAMS?
JET.
HUH?
SHE HATED HER NAME.
EVERYONE CALLED HER JET.
SO, YOU WERE FRIENDS?
YES. WE GREW UP TOGETHER.
I'M SORRY.
IF IT'S ANY COMFORT, THE MEDICAL EXAMINER SAYS SHE DIED INSTANTLY, ON IMPACT. SO...
NO, SHE WAS ALIVE AFTER THE CRASH.
SHE TALKED TO ME.
THEN SHE DIED—
IN MY ARMS.

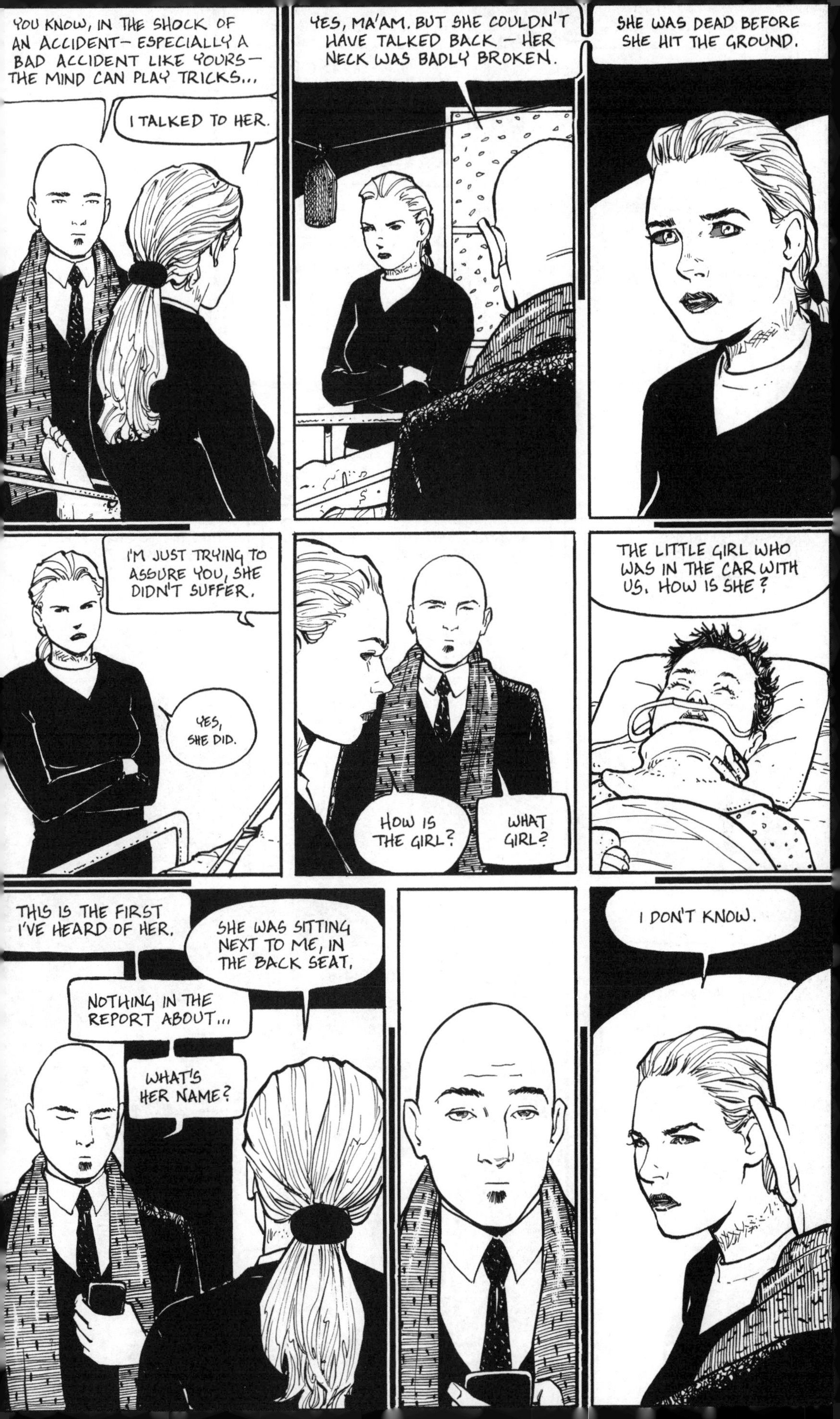
YOU KNOW, IN THE SHOCK OF AN ACCIDENT— ESPECIALLY A BAD ACCIDENT LIKE YOURS— THE MIND CAN PLAY TRICKS...
I TALKED TO HER.
YES, MA'AM. BUT SHE COULDN'T HAVE TALKED BACK — HER NECK WAS BADLY BROKEN.
SHE WAS DEAD BEFORE SHE HIT THE GROUND.
I'M JUST TRYING TO ASSURE YOU, SHE DIDN'T SUFFER.
YES, SHE DID.
HOW IS THE GIRL?
WHAT GIRL?
THE LITTLE GIRL WHO WAS IN THE CAR WITH US. HOW IS SHE?
THIS IS THE FIRST I'VE HEARD OF HER.
SHE WAS SITTING NEXT TO ME, IN THE BACK SEAT.
NOTHING IN THE REPORT ABOUT...
WHAT'S HER NAME?
I DON'T KNOW.

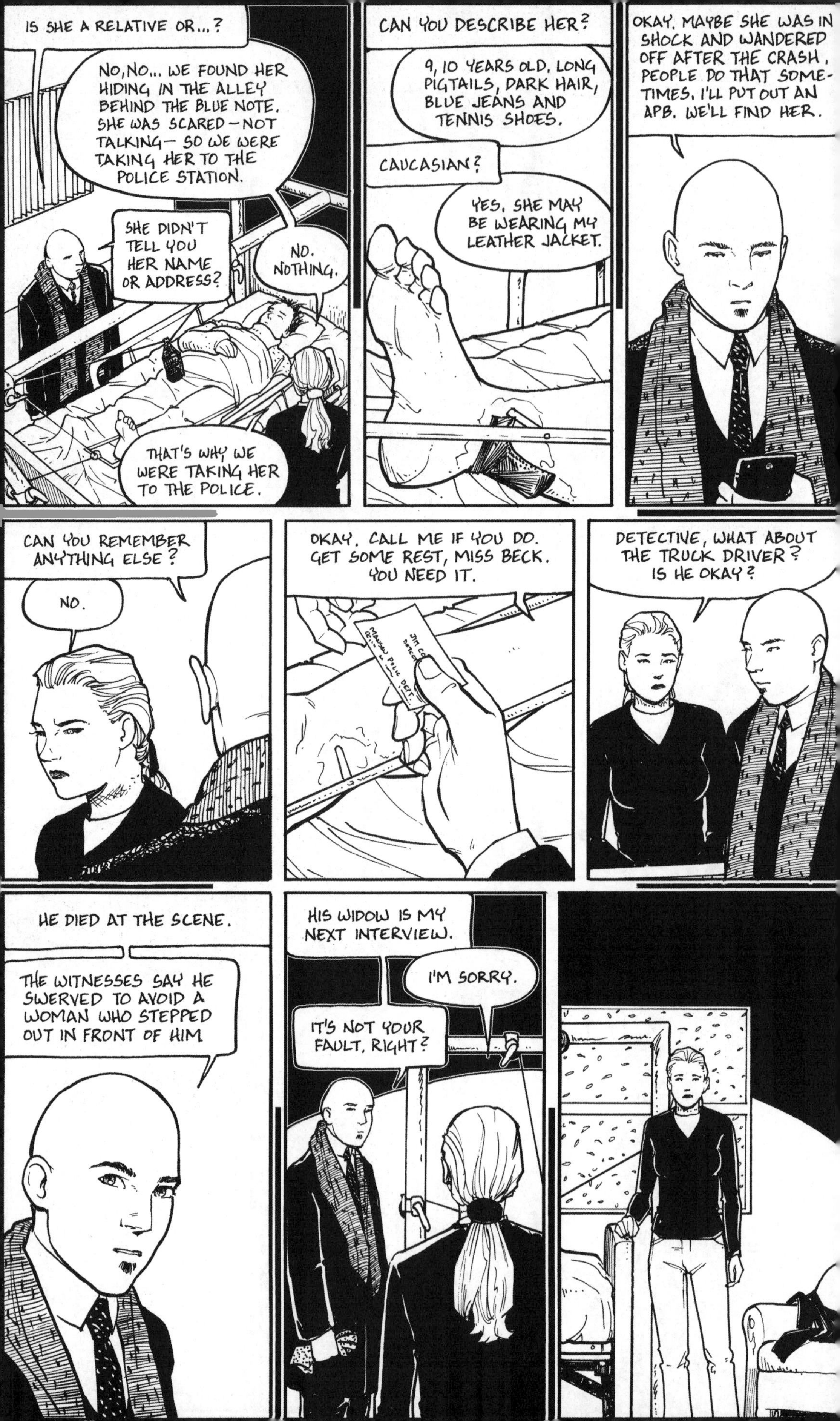
IS SHE A RELATIVE OR...?
NO, NO... WE FOUND HER HIDING IN THE ALLEY BEHIND THE BLUE NOTE. SHE WAS SCARED—NOT TALKING— SO WE WERE TAKING HER TO THE POLICE STATION.
SHE DIDN'T TELL YOU HER NAME OR ADDRESS?
NO. NOTHING.
THAT'S WHY WE WERE TAKING HER TO THE POLICE.
CAN YOU DESCRIBE HER?
9, 10 YEARS OLD, LONG PIGTAILS, DARK HAIR, BLUE JEANS AND TENNIS SHOES.
CAUCASIAN?
YES. SHE MAY BE WEARING MY LEATHER JACKET.
OKAY. MAYBE SHE WAS IN SHOCK AND WANDERED OFF AFTER THE CRASH. PEOPLE DO THAT SOMETIMES. I'LL PUT OUT AN APB. WE'LL FIND HER.
CAN YOU REMEMBER ANYTHING ELSE?
NO.
OKAY. CALL ME IF YOU DO. GET SOME REST, MISS BECK. YOU NEED IT.
DETECTIVE, WHAT ABOUT THE TRUCK DRIVER? IS HE OKAY?
HE DIED AT THE SCENE.
THE WITNESSES SAY HE SWERVED TO AVOID A WOMAN WHO STEPPED OUT IN FRONT OF HIM
HIS WIDOW IS MY NEXT INTERVIEW.
I'M SORRY.
IT'S NOT YOUR FAULT, RIGHT?

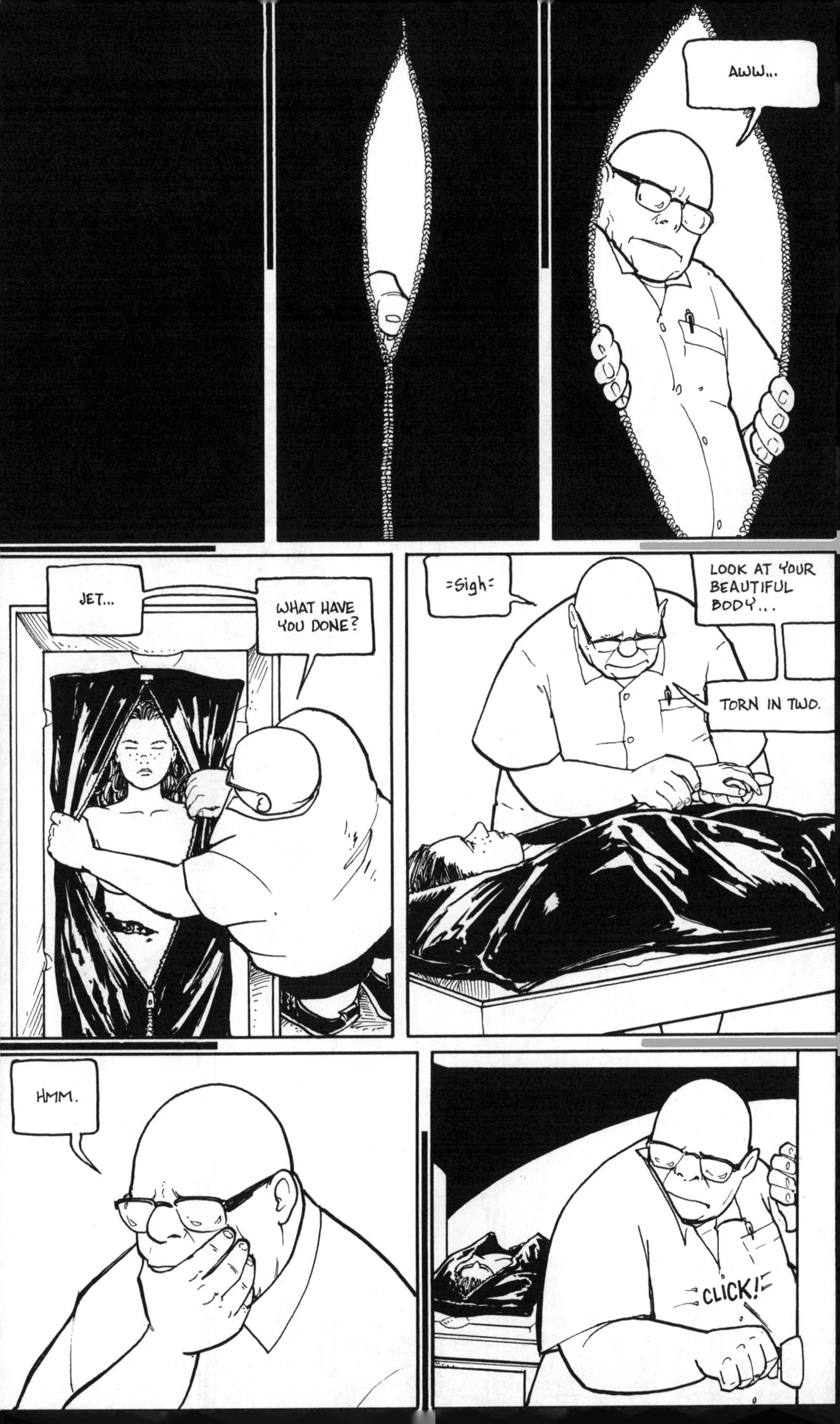
AWW...
JET...
WHAT HAVE YOU DONE?
=Sigh=
LOOK AT YOUR BEAUTIFUL BODY...
TORN IN TWO.
HMM.
CLICK!

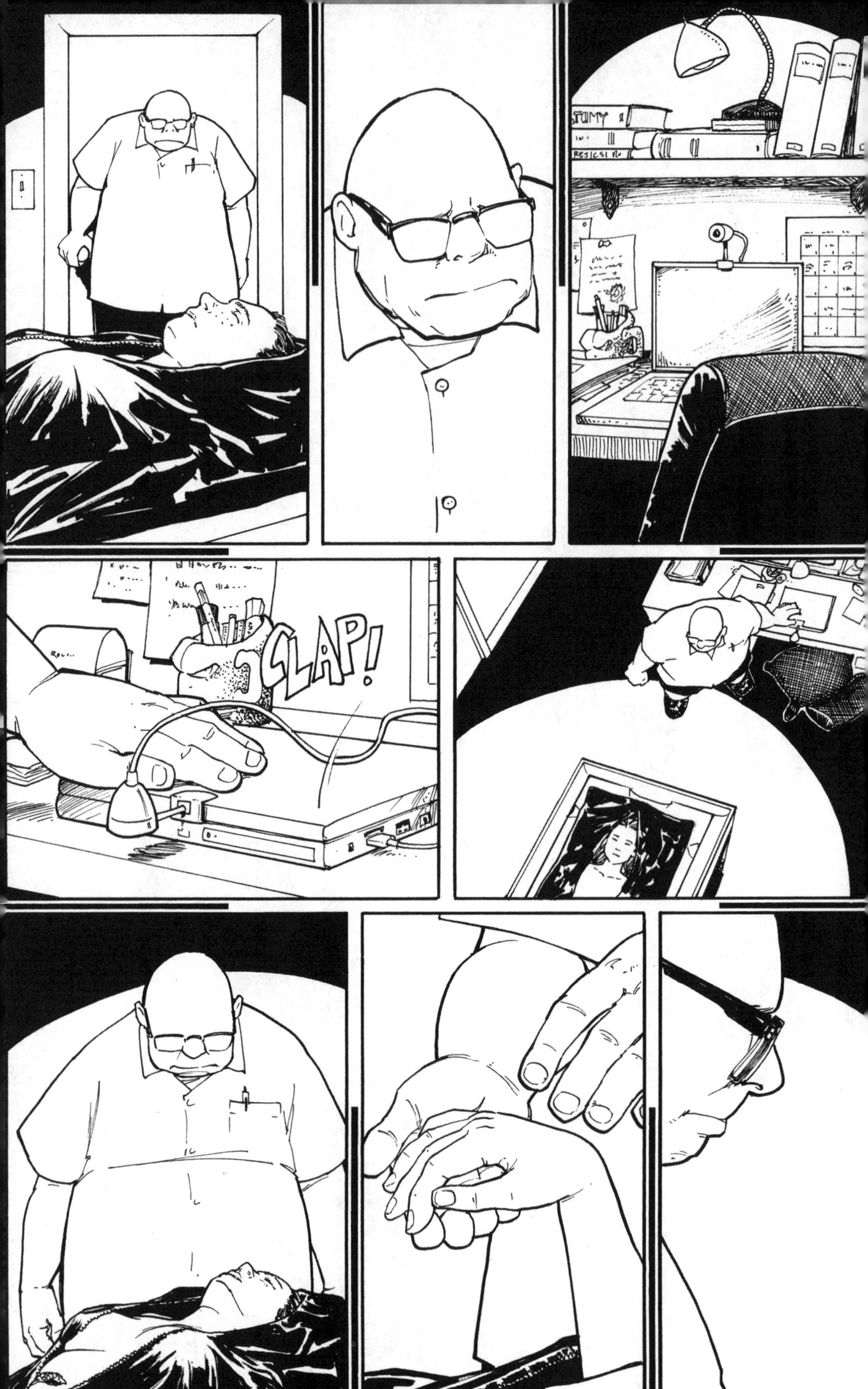
CLAP!

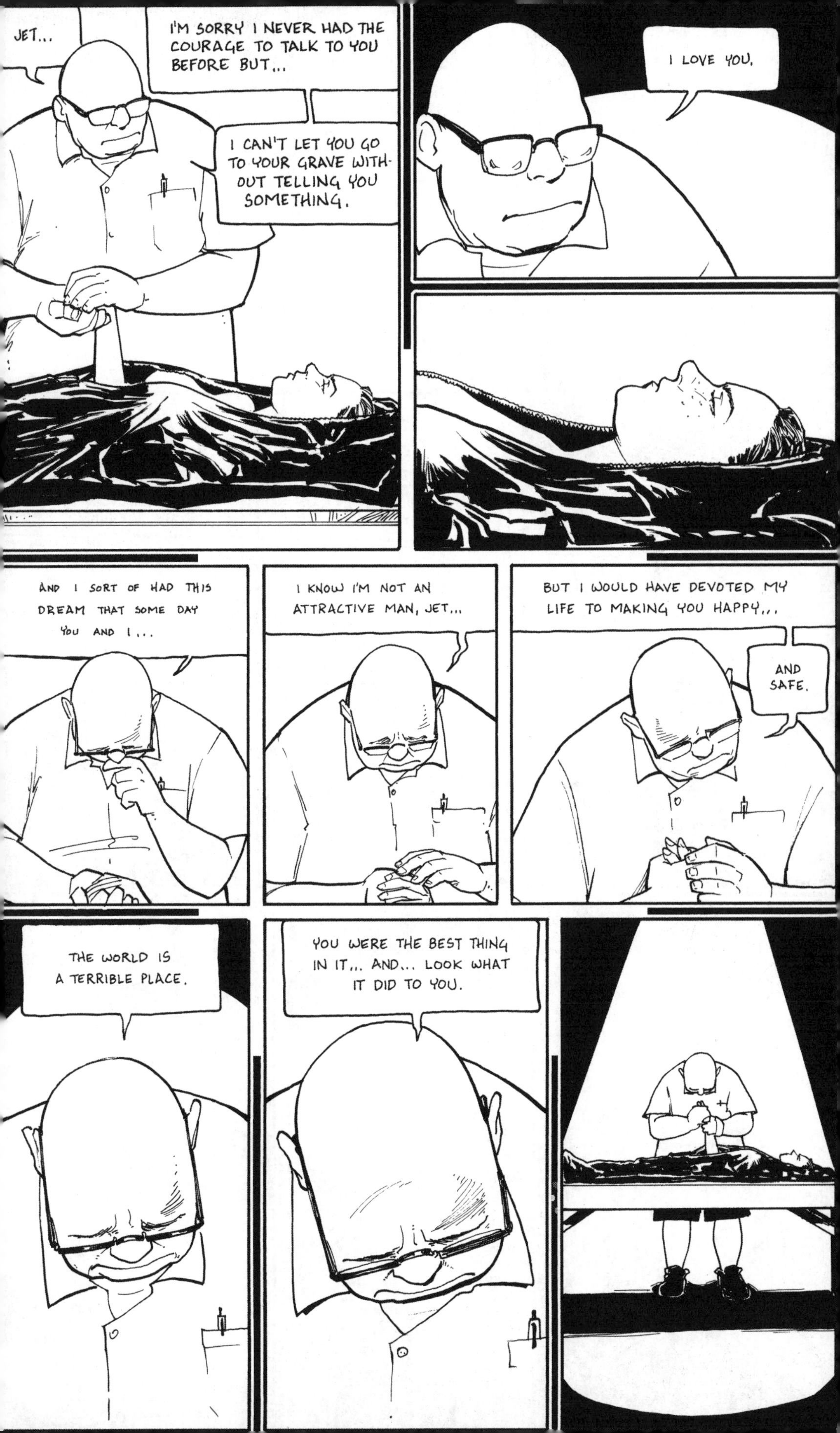
JET...
I'M SORRY I NEVER HAD THE COURAGE TO TALK TO YOU BEFORE BUT...
I CAN'T LET YOU GO TO YOUR GRAVE WITH-OUT TELLING YOU SOMETHING.
I LOVE YOU.
AND I SORT OF HAD THIS DREAM THAT SOME DAY YOU AND I...
I KNOW I'M NOT AN ATTRACTIVE MAN, JET...
BUT I WOULD HAVE DEVOTED MY LIFE TO MAKING YOU HAPPY...
AND SAFE.
THE WORLD IS A TERRIBLE PLACE.
YOU WERE THE BEST THING IN IT... AND... LOOK WHAT IT DID TO YOU.

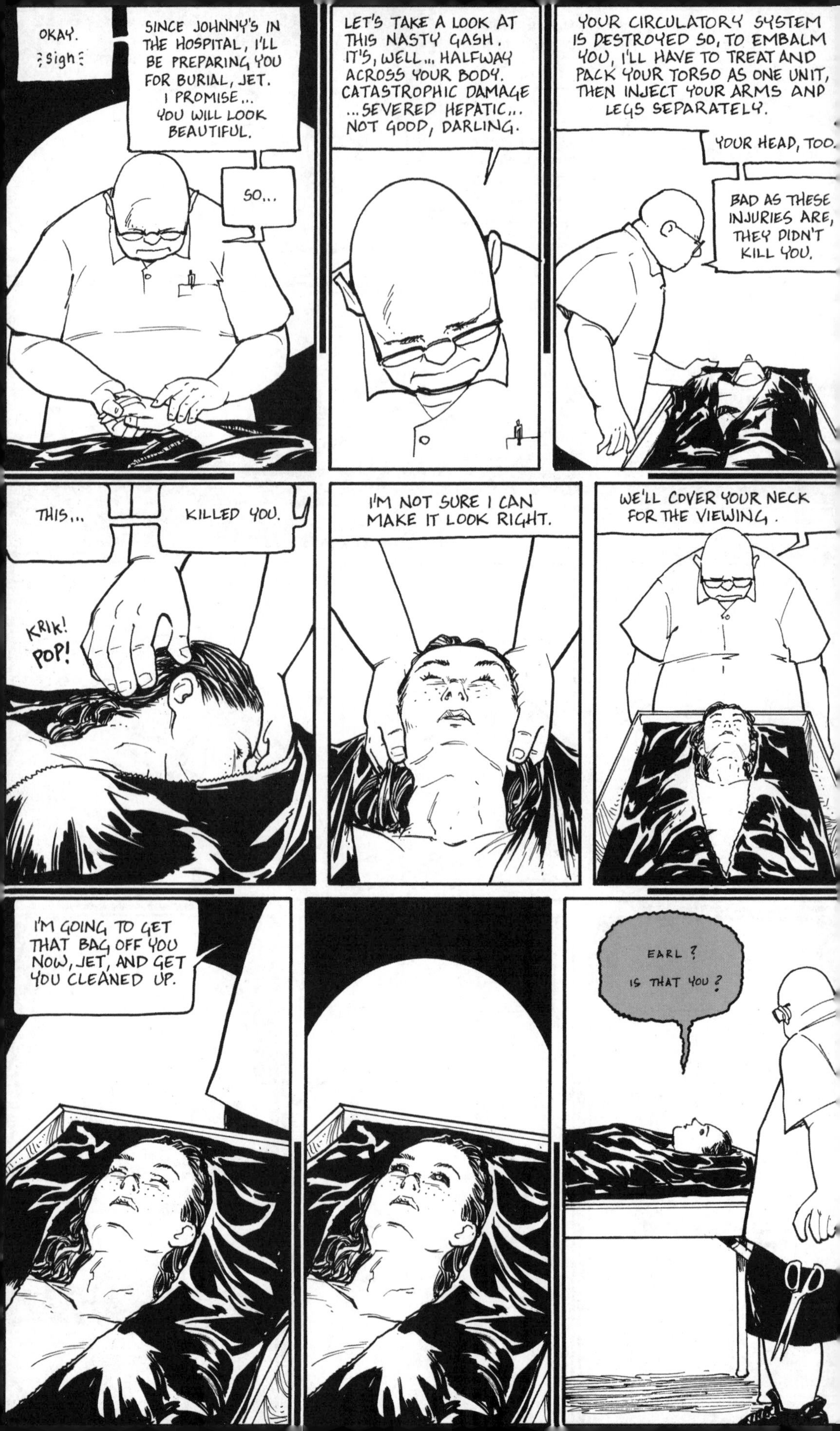
OKAY.
⁝sigh⁝
SINCE JOHNNY'S IN THE HOSPITAL, I'LL BE PREPARING YOU FOR BURIAL, JET. I PROMISE... YOU WILL LOOK BEAUTIFUL.
SO...
LET'S TAKE A LOOK AT THIS NASTY GASH. IT'S, WELL... HALFWAY ACROSS YOUR BODY. CATASTROPHIC DAMAGE ...SEVERED HEPATIC... NOT GOOD, DARLING.
YOUR CIRCULATORY SYSTEM IS DESTROYED SO, TO EMBALM YOU, I'LL HAVE TO TREAT AND PACK YOUR TORSO AS ONE UNIT, THEN INJECT YOUR ARMS AND LEGS SEPARATELY.
YOUR HEAD, TOO.
BAD AS THESE INJURIES ARE, THEY DIDN'T KILL YOU.
THIS...
KILLED YOU.
KRIK! POP!
I'M NOT SURE I CAN MAKE IT LOOK RIGHT.
WE'LL COVER YOUR NECK FOR THE VIEWING.
I'M GOING TO GET THAT BAG OFF YOU NOW, JET, AND GET YOU CLEANED UP.
EARL? IS THAT YOU?

JET! YOU'RE DEAD!
I'M NOT DEAD. I JUST... CAN'T MOVE.
NO, YOU CAN'T BE ALIVE — YOU'RE ALL TORN UP!
YOU'RE DEAD.
BUMMER.
WHAT HAPPENED?
YOU WERE IN AN ACCIDENT.
AN ACCIDENT?
AN 18-WHEELER JACK-KNIFED INTO YOUR CAR.
IT WAS BAD.
DO I LOOK... AWFUL?
NO, YOU'RE STILL BEAUTIFUL. BUT, YOU'RE CUT BAD—ALMOST IN TWO—AND YOUR NECK IS BROKEN. I DON'T UNDERSTAND WHAT'S HAPPENING HERE.
WHAT AM I WEARING?
A BODY BAG.
OH GRRROSS! GET ME OUT OF HERE! GOD ALMIGHTY!
ALL RIGHT. PLEASE DON'T GET UPSET. I'LL CUT THE BAG OFF.
WAIT, AM I NAKED?
YES. I WAS ABOUT TO EMBALM YOU.
GOD ALMIGHTY, EARL!

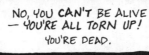

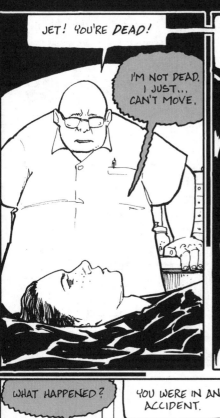

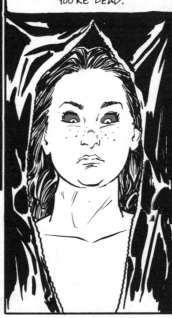

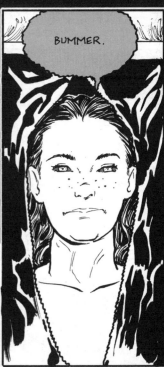

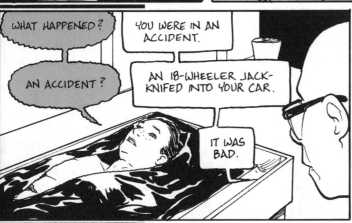

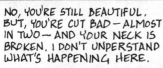

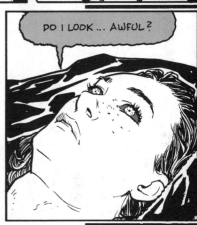

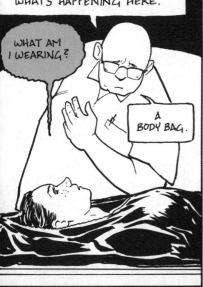

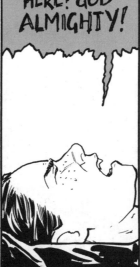

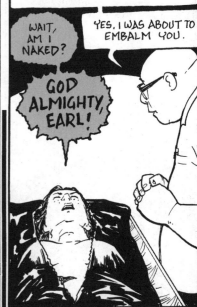

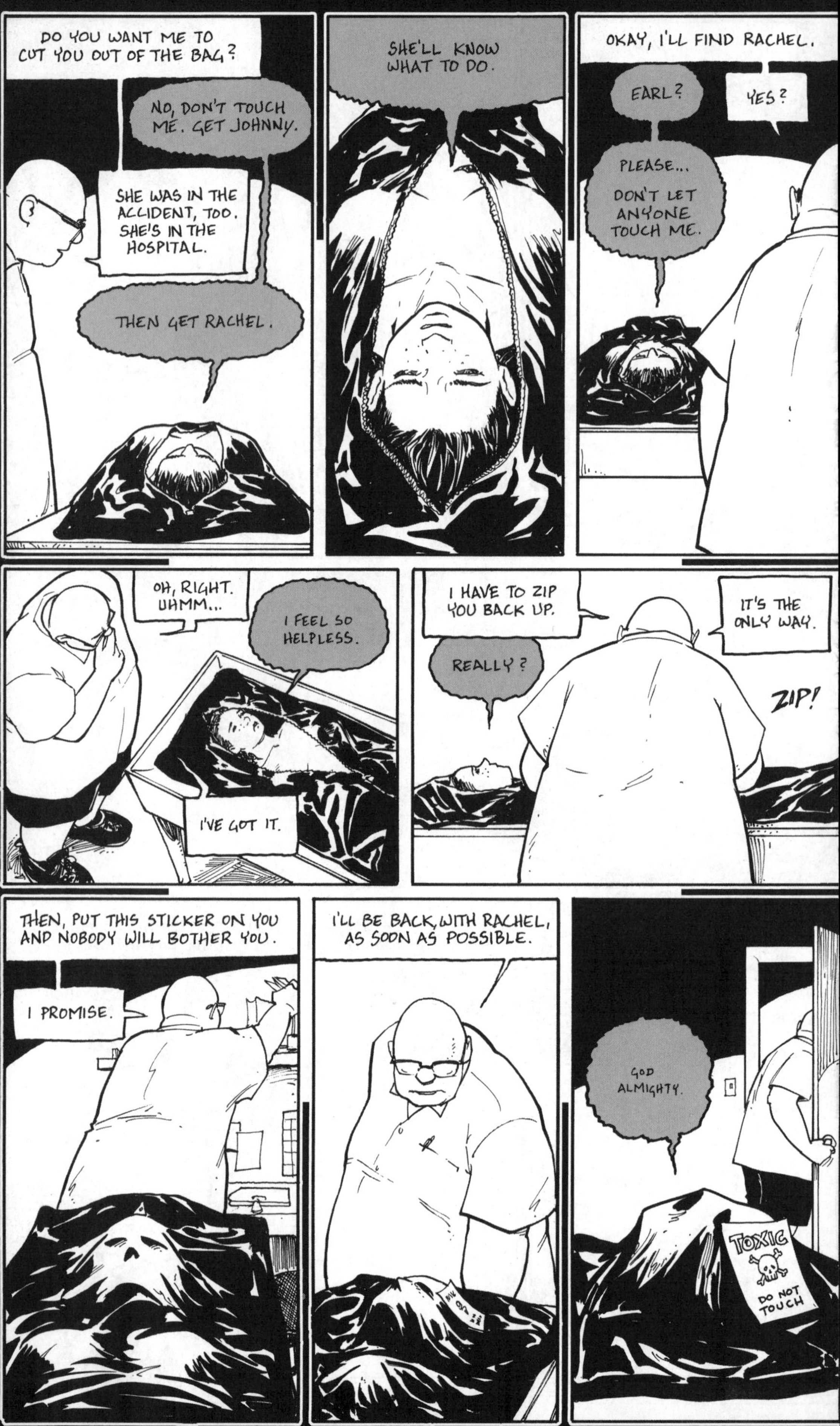
DO YOU WANT ME TO CUT YOU OUT OF THE BAG?
NO, DON'T TOUCH ME. GET JOHNNY.
SHE WAS IN THE ACCIDENT, TOO. SHE'S IN THE HOSPITAL.
THEN GET RACHEL.
SHE'LL KNOW WHAT TO DO.
OKAY, I'LL FIND RACHEL.
EARL?
YES?
PLEASE... DON'T LET ANYONE TOUCH ME.
OH, RIGHT. UHMM...
I FEEL SO HELPLESS.
I'VE GOT IT.
I HAVE TO ZIP YOU BACK UP.
IT'S THE ONLY WAY.
REALLY?
ZIP!
THEN, PUT THIS STICKER ON YOU AND NOBODY WILL BOTHER YOU.
I PROMISE.
I'LL BE BACK, WITH RACHEL, AS SOON AS POSSIBLE.
GOD ALMIGHTY.
TOXIC
DO NOT TOUCH

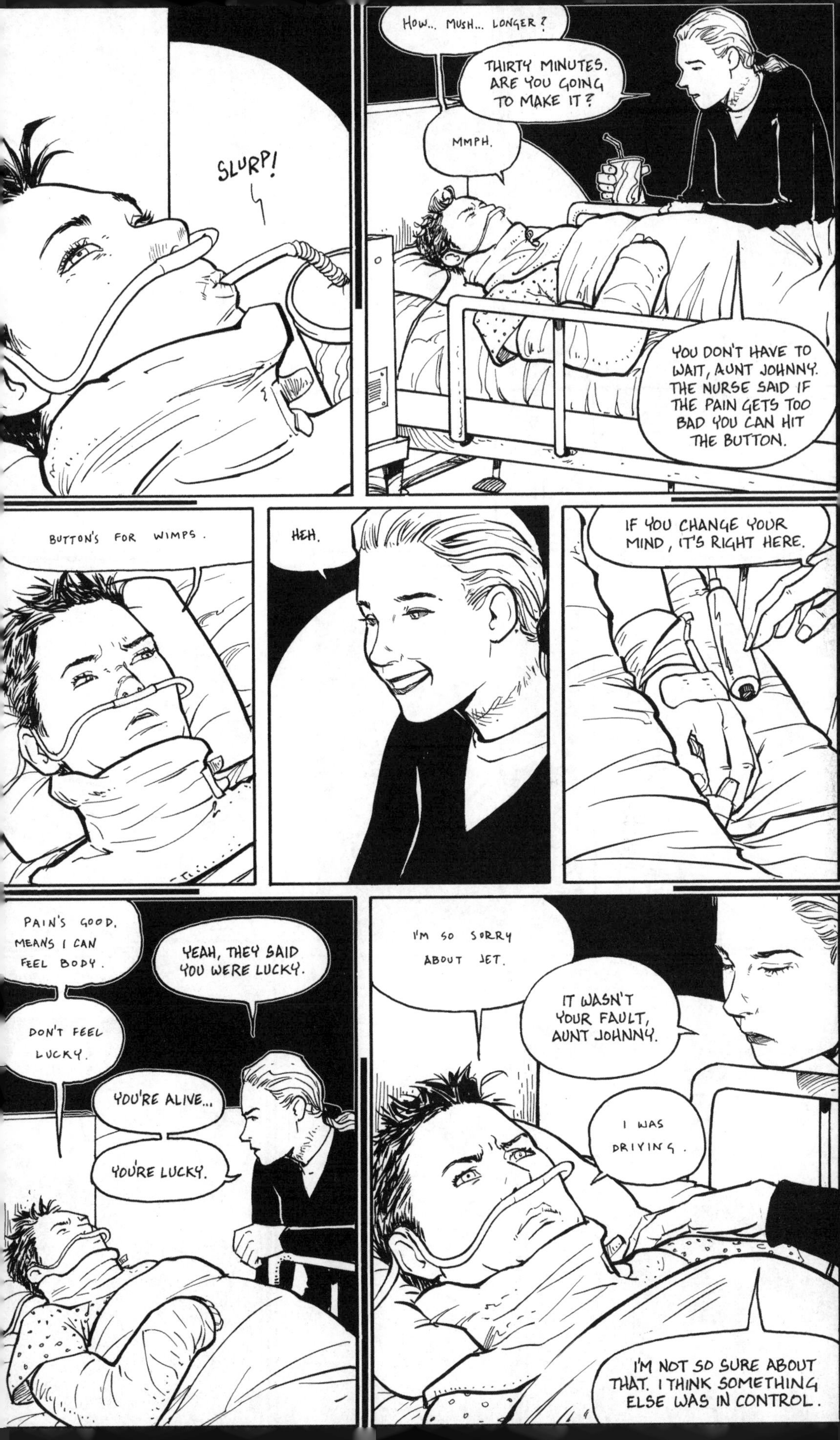
SLURP!
HOW... MUSH... LONGER?
THIRTY MINUTES. ARE YOU GOING TO MAKE IT?
MMPH.
YOU DON'T HAVE TO WAIT, AUNT JOHNNY. THE NURSE SAID IF THE PAIN GETS TOO BAD YOU CAN HIT THE BUTTON.
BUTTON'S FOR WIMPS.
HEH.
IF YOU CHANGE YOUR MIND, IT'S RIGHT HERE.
PAIN'S GOOD. MEANS I CAN FEEL BODY.
YEAH, THEY SAID YOU WERE LUCKY.
DON'T FEEL LUCKY.
YOU'RE ALIVE...
YOU'RE LUCKY.
I'M SO SORRY ABOUT JET.
IT WASN'T YOUR FAULT, AUNT JOHNNY.
I WAS DRIVING.
I'M NOT SO SURE ABOUT THAT. I THINK SOMETHING ELSE WAS IN CONTROL.

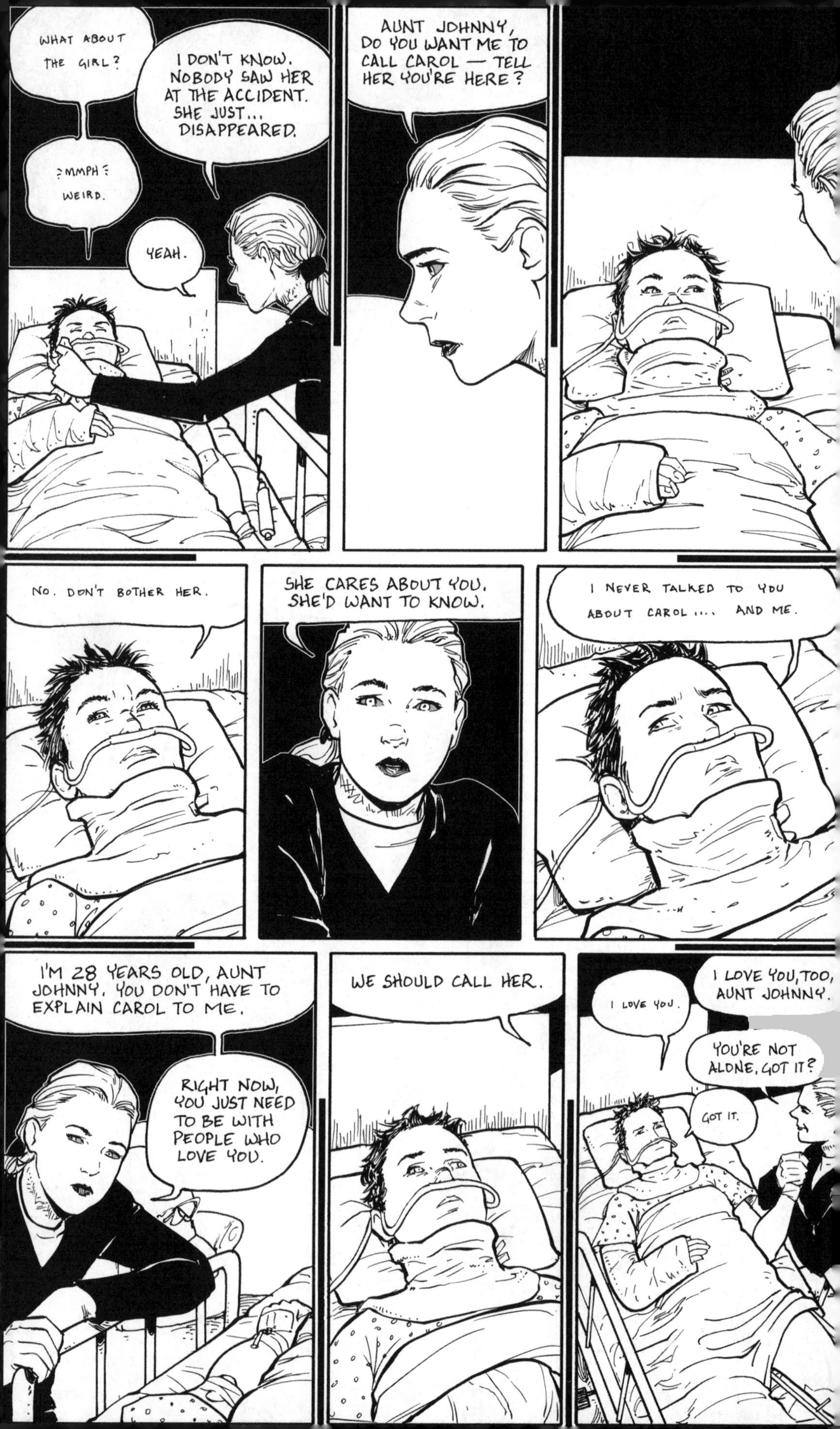
WHAT ABOUT THE GIRL?
I DON'T KNOW. NOBODY SAW HER AT THE ACCIDENT. SHE JUST... DISAPPEARED.
MMPH WEIRD.
YEAH.
AUNT JOHNNY, DO YOU WANT ME TO CALL CAROL — TELL HER YOU'RE HERE?
NO. DON'T BOTHER HER.
SHE CARES ABOUT YOU. SHE'D WANT TO KNOW.
I NEVER TALKED TO YOU ABOUT CAROL.... AND ME.
I'M 28 YEARS OLD, AUNT JOHNNY. YOU DON'T HAVE TO EXPLAIN CAROL TO ME.
RIGHT NOW, YOU JUST NEED TO BE WITH PEOPLE WHO LOVE YOU.
WE SHOULD CALL HER.
I LOVE YOU.
I LOVE YOU, TOO, AUNT JOHNNY.
YOU'RE NOT ALONE, GOT IT?
GOT IT.

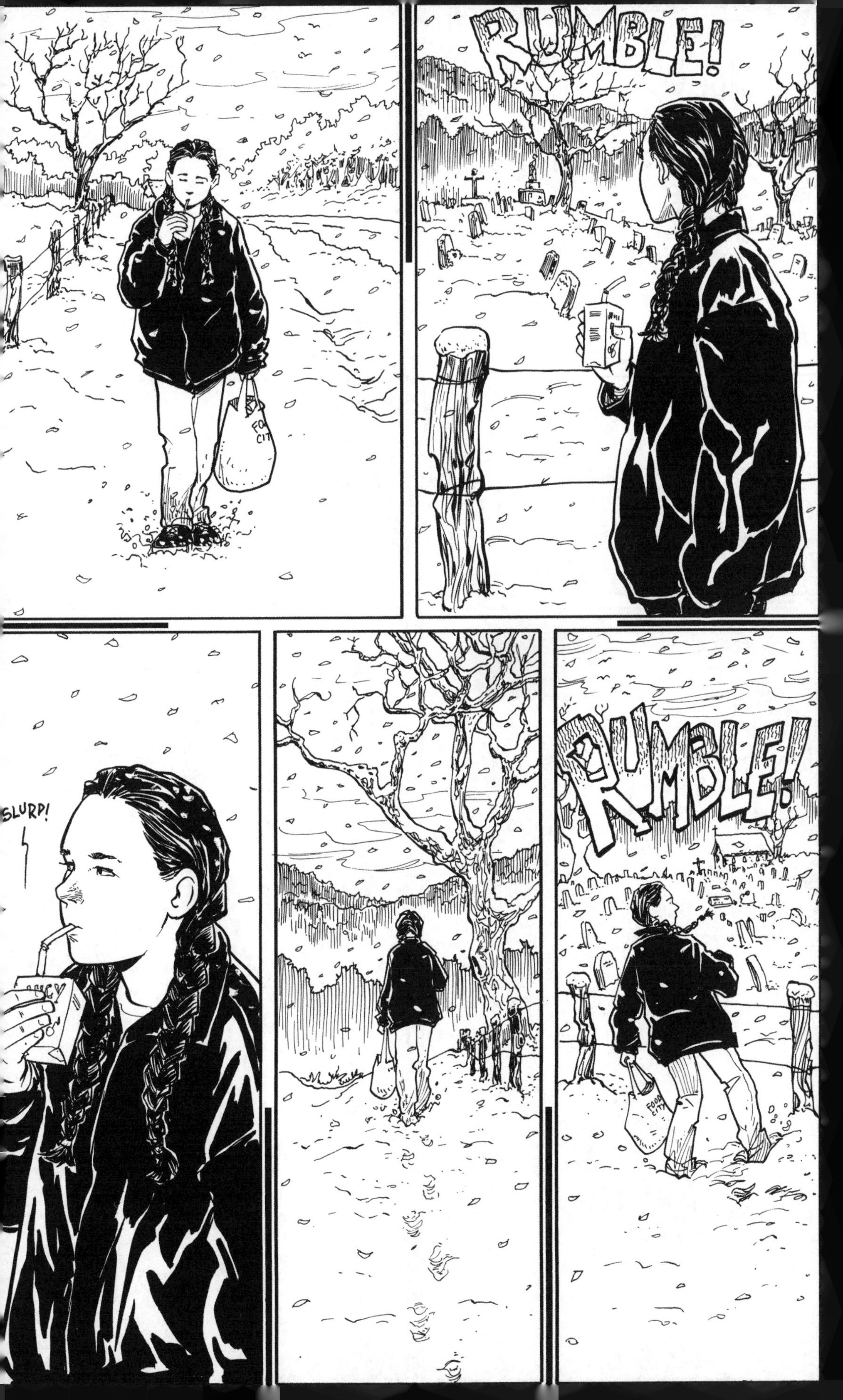
RUMBLE!
SLURP!
RUMBLE!

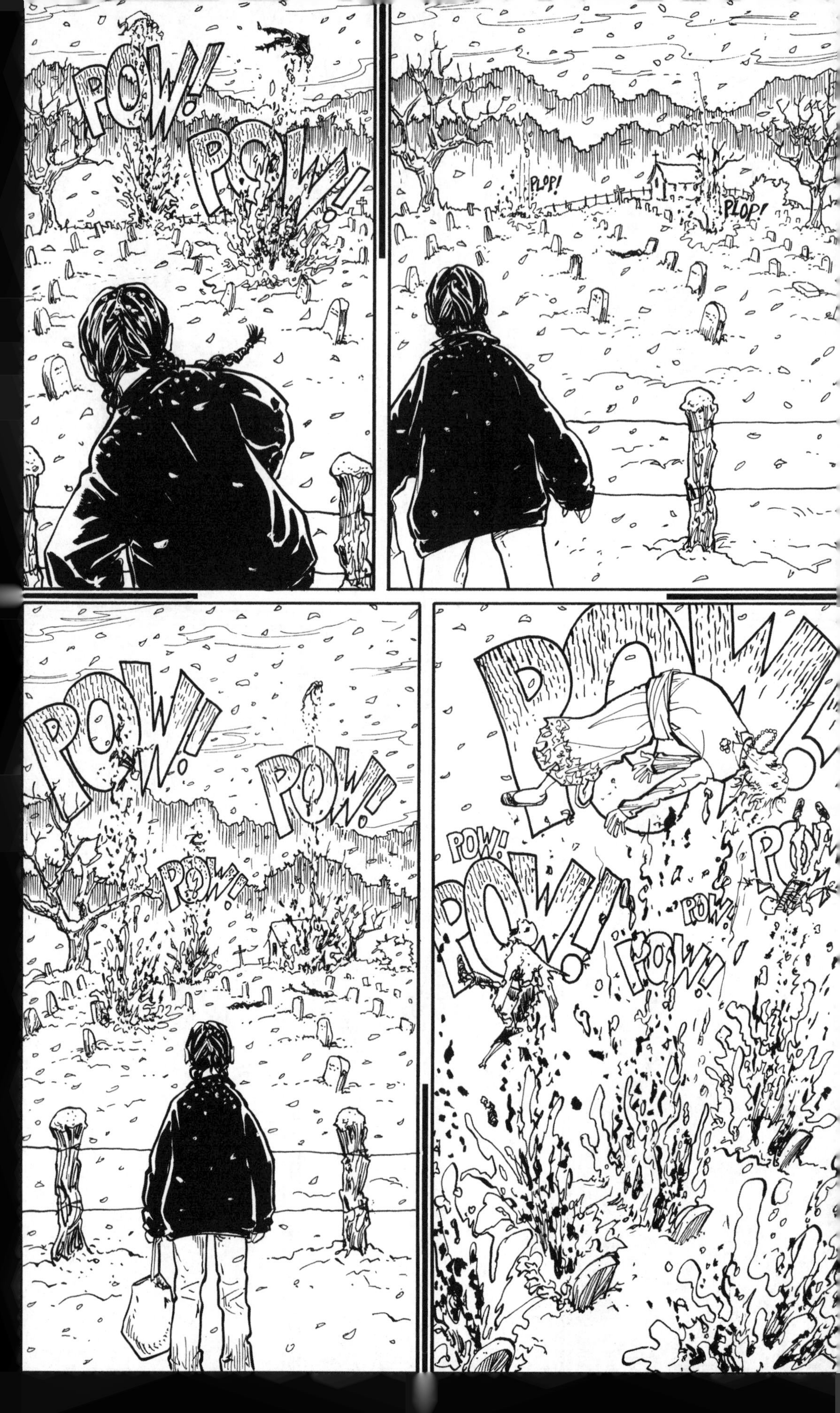
POW!
POW!
PLOP!
PLOP!
POW!
POW!
POW!
POW!
POW!
POW!
POW!
POW!
POW!

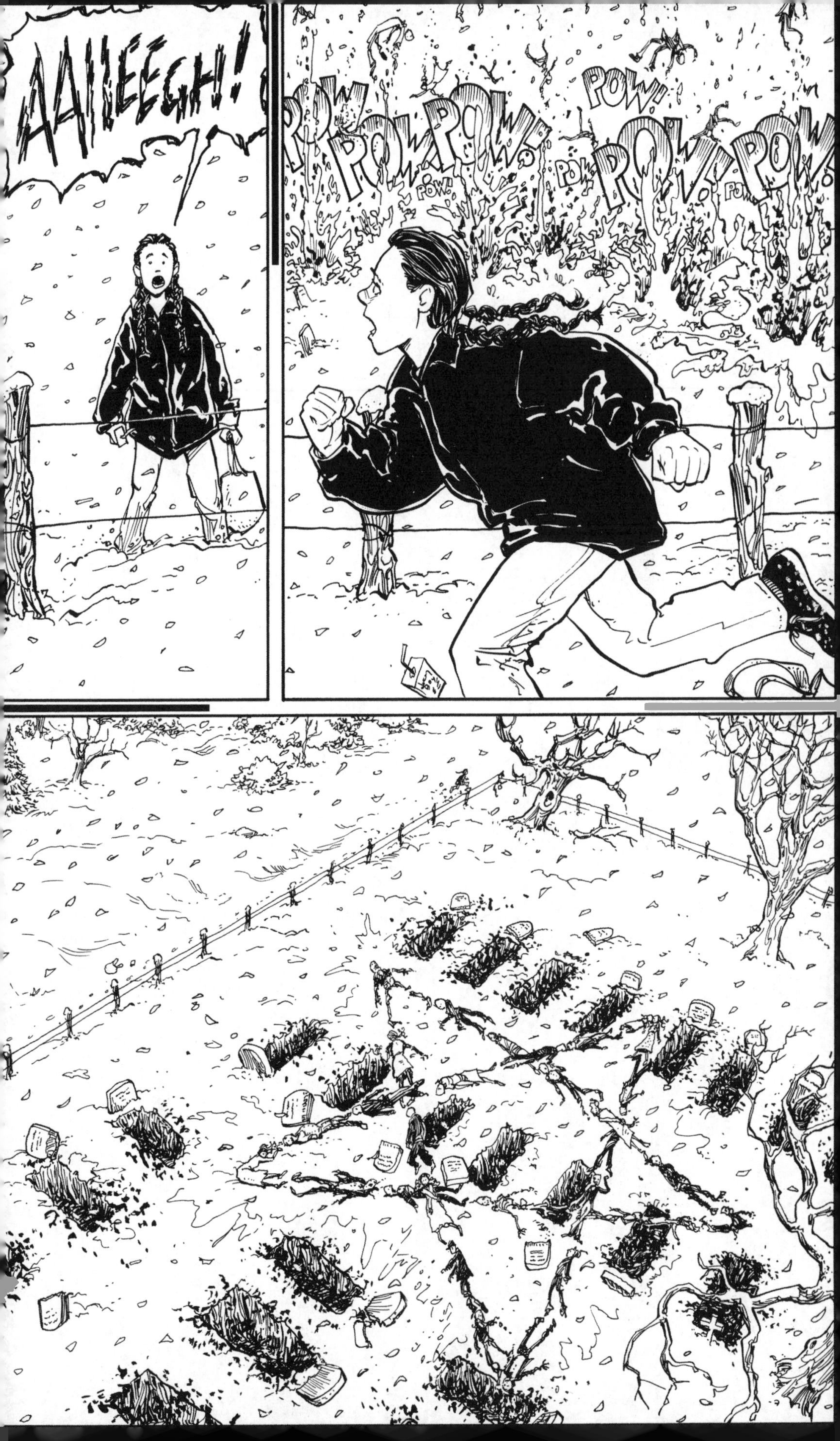

AAIIEEGH!!
POW! POW! POW! POW! POW! POW! POW! POW! POW! POW!

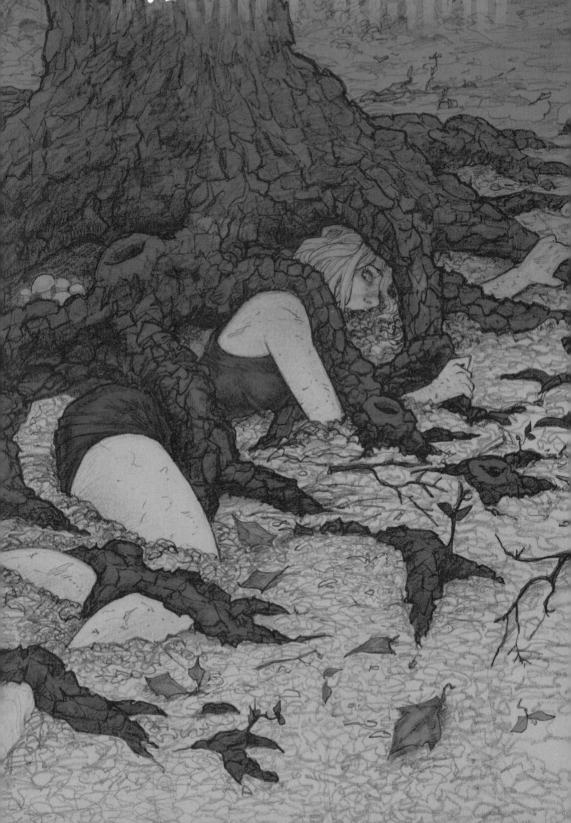

TERRY MOORE

RACHEL RISING

ABSTRACT STUDIO

ISSUE No.

8

3.99 US

FEAR NOT DEATH FOR THE SOONER WE DIE,
THE LONGER WE SHALL BE IMMORTAL.

—BENJAMIN FRANKLIN

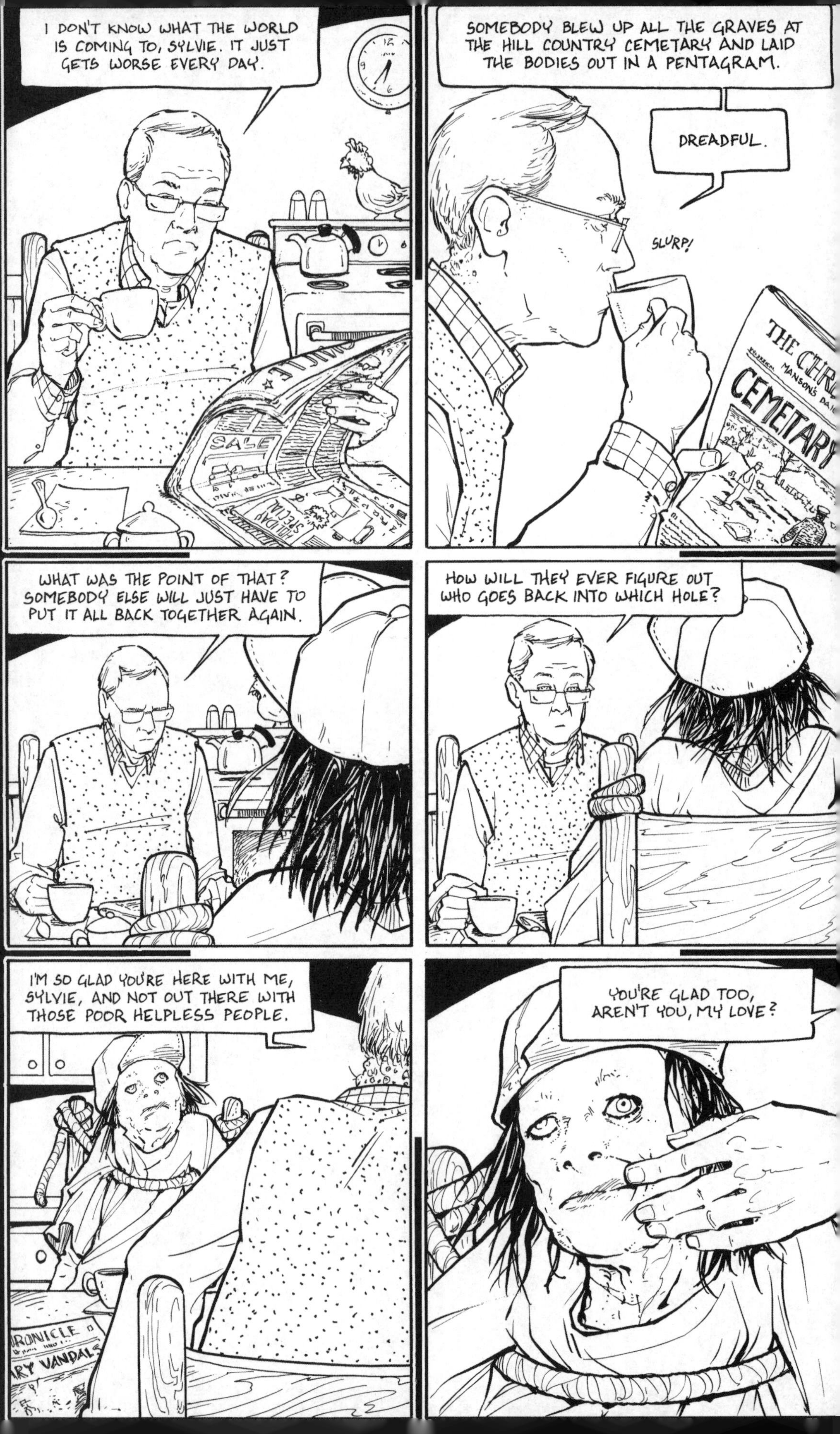
I DON'T KNOW WHAT THE WORLD IS COMING TO, SYLVIE. IT JUST GETS WORSE EVERY DAY.
SALE
SOMEBODY BLEW UP ALL THE GRAVES AT THE HILL COUNTRY CEMETARY AND LAID THE BODIES OUT IN A PENTAGRAM.
DREADFUL.
SLURP!
CEMETARY
WHAT WAS THE POINT OF THAT? SOMEBODY ELSE WILL JUST HAVE TO PUT IT ALL BACK TOGETHER AGAIN.
HOW WILL THEY EVER FIGURE OUT WHO GOES BACK INTO WHICH HOLE?
I'M SO GLAD YOU'RE HERE WITH ME, SYLVIE, AND NOT OUT THERE WITH THOSE POOR HELPLESS PEOPLE.
YOU'RE GLAD TOO, AREN'T YOU, MY LOVE?

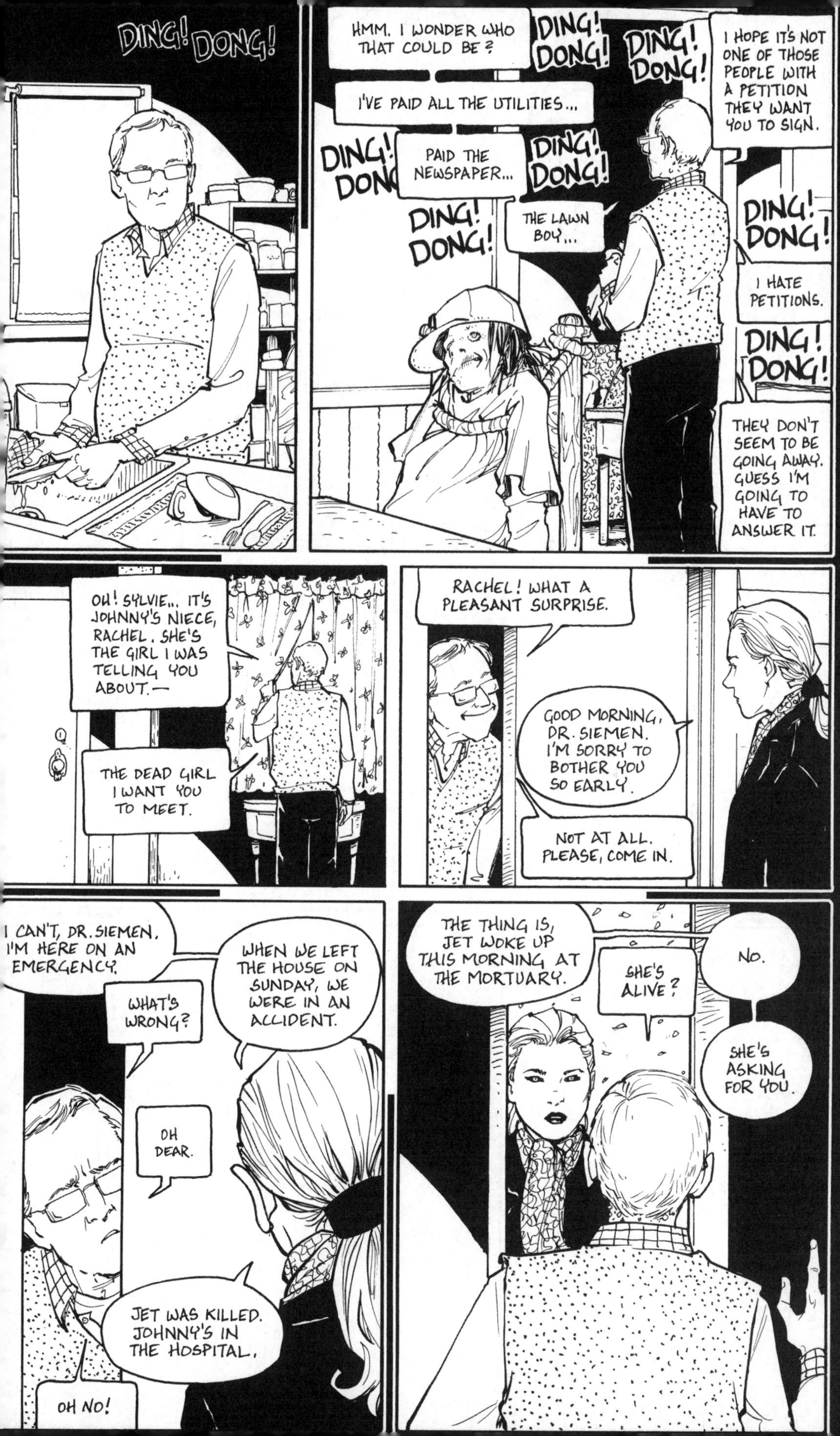
DING! DONG!
HMM. I WONDER WHO THAT COULD BE?
DING! DONG!
DING! DONG!
I'VE PAID ALL THE UTILITIES...
DING! DONG
PAID THE NEWSPAPER...
DING! DONG!
DING! DONG!
THE LAWN BOY...
I HOPE IT'S NOT ONE OF THOSE PEOPLE WITH A PETITION THEY WANT YOU TO SIGN.
DING! DONG!
I HATE PETITIONS.
DING! DONG!
THEY DON'T SEEM TO BE GOING AWAY. GUESS I'M GOING TO HAVE TO ANSWER IT.
OH! SYLVIE... IT'S JOHNNY'S NIECE, RACHEL. SHE'S THE GIRL I WAS TELLING YOU ABOUT.—
THE DEAD GIRL I WANT YOU TO MEET.
RACHEL! WHAT A PLEASANT SURPRISE.
GOOD MORNING, DR. SIEMEN. I'M SORRY TO BOTHER YOU SO EARLY.
NOT AT ALL. PLEASE, COME IN.
I CAN'T, DR. SIEMEN. I'M HERE ON AN EMERGENCY.
WHAT'S WRONG?
WHEN WE LEFT THE HOUSE ON SUNDAY, WE WERE IN AN ACCIDENT.
OH DEAR.
JET WAS KILLED. JOHNNY'S IN THE HOSPITAL.
OH NO!
THE THING IS, JET WOKE UP THIS MORNING AT THE MORTUARY.
SHE'S ALIVE?
NO.
SHE'S ASKING FOR YOU.

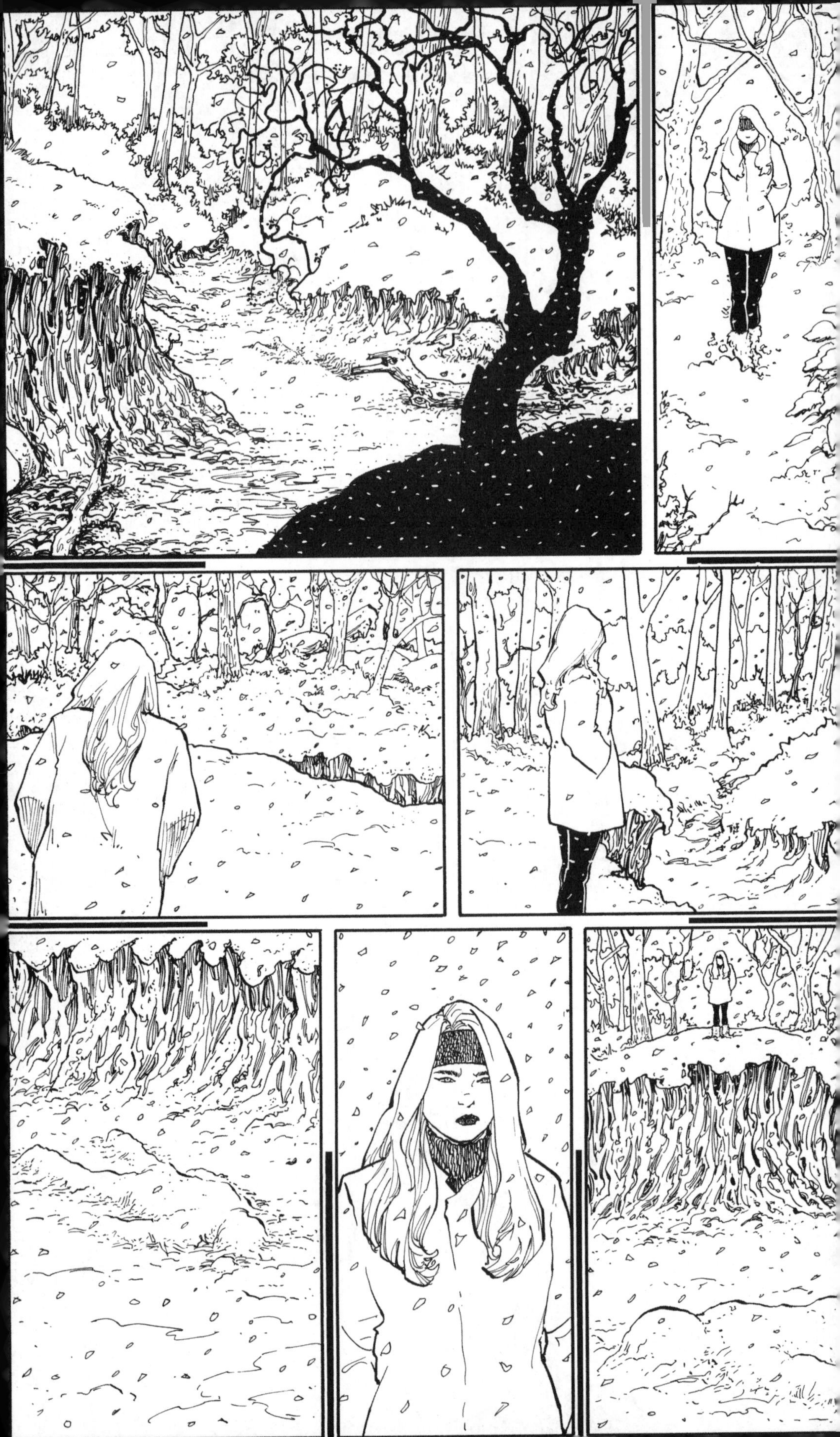

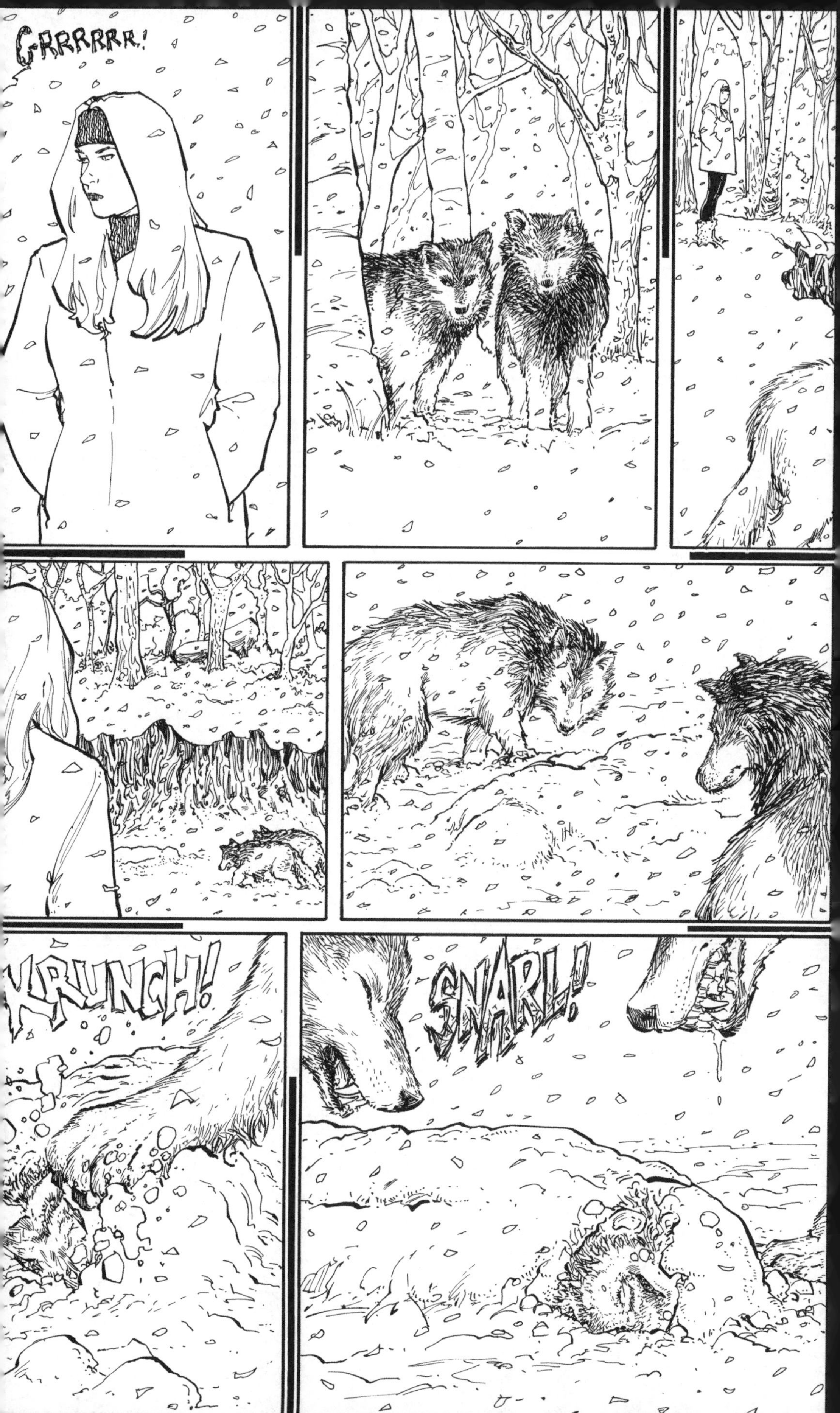
GRRRRRR!
KRUNCH!
SNARL!

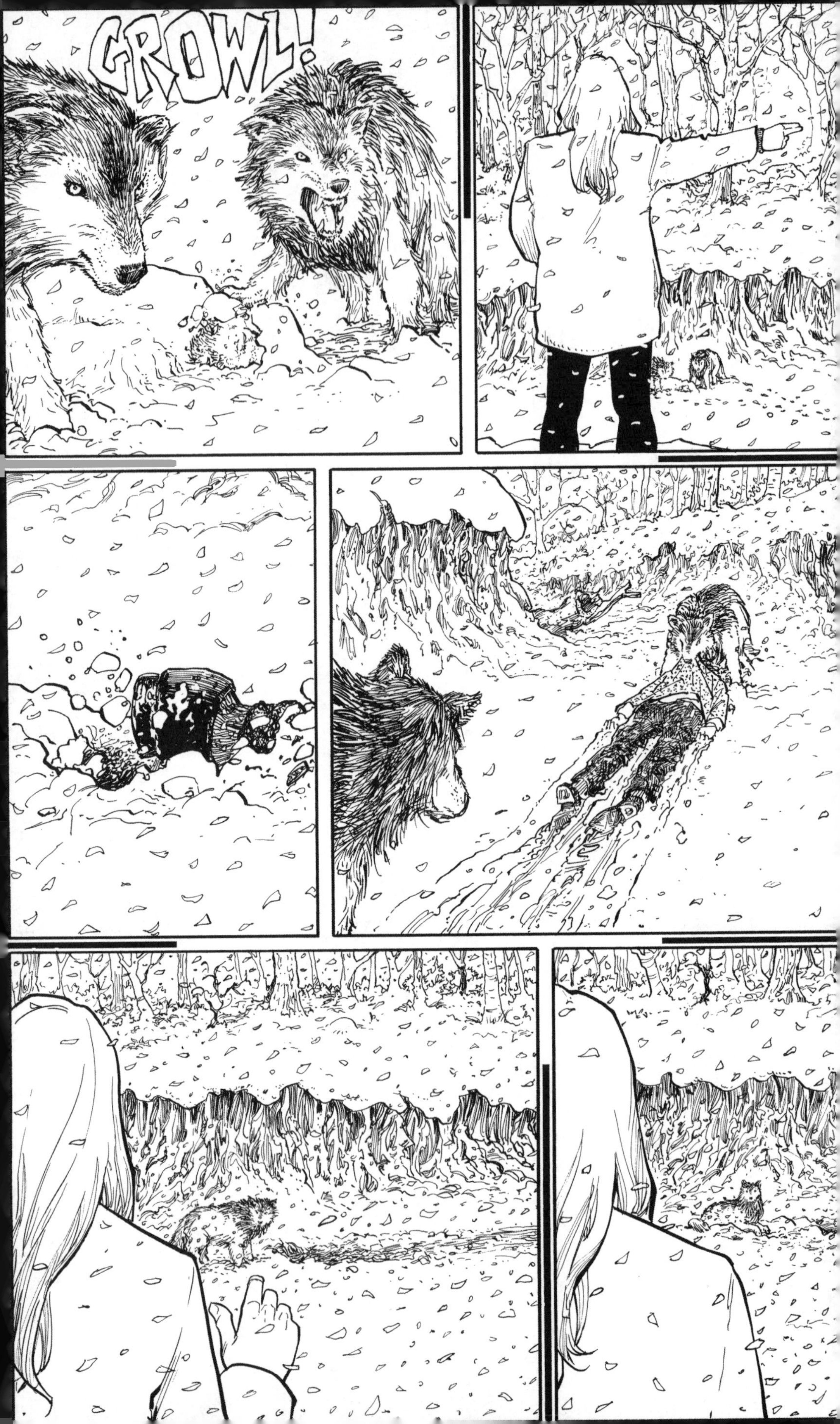
GROWL!

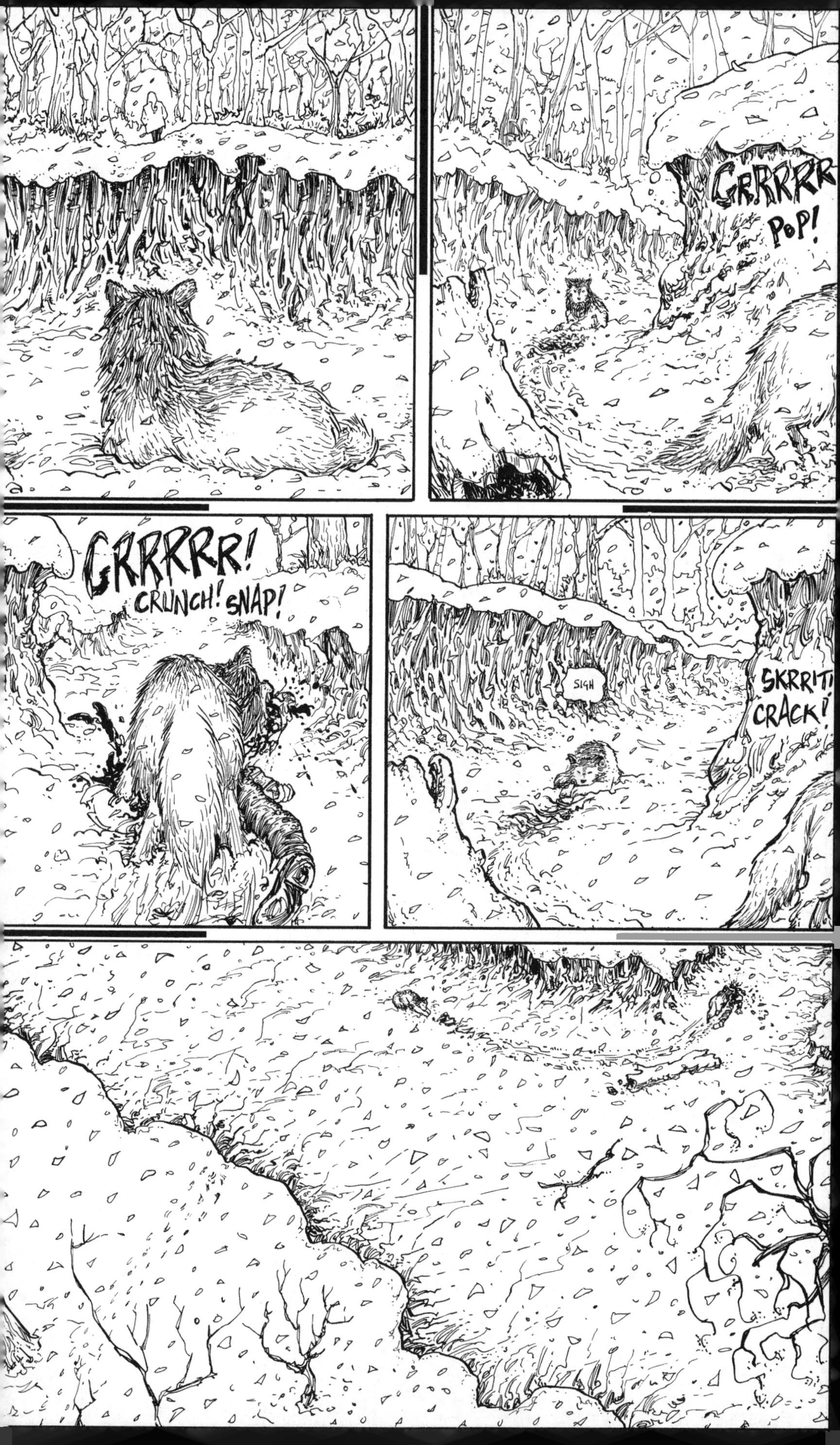
GRRRRR
POP!
GRRRRR!
CRUNCH! SNAP!
SIGH
SKRRITI
CRACK!

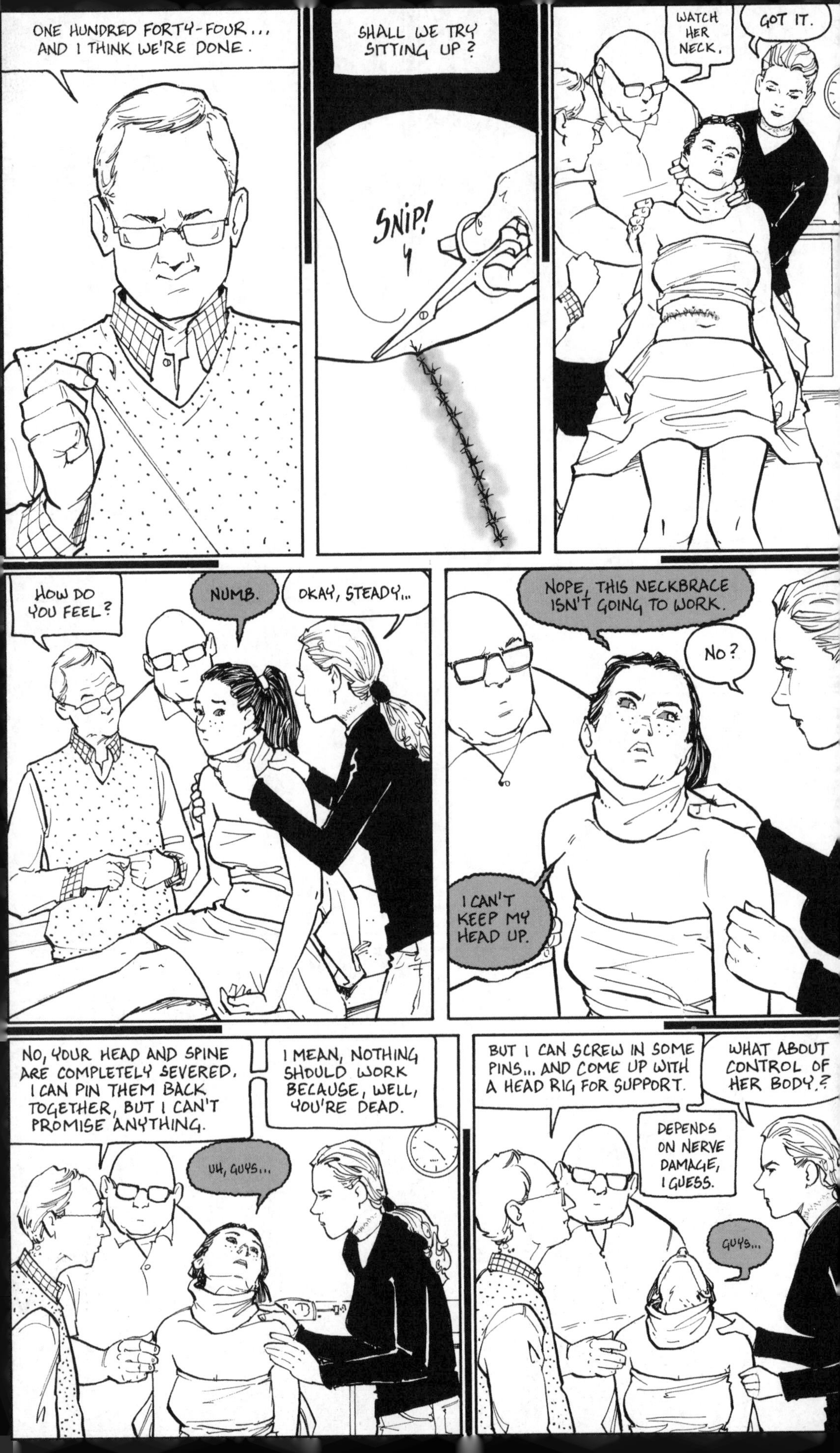
ONE HUNDRED FORTY-FOUR... AND I THINK WE'RE DONE.
SHALL WE TRY SITTING UP?
SNIP!
WATCH HER NECK.
GOT IT.
HOW DO YOU FEEL?
NUMB.
OKAY, STEADY...
NOPE, THIS NECKBRACE ISN'T GOING TO WORK.
NO?
I CAN'T KEEP MY HEAD UP.
NO, YOUR HEAD AND SPINE ARE COMPLETELY SEVERED. I CAN PIN THEM BACK TOGETHER, BUT I CAN'T PROMISE ANYTHING.
I MEAN, NOTHING SHOULD WORK BECAUSE, WELL, YOU'RE DEAD.
UH, GUYS...
BUT I CAN SCREW IN SOME PINS... AND COME UP WITH A HEAD RIG FOR SUPPORT.
WHAT ABOUT CONTROL OF HER BODY?
DEPENDS ON NERVE DAMAGE, I GUESS.
GUYS...

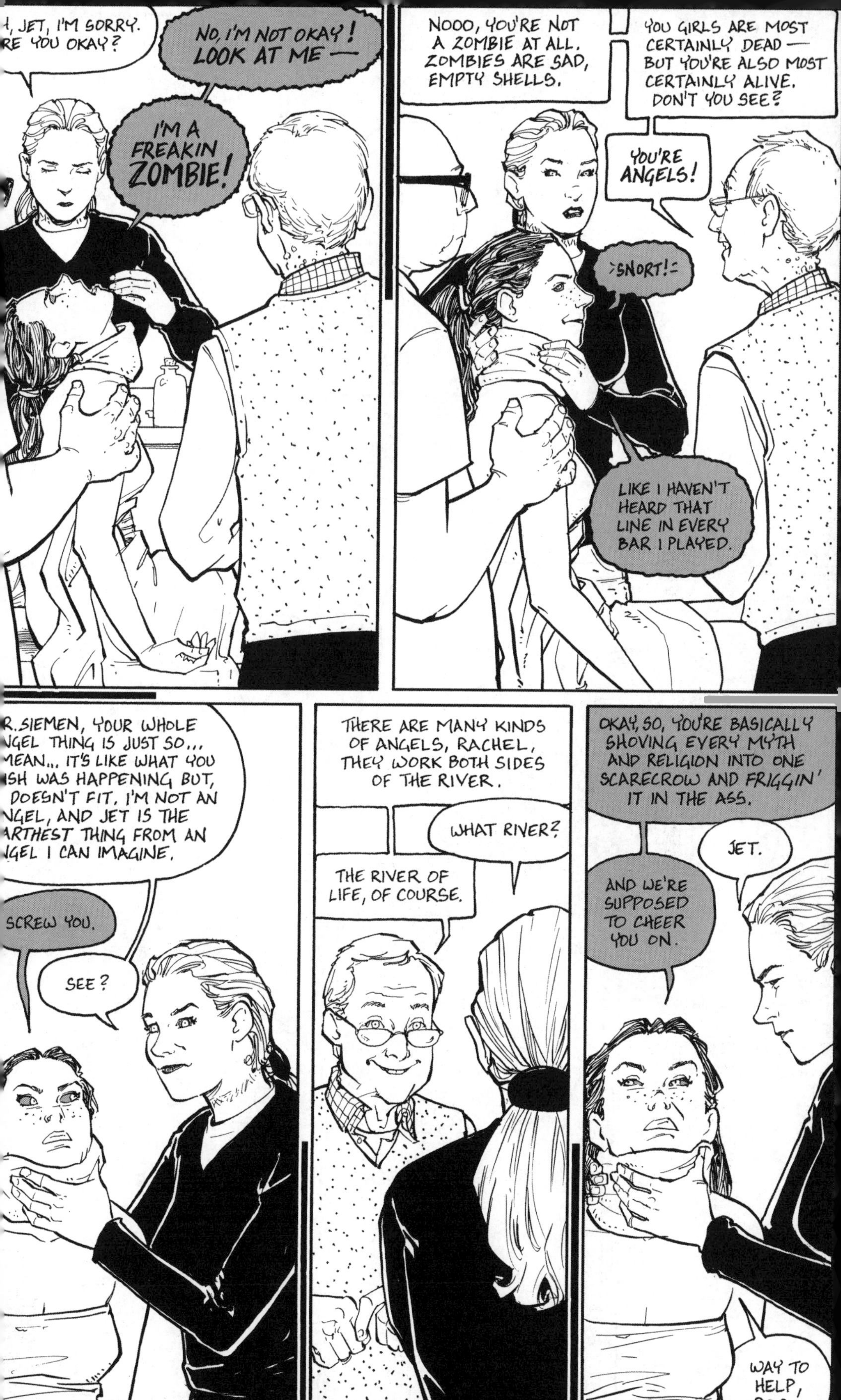

H, JET, I'M SORRY. RE YOU OKAY?
NO, I'M NOT OKAY! LOOK AT ME —
I'M A FREAKIN ZOMBIE!
NOOO, YOU'RE NOT A ZOMBIE AT ALL. ZOMBIES ARE SAD, EMPTY SHELLS.
YOU GIRLS ARE MOST CERTAINLY DEAD — BUT YOU'RE ALSO MOST CERTAINLY ALIVE. DON'T YOU SEE?
YOU'RE ANGELS!
>SNORT!<
LIKE I HAVEN'T HEARD THAT LINE IN EVERY BAR I PLAYED.
R. SIEMEN, YOUR WHOLE NGEL THING IS JUST SO... MEAN... IT'S LIKE WHAT YOU ISH WAS HAPPENING BUT, DOESN'T FIT. I'M NOT AN NGEL, AND JET IS THE ARTHEST THING FROM AN NGEL I CAN IMAGINE.
SCREW YOU.
SEE?
THERE ARE MANY KINDS OF ANGELS, RACHEL. THEY WORK BOTH SIDES OF THE RIVER.
WHAT RIVER?
THE RIVER OF LIFE, OF COURSE.
OKAY, SO, YOU'RE BASICALLY SHOVING EVERY MYTH AND RELIGION INTO ONE SCARECROW AND FRIGGIN' IT IN THE ASS.
JET.
AND WE'RE SUPPOSED TO CHEER YOU ON.
WAY TO HELP, DOC.

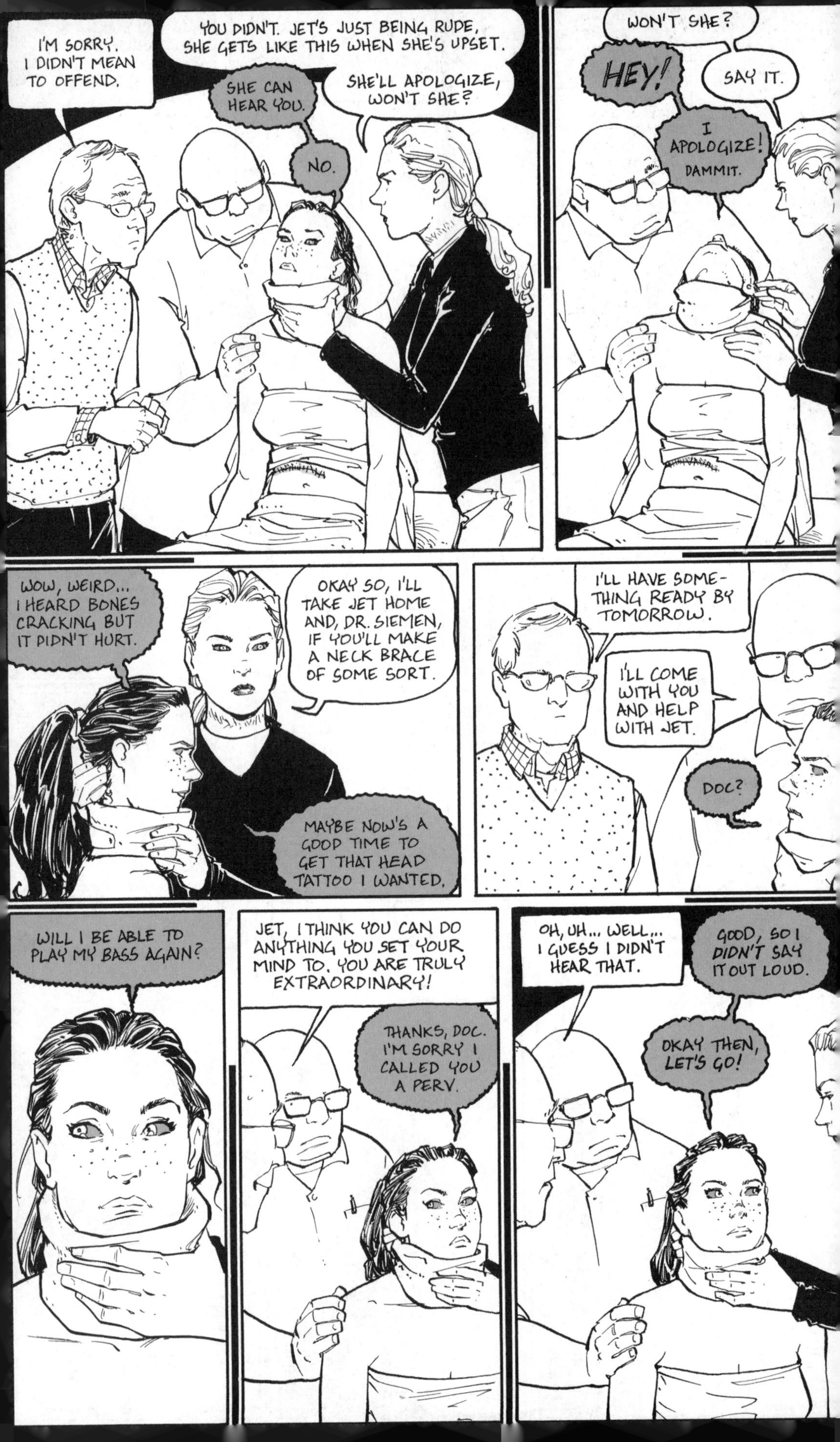
I'M SORRY. I DIDN'T MEAN TO OFFEND.
YOU DIDN'T. JET'S JUST BEING RUDE, SHE GETS LIKE THIS WHEN SHE'S UPSET.
SHE CAN HEAR YOU.
SHE'LL APOLOGIZE, WON'T SHE?
NO.
WON'T SHE?
HEY!
SAY IT.
I APOLOGIZE! DAMMIT.
WOW, WEIRD... I HEARD BONES CRACKING BUT IT DIDN'T HURT.
OKAY SO, I'LL TAKE JET HOME AND, DR. SIEMEN, IF YOU'LL MAKE A NECK BRACE OF SOME SORT.
MAYBE NOW'S A GOOD TIME TO GET THAT HEAD TATTOO I WANTED.
I'LL HAVE SOME-THING READY BY TOMORROW.
I'LL COME WITH YOU AND HELP WITH JET.
DOC?
WILL I BE ABLE TO PLAY MY BASS AGAIN?
JET, I THINK YOU CAN DO ANYTHING YOU SET YOUR MIND TO. YOU ARE TRULY EXTRAORDINARY!
THANKS, DOC. I'M SORRY I CALLED YOU A PERV.
OH, UH... WELL... I GUESS I DIDN'T HEAR THAT.
GOOD, SO I DIDN'T SAY IT OUT LOUD.
OKAY THEN, LET'S GO!

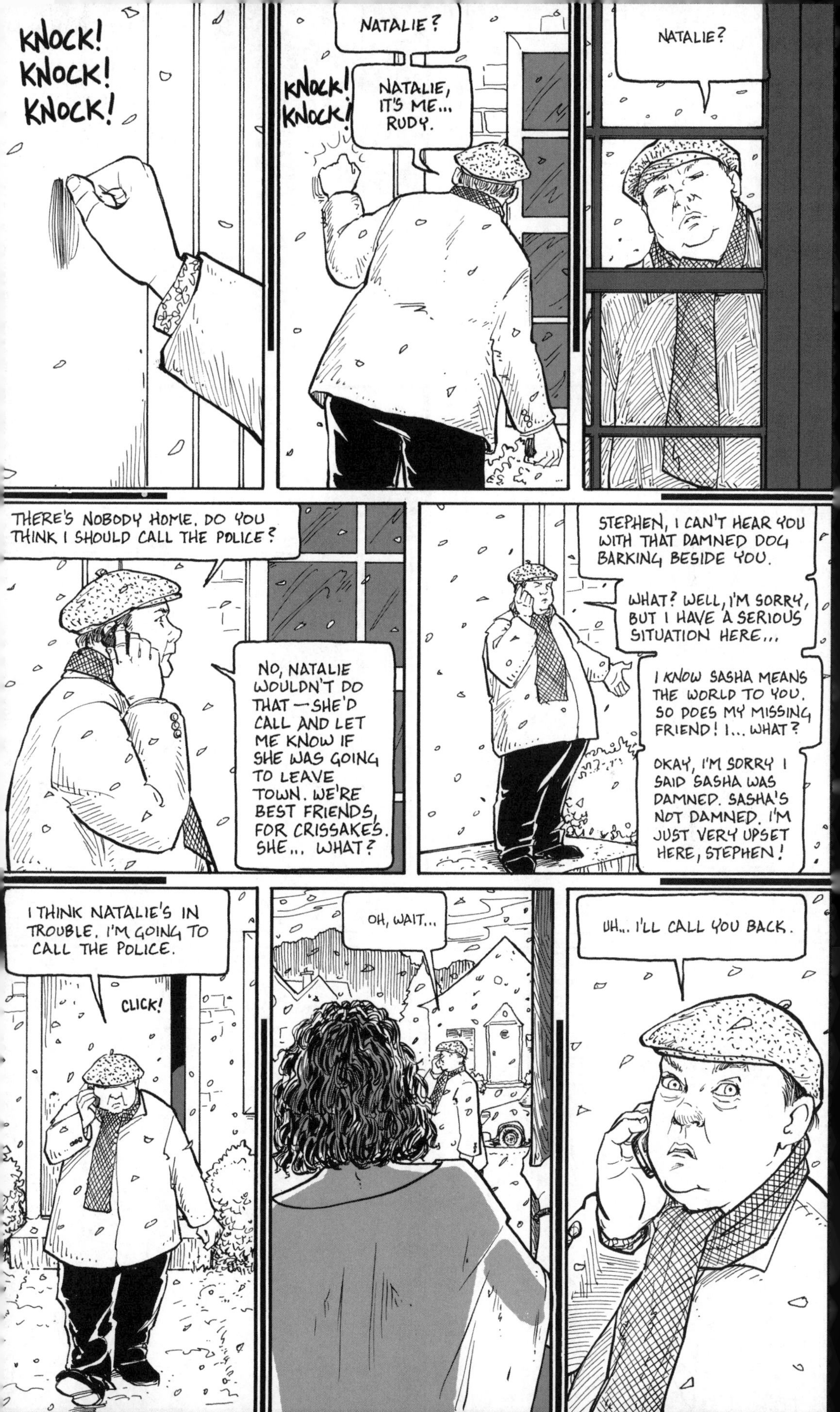
KNOCK! KNOCK! KNOCK!
NATALIE?
KNOCK! KNOCK!
NATALIE, IT'S ME... RUDY.
NATALIE?
THERE'S NOBODY HOME. DO YOU THINK I SHOULD CALL THE POLICE?
NO, NATALIE WOULDN'T DO THAT—SHE'D CALL AND LET ME KNOW IF SHE WAS GOING TO LEAVE TOWN. WE'RE BEST FRIENDS, FOR CRISSAKES. SHE... WHAT?
STEPHEN, I CAN'T HEAR YOU WITH THAT DAMNED DOG BARKING BESIDE YOU.
WHAT? WELL, I'M SORRY, BUT I HAVE A SERIOUS SITUATION HERE...
I KNOW SASHA MEANS THE WORLD TO YOU. SO DOES MY MISSING FRIEND! I... WHAT?
OKAY, I'M SORRY I SAID SASHA WAS DAMNED. SASHA'S NOT DAMNED. I'M JUST VERY UPSET HERE, STEPHEN!
I THINK NATALIE'S IN TROUBLE. I'M GOING TO CALL THE POLICE.
CLICK!
OH, WAIT...
UH... I'LL CALL YOU BACK.

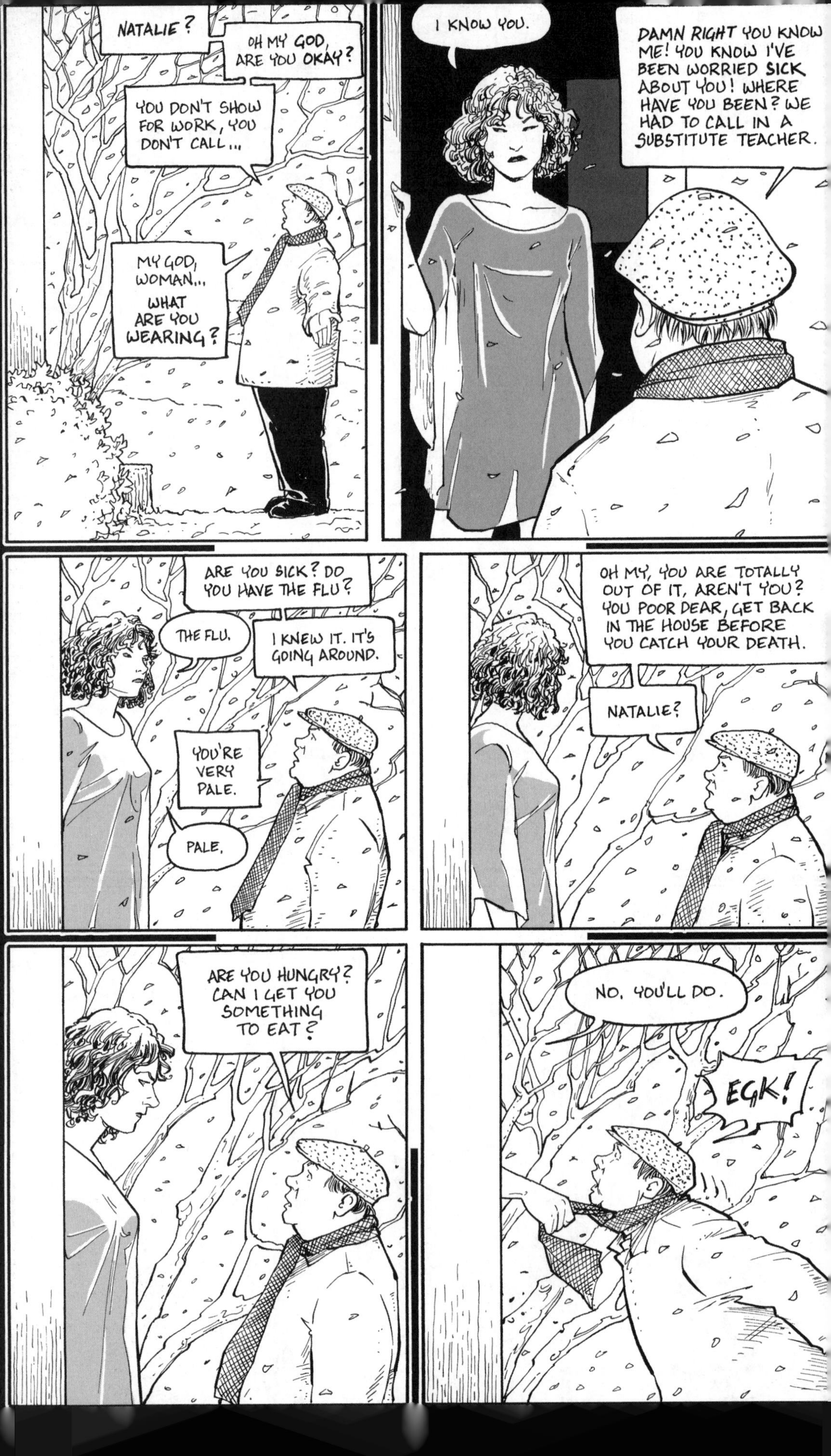
NATALIE?
OH MY GOD, ARE YOU OKAY?
YOU DON'T SHOW FOR WORK, YOU DON'T CALL...
MY GOD, WOMAN... WHAT ARE YOU WEARING?
I KNOW YOU.
DAMN RIGHT YOU KNOW ME! YOU KNOW I'VE BEEN WORRIED SICK ABOUT YOU! WHERE HAVE YOU BEEN? WE HAD TO CALL IN A SUBSTITUTE TEACHER.
ARE YOU SICK? DO YOU HAVE THE FLU?
THE FLU.
I KNEW IT. IT'S GOING AROUND.
YOU'RE VERY PALE.
PALE.
OH MY, YOU ARE TOTALLY OUT OF IT, AREN'T YOU? YOU POOR DEAR, GET BACK IN THE HOUSE BEFORE YOU CATCH YOUR DEATH.
NATALIE?
ARE YOU HUNGRY? CAN I GET YOU SOMETHING TO EAT?
NO. YOU'LL DO.
EGK!

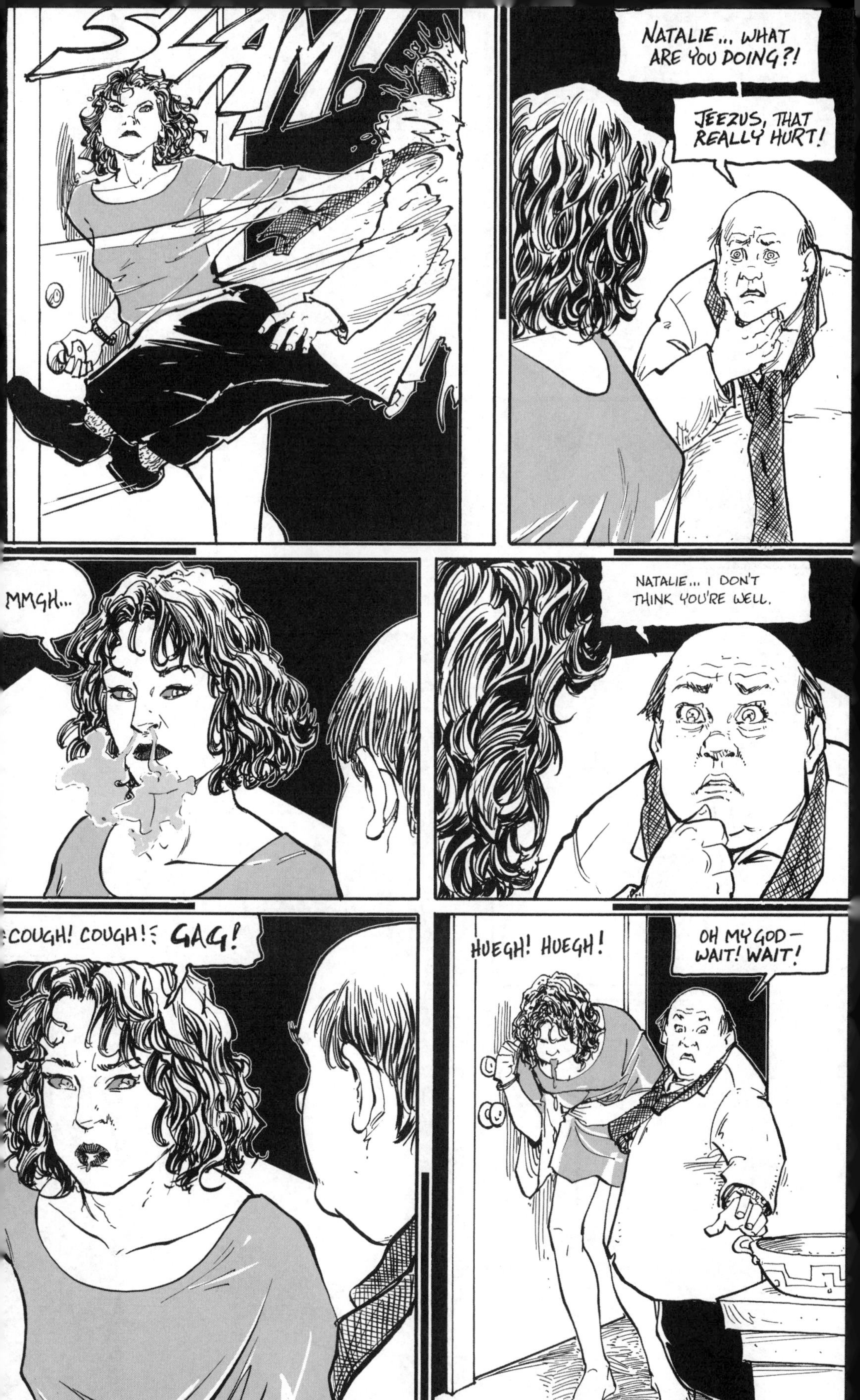
SLAM!
NATALIE... WHAT ARE YOU DOING?!
JEEZUS, THAT REALLY HURT!
MMGH...
NATALIE... I DON'T THINK YOU'RE WELL.
COUGH! COUGH! GAG!
HUEGH! HUEGH!
OH MY GOD— WAIT! WAIT!

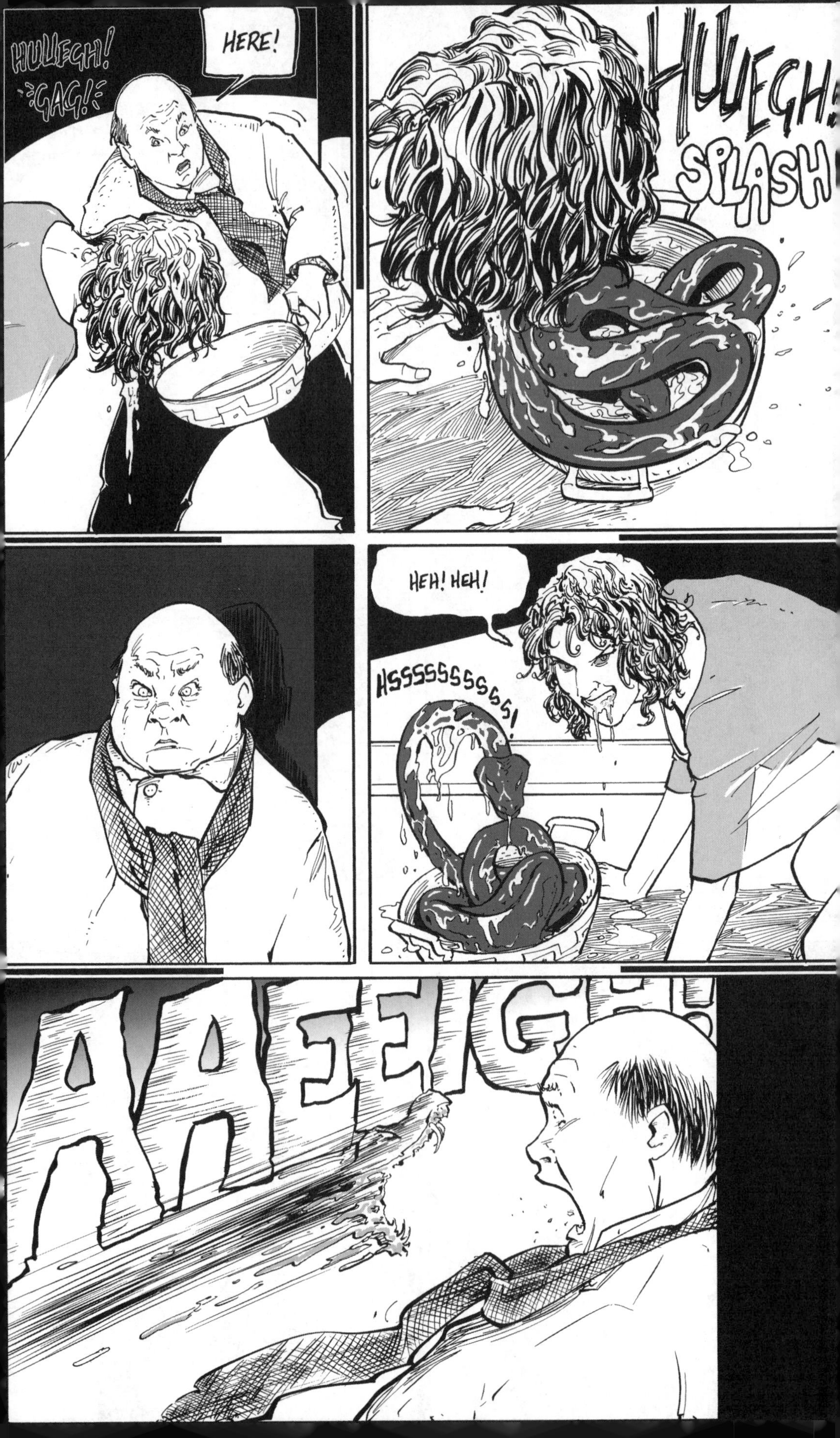

HULLEGH!
GAG!
HERE!
HULLEGH!
SPLASH
HEH! HEH!
HSSSSSSSSSSS!
AAEEIGH!

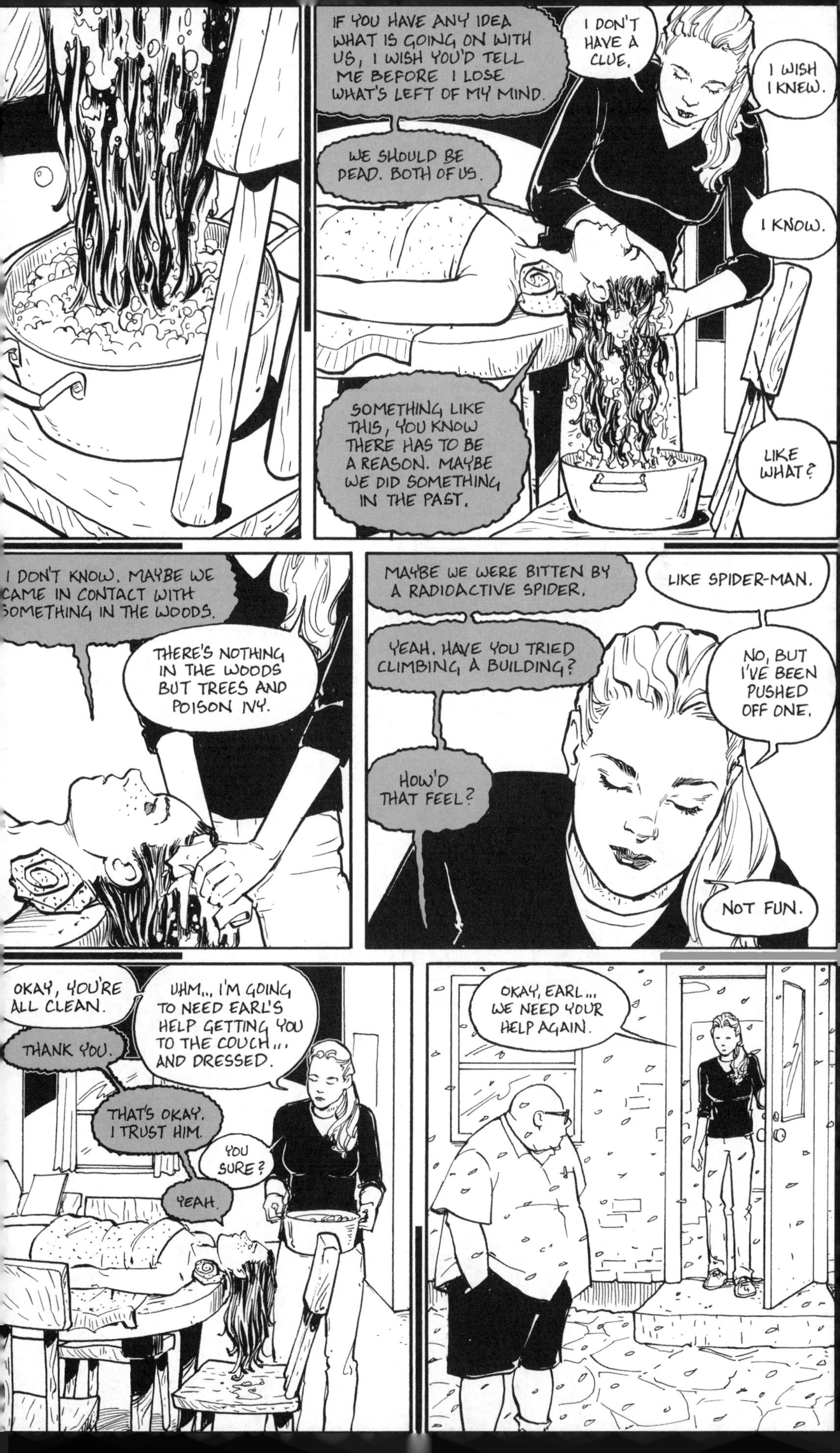
IF YOU HAVE ANY IDEA WHAT IS GOING ON WITH US, I WISH YOU'D TELL ME BEFORE I LOSE WHAT'S LEFT OF MY MIND.
I DON'T HAVE A CLUE.
I WISH I KNEW.
WE SHOULD BE DEAD. BOTH OF US.
I KNOW.
SOMETHING LIKE THIS, YOU KNOW THERE HAS TO BE A REASON. MAYBE WE DID SOMETHING IN THE PAST.
LIKE WHAT?
I DON'T KNOW. MAYBE WE CAME IN CONTACT WITH SOMETHING IN THE WOODS.
THERE'S NOTHING IN THE WOODS BUT TREES AND POISON IVY.
MAYBE WE WERE BITTEN BY A RADIOACTIVE SPIDER.
LIKE SPIDER-MAN.
YEAH. HAVE YOU TRIED CLIMBING A BUILDING?
NO, BUT I'VE BEEN PUSHED OFF ONE.
HOW'D THAT FEEL?
NOT FUN.
OKAY, YOU'RE ALL CLEAN.
UHM... I'M GOING TO NEED EARL'S HELP GETTING YOU TO THE COUCH... AND DRESSED.
THANK YOU.
THAT'S OKAY. I TRUST HIM.
YOU SURE?
YEAH.
OKAY, EARL... WE NEED YOUR HELP AGAIN.

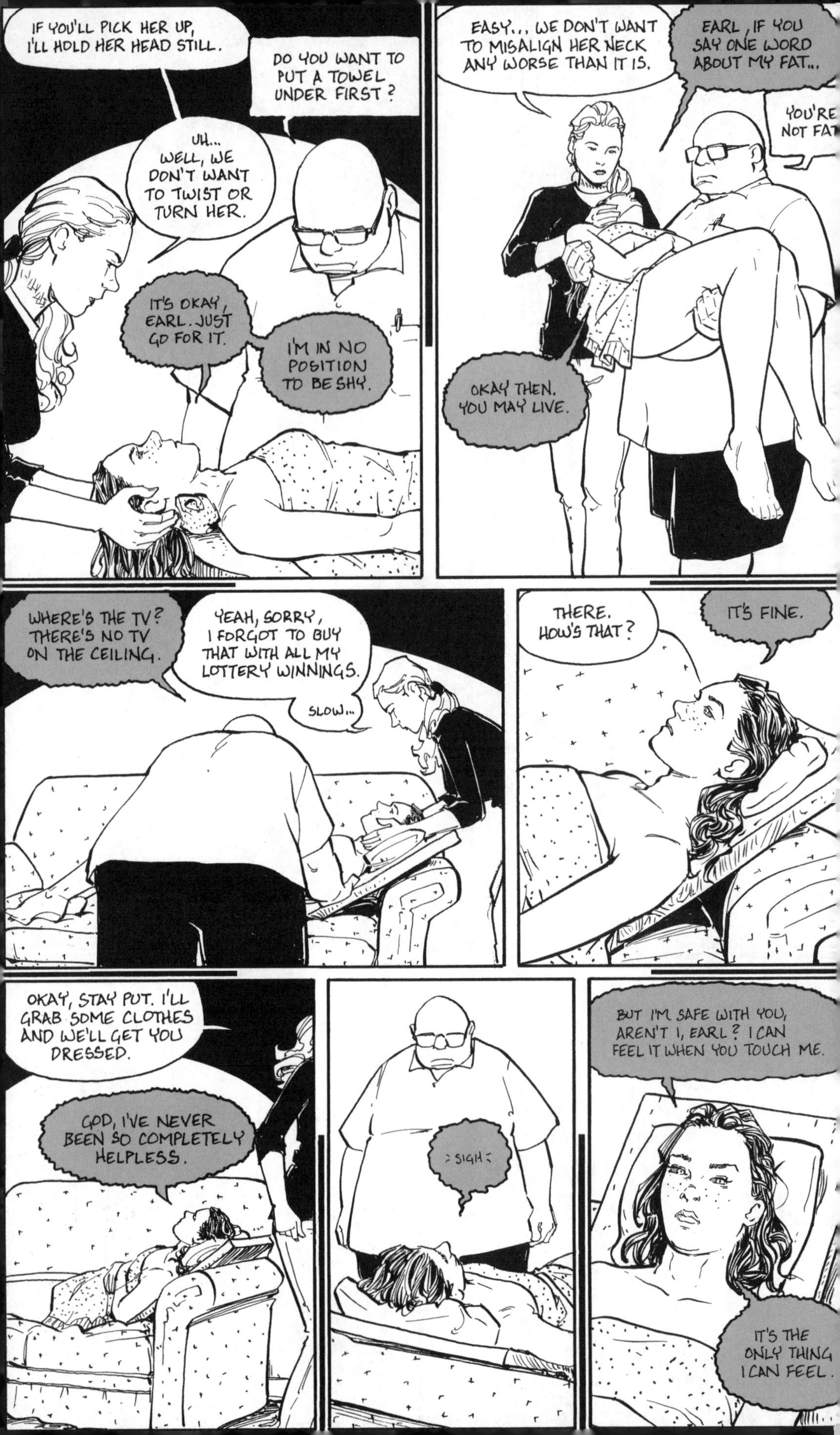
IF YOU'LL PICK HER UP, I'LL HOLD HER HEAD STILL.
DO YOU WANT TO PUT A TOWEL UNDER FIRST?
UH... WELL, WE DON'T WANT TO TWIST OR TURN HER.
IT'S OKAY, EARL. JUST GO FOR IT.
I'M IN NO POSITION TO BE SHY.
EASY... WE DON'T WANT TO MISALIGN HER NECK ANY WORSE THAN IT IS.
EARL, IF YOU SAY ONE WORD ABOUT MY FAT...
YOU'RE NOT FAT
OKAY THEN. YOU MAY LIVE.
WHERE'S THE TV? THERE'S NO TV ON THE CEILING.
YEAH, SORRY, I FORGOT TO BUY THAT WITH ALL MY LOTTERY WINNINGS.
SLOW...
THERE. HOW'S THAT?
IT'S FINE.
OKAY, STAY PUT. I'LL GRAB SOME CLOTHES AND WE'LL GET YOU DRESSED.
GOD, I'VE NEVER BEEN SO COMPLETELY HELPLESS.
SIGH
BUT I'M SAFE WITH YOU, AREN'T I, EARL? I CAN FEEL IT WHEN YOU TOUCH ME.
IT'S THE ONLY THING I CAN FEEL.

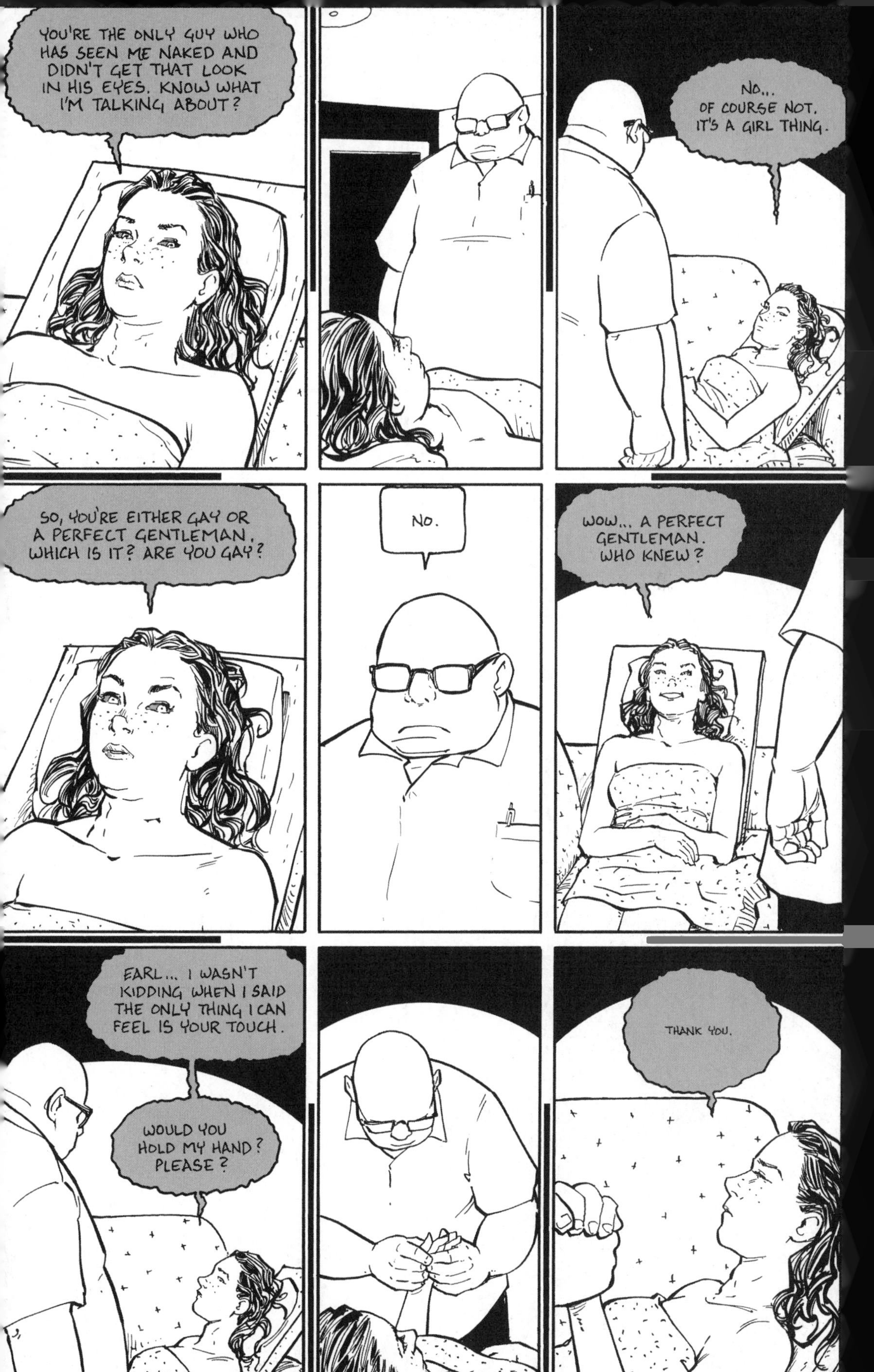
YOU'RE THE ONLY GUY WHO HAS SEEN ME NAKED AND DIDN'T GET THAT LOOK IN HIS EYES. KNOW WHAT I'M TALKING ABOUT?
NO... OF COURSE NOT. IT'S A GIRL THING.
SO, YOU'RE EITHER GAY OR A PERFECT GENTLEMAN. WHICH IS IT? ARE YOU GAY?
NO.
WOW... A PERFECT GENTLEMAN. WHO KNEW?
EARL... I WASN'T KIDDING WHEN I SAID THE ONLY THING I CAN FEEL IS YOUR TOUCH.
WOULD YOU HOLD MY HAND? PLEASE?
THANK YOU.

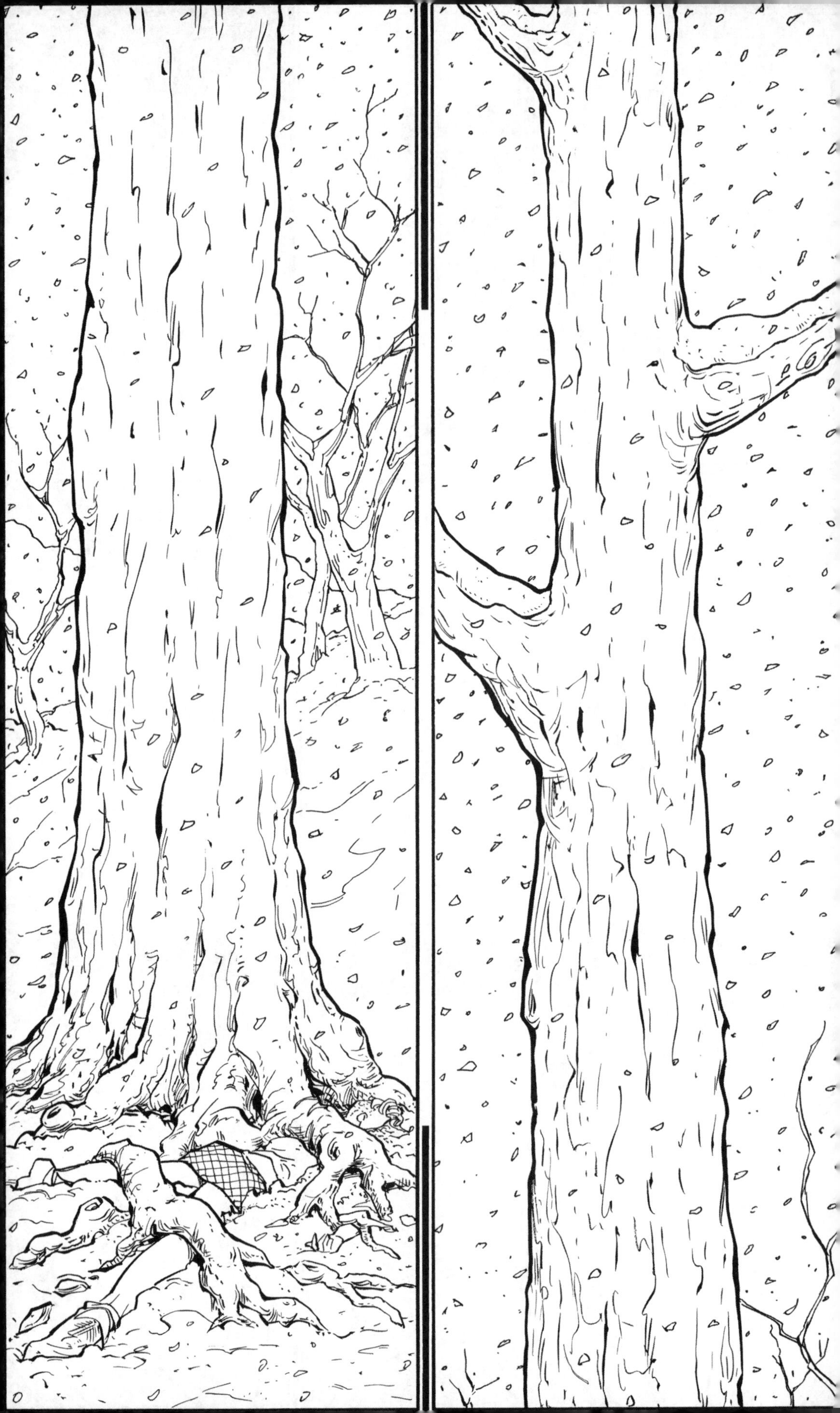

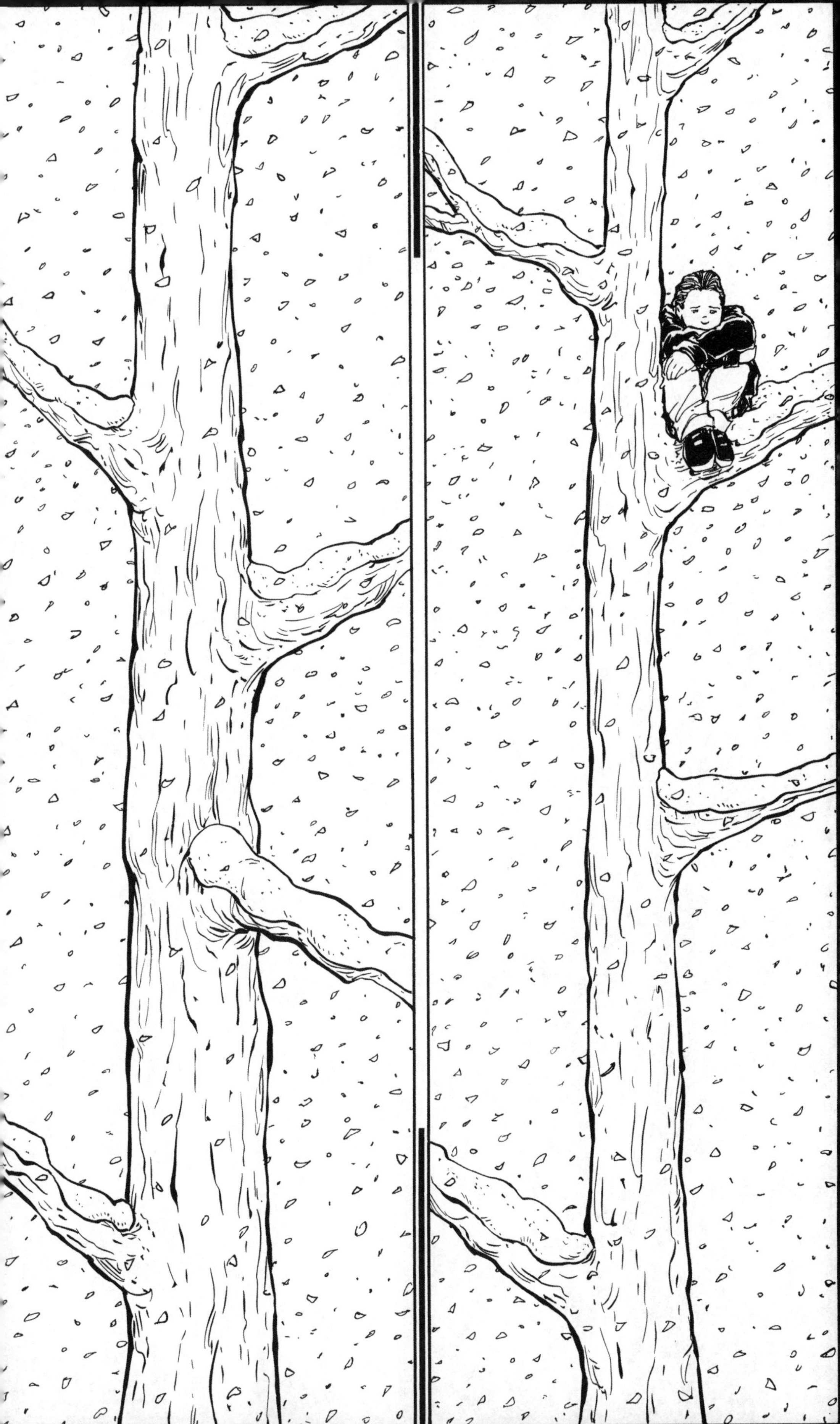

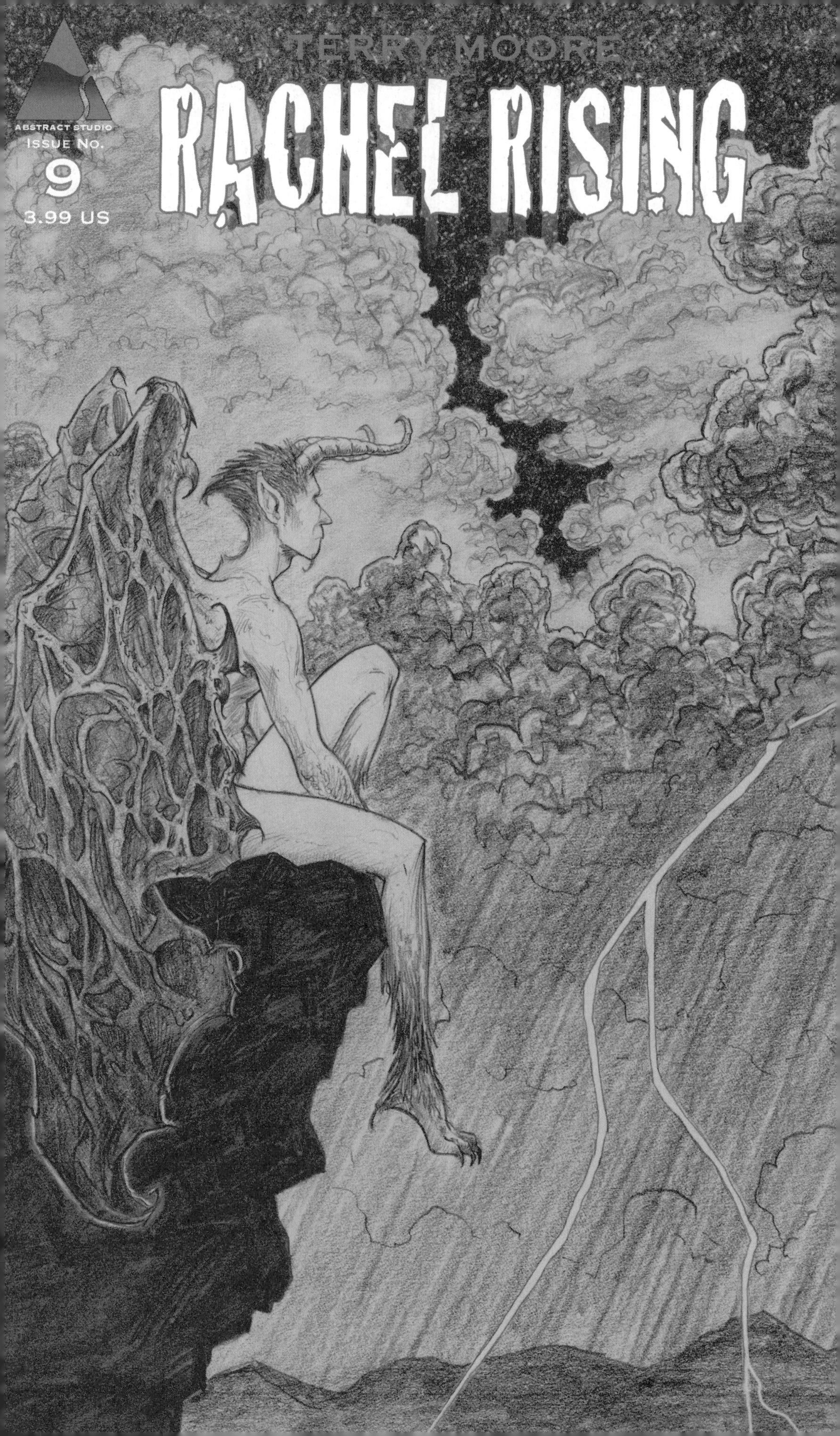

TERRY MOORE
RACHEL RISING
ABSTRACT STUDIO
ISSUE NO.
9
3.99 US

"HELL IS EMPTY AND
ALL THE DEVILS ARE HERE."

—WILLIAM SHAKESPEARE

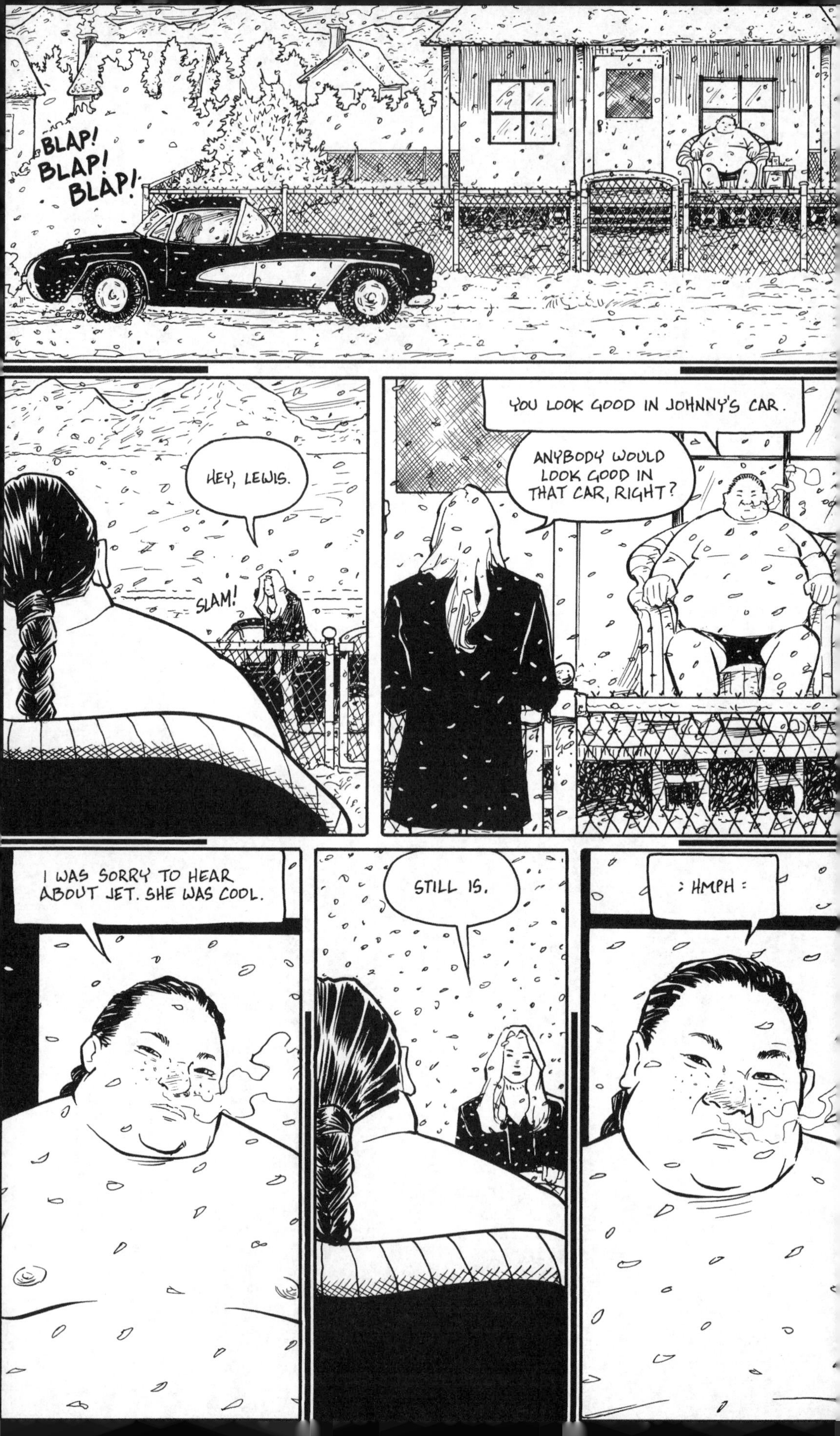
BLAP! BLAP! BLAP!
HEY, LEWIS.
SLAM!
YOU LOOK GOOD IN JOHNNY'S CAR.
ANYBODY WOULD LOOK GOOD IN THAT CAR, RIGHT?
I WAS SORRY TO HEAR ABOUT JET. SHE WAS COOL.
STILL IS.
: HMPH :

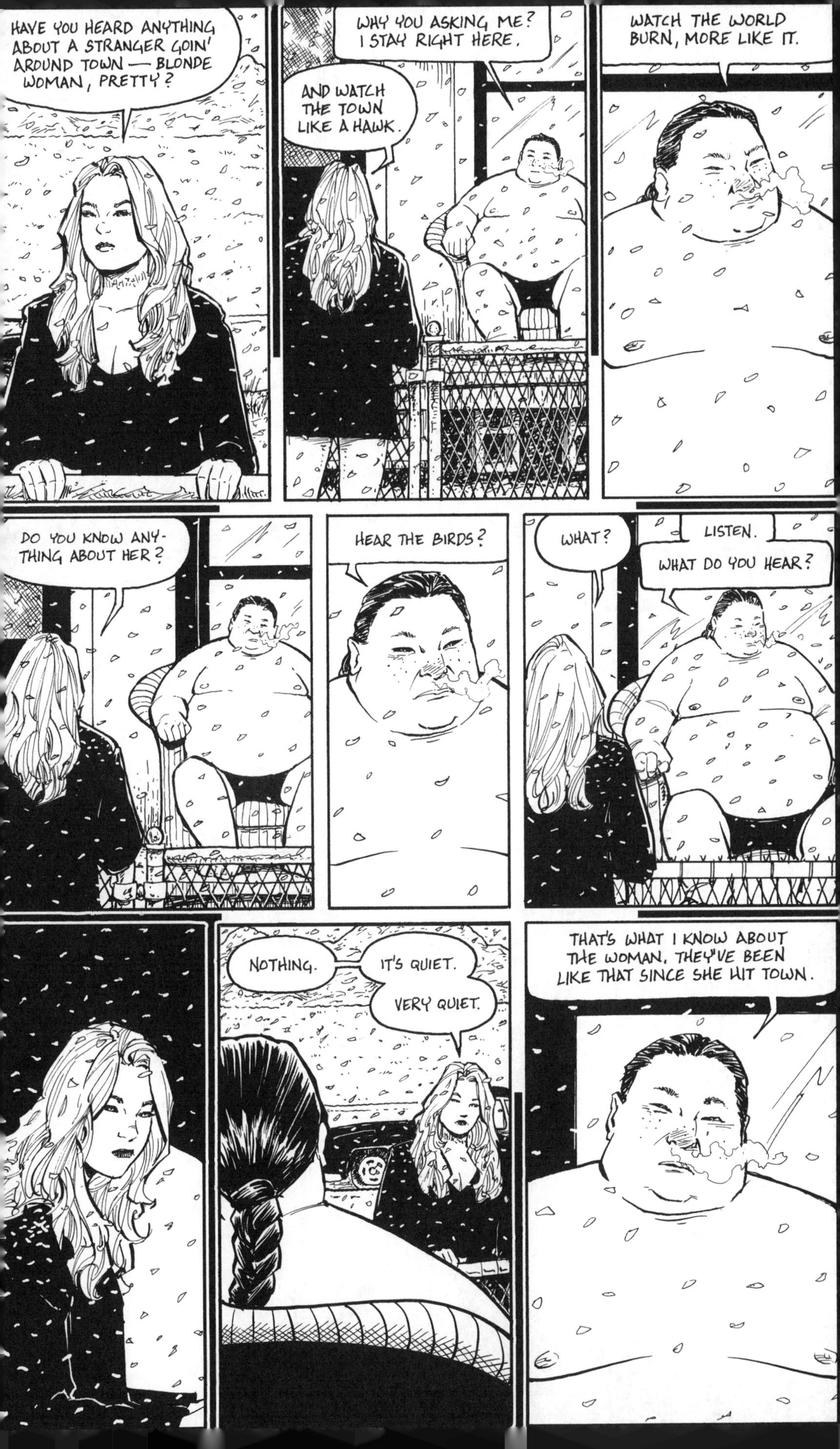
HAVE YOU HEARD ANYTHING ABOUT A STRANGER GOIN' AROUND TOWN — BLONDE WOMAN, PRETTY?
WHY YOU ASKING ME? I STAY RIGHT HERE.
AND WATCH THE TOWN LIKE A HAWK.
WATCH THE WORLD BURN, MORE LIKE IT.
DO YOU KNOW ANYTHING ABOUT HER?
HEAR THE BIRDS?
WHAT?
LISTEN.
WHAT DO YOU HEAR?
NOTHING.
IT'S QUIET.
VERY QUIET.
THAT'S WHAT I KNOW ABOUT THE WOMAN. THEY'VE BEEN LIKE THAT SINCE SHE HIT TOWN.

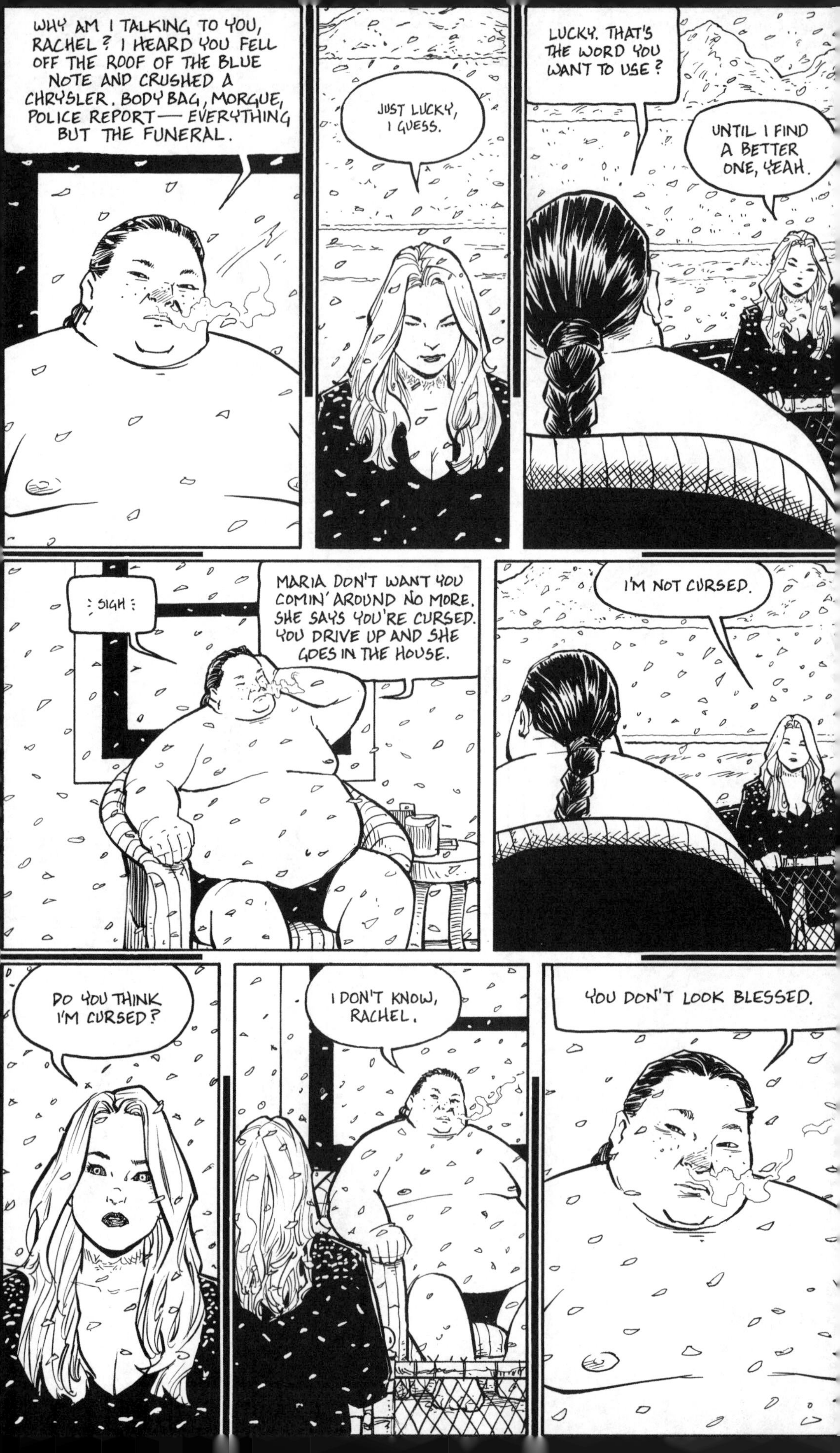
WHY AM I TALKING TO YOU, RACHEL? I HEARD YOU FELL OFF THE ROOF OF THE BLUE NOTE AND CRUSHED A CHRYSLER. BODY BAG, MORGUE, POLICE REPORT— EVERYTHING BUT THE FUNERAL.
JUST LUCKY, I GUESS.
LUCKY. THAT'S THE WORD YOU WANT TO USE?
UNTIL I FIND A BETTER ONE, YEAH.
:SIGH:
MARIA DON'T WANT YOU COMIN' AROUND NO MORE. SHE SAYS YOU'RE CURSED. YOU DRIVE UP AND SHE GOES IN THE HOUSE.
I'M NOT CURSED.
DO YOU THINK I'M CURSED?
I DON'T KNOW, RACHEL.
YOU DON'T LOOK BLESSED.

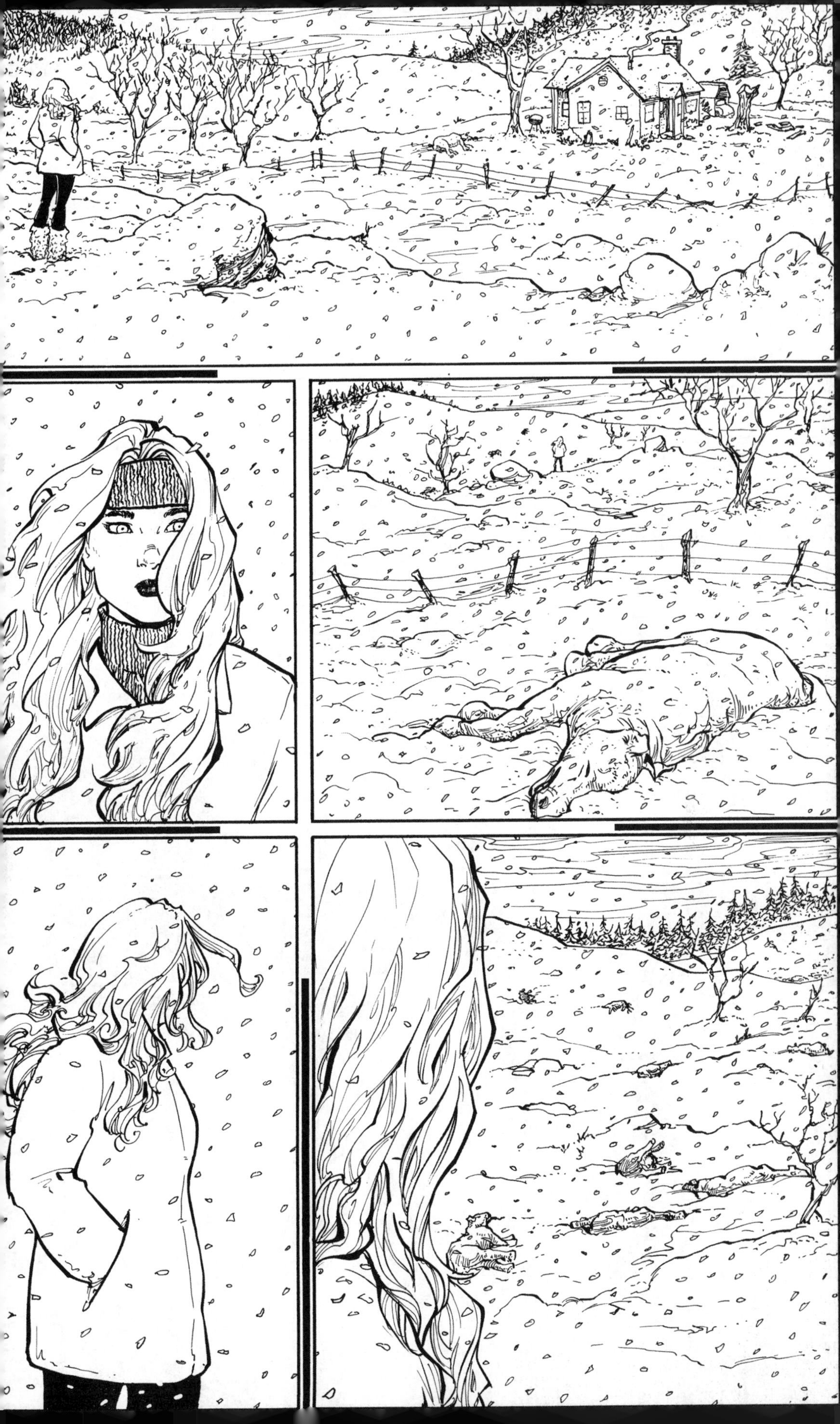

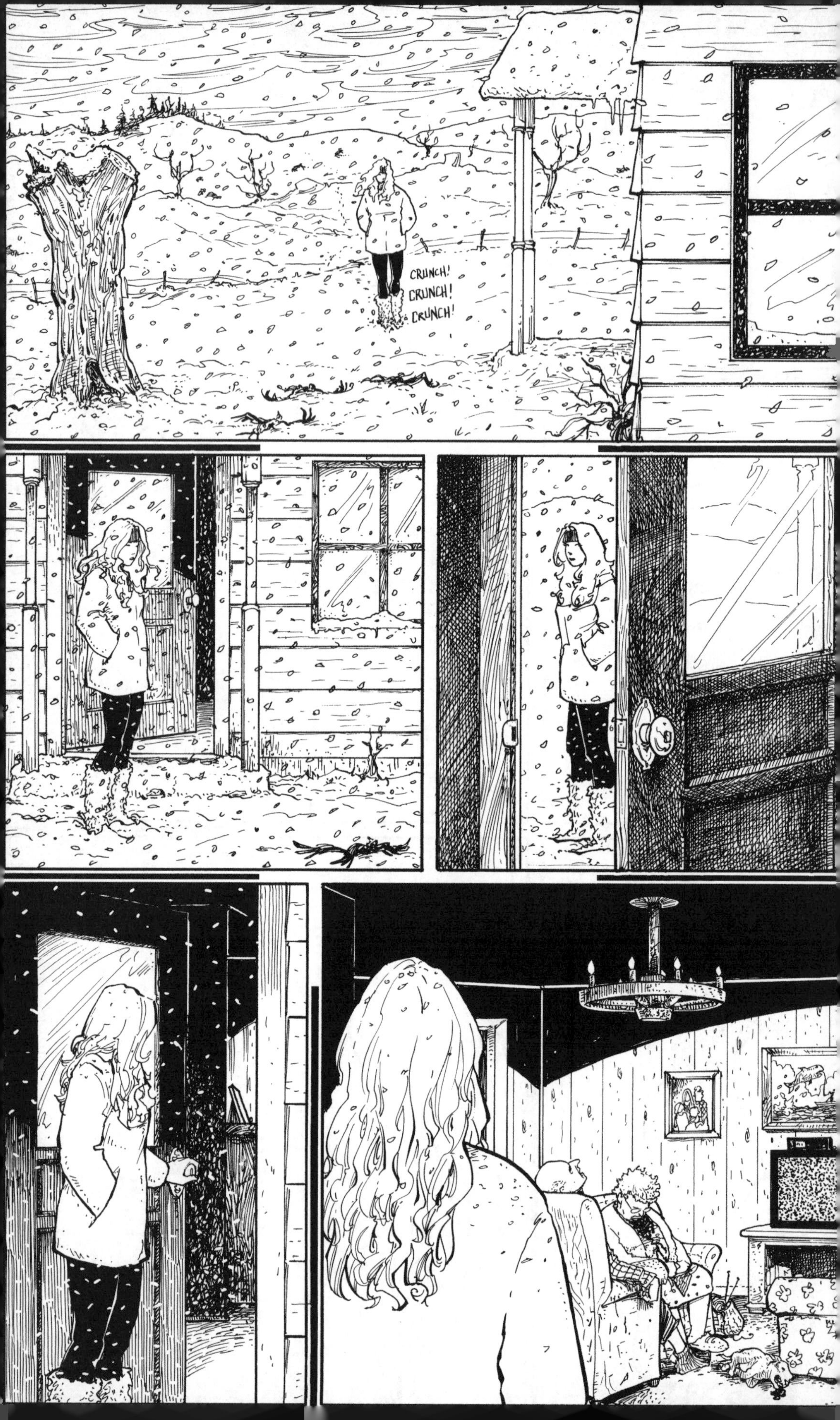
CRUNCH!
CRUNCH!
CRUNCH!

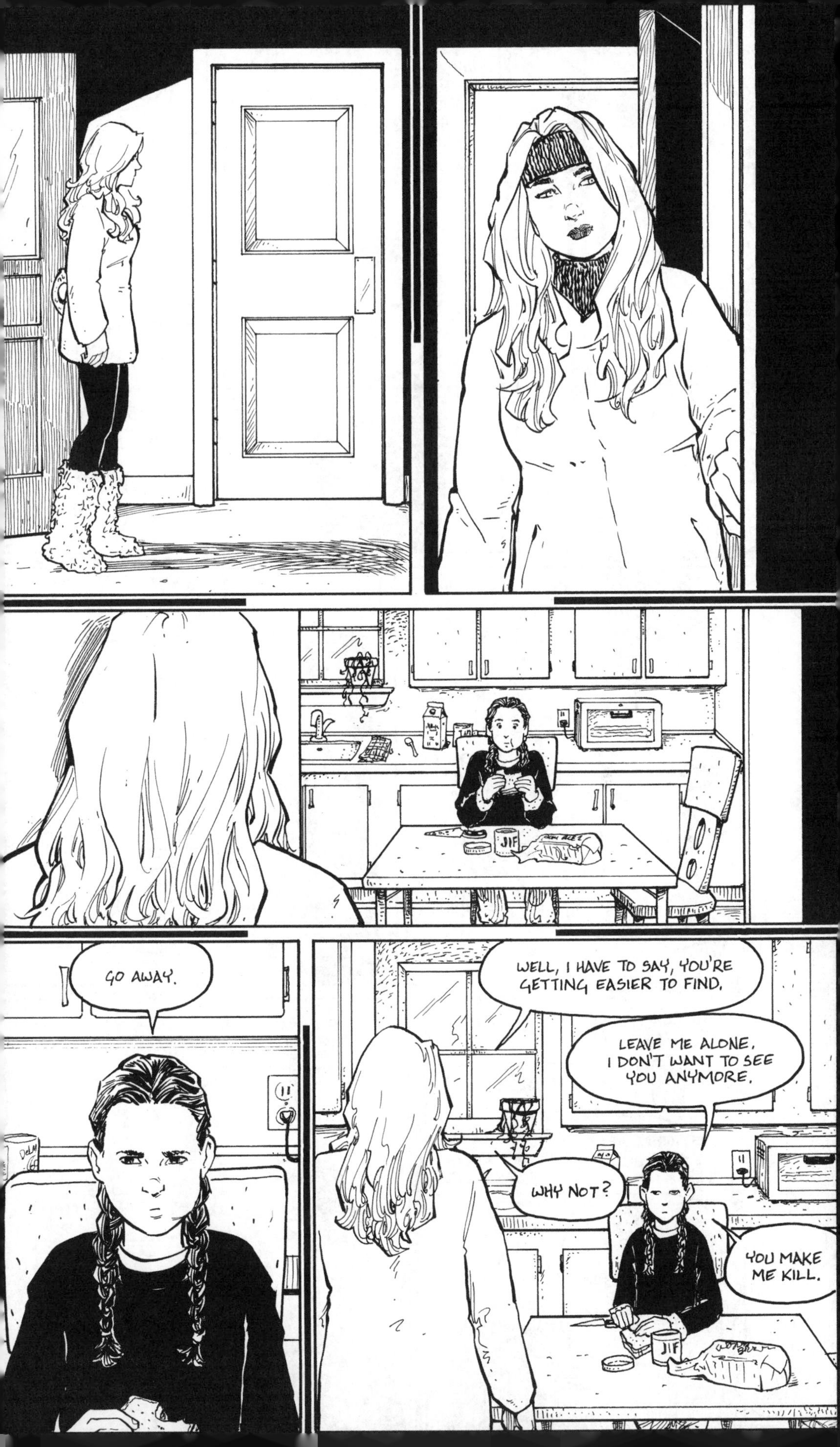
GO AWAY.
WELL, I HAVE TO SAY, YOU'RE GETTING EASIER TO FIND.
LEAVE ME ALONE. I DON'T WANT TO SEE YOU ANYMORE.
WHY NOT?
YOU MAKE ME KILL.
JIF

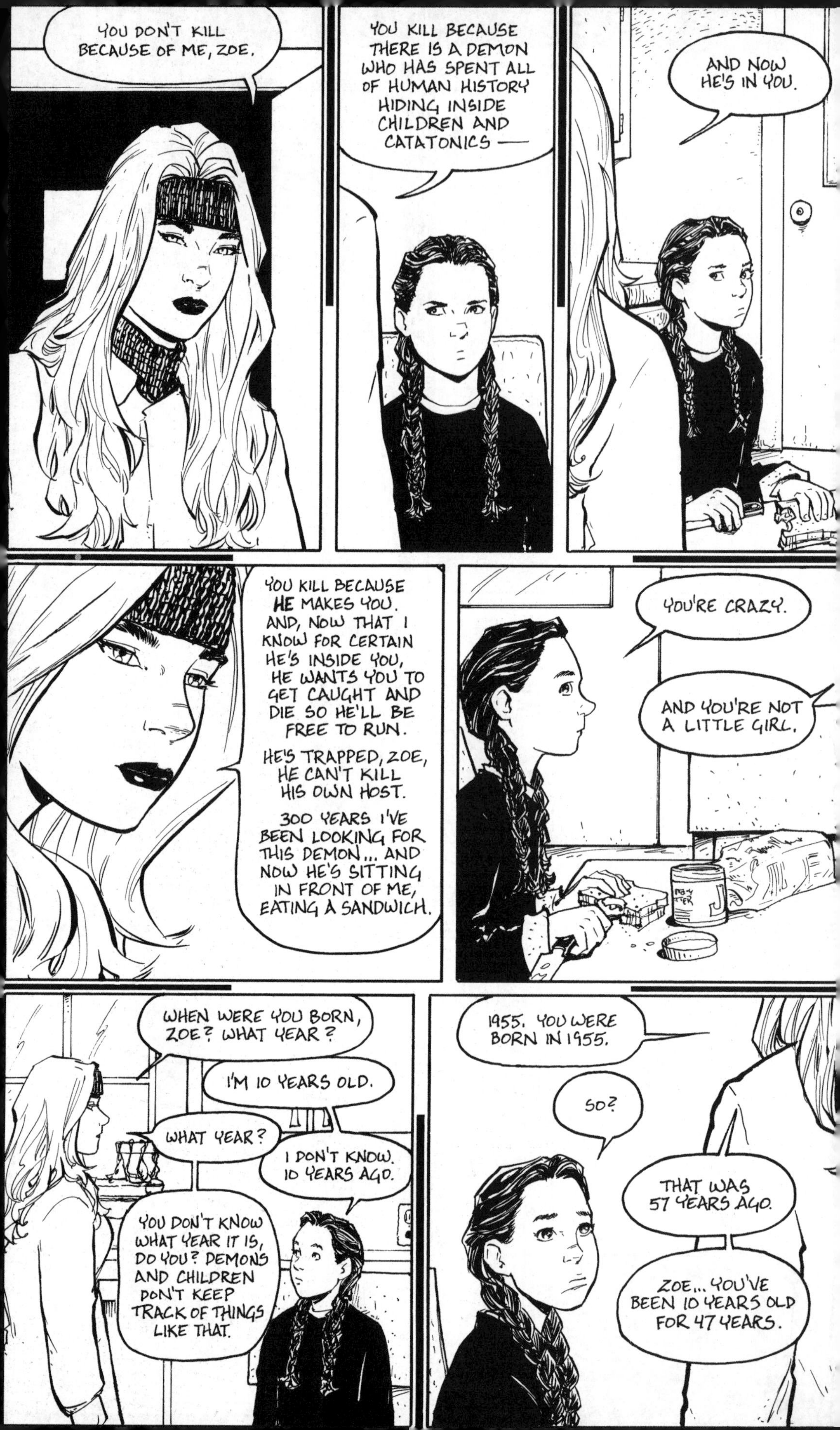
YOU DON'T KILL BECAUSE OF ME, ZOE.
YOU KILL BECAUSE THERE IS A DEMON WHO HAS SPENT ALL OF HUMAN HISTORY HIDING INSIDE CHILDREN AND CATATONICS —
AND NOW HE'S IN YOU.
YOU KILL BECAUSE **HE** MAKES YOU. AND, NOW THAT I KNOW FOR CERTAIN HE'S INSIDE YOU, HE WANTS YOU TO GET CAUGHT AND DIE SO HE'LL BE FREE TO RUN.
HE'S TRAPPED, ZOE, HE CAN'T KILL HIS OWN HOST.
300 YEARS I'VE BEEN LOOKING FOR THIS DEMON... AND NOW HE'S SITTING IN FRONT OF ME, EATING A SANDWICH.
YOU'RE CRAZY.
AND YOU'RE NOT A LITTLE GIRL.
WHEN WERE YOU BORN, ZOE? WHAT YEAR?
I'M 10 YEARS OLD.
WHAT YEAR?
I DON'T KNOW. 10 YEARS AGO.
YOU DON'T KNOW WHAT YEAR IT IS, DO YOU? DEMONS AND CHILDREN DON'T KEEP TRACK OF THINGS LIKE THAT.
1955. YOU WERE BORN IN 1955.
SO?
THAT WAS 57 YEARS AGO.
ZOE... YOU'VE BEEN 10 YEARS OLD FOR 47 YEARS.

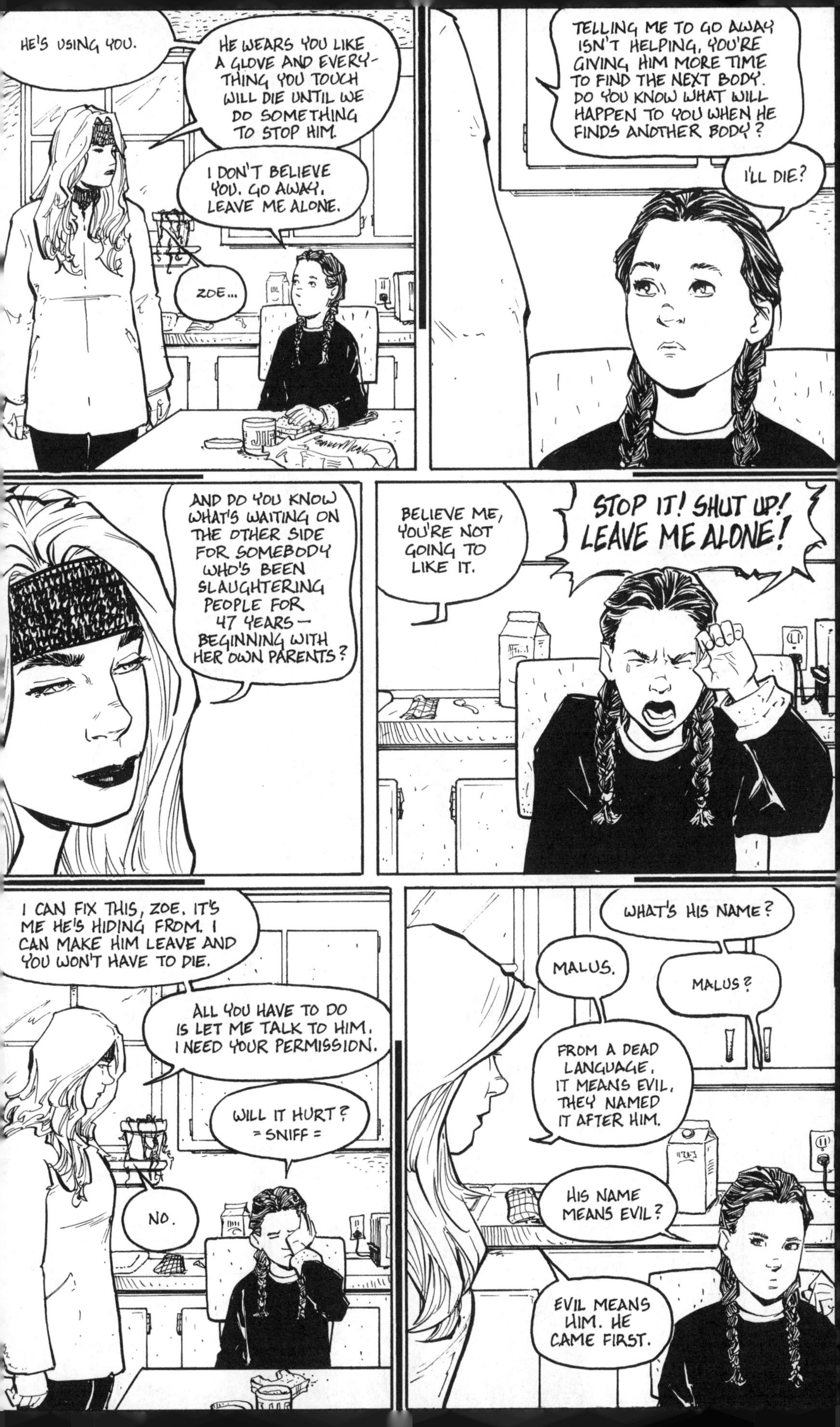
HE'S USING YOU.
HE WEARS YOU LIKE A GLOVE AND EVERY-THING YOU TOUCH WILL DIE UNTIL WE DO SOMETHING TO STOP HIM.
I DON'T BELIEVE YOU. GO AWAY. LEAVE ME ALONE.
ZOE...
TELLING ME TO GO AWAY ISN'T HELPING. YOU'RE GIVING HIM MORE TIME TO FIND THE NEXT BODY. DO YOU KNOW WHAT WILL HAPPEN TO YOU WHEN HE FINDS ANOTHER BODY?
I'LL DIE?
AND DO YOU KNOW WHAT'S WAITING ON THE OTHER SIDE FOR SOMEBODY WHO'S BEEN SLAUGHTERING PEOPLE FOR 47 YEARS — BEGINNING WITH HER OWN PARENTS?
BELIEVE ME, YOU'RE NOT GOING TO LIKE IT.
STOP IT! SHUT UP! LEAVE ME ALONE!
I CAN FIX THIS, ZOE. IT'S ME HE'S HIDING FROM. I CAN MAKE HIM LEAVE AND YOU WON'T HAVE TO DIE.
ALL YOU HAVE TO DO IS LET ME TALK TO HIM. I NEED YOUR PERMISSION.
WILL IT HURT? =SNIFF=
NO.
WHAT'S HIS NAME?
MALUS.
MALUS?
FROM A DEAD LANGUAGE. IT MEANS EVIL. THEY NAMED IT AFTER HIM.
HIS NAME MEANS EVIL?
EVIL MEANS HIM. HE CAME FIRST.

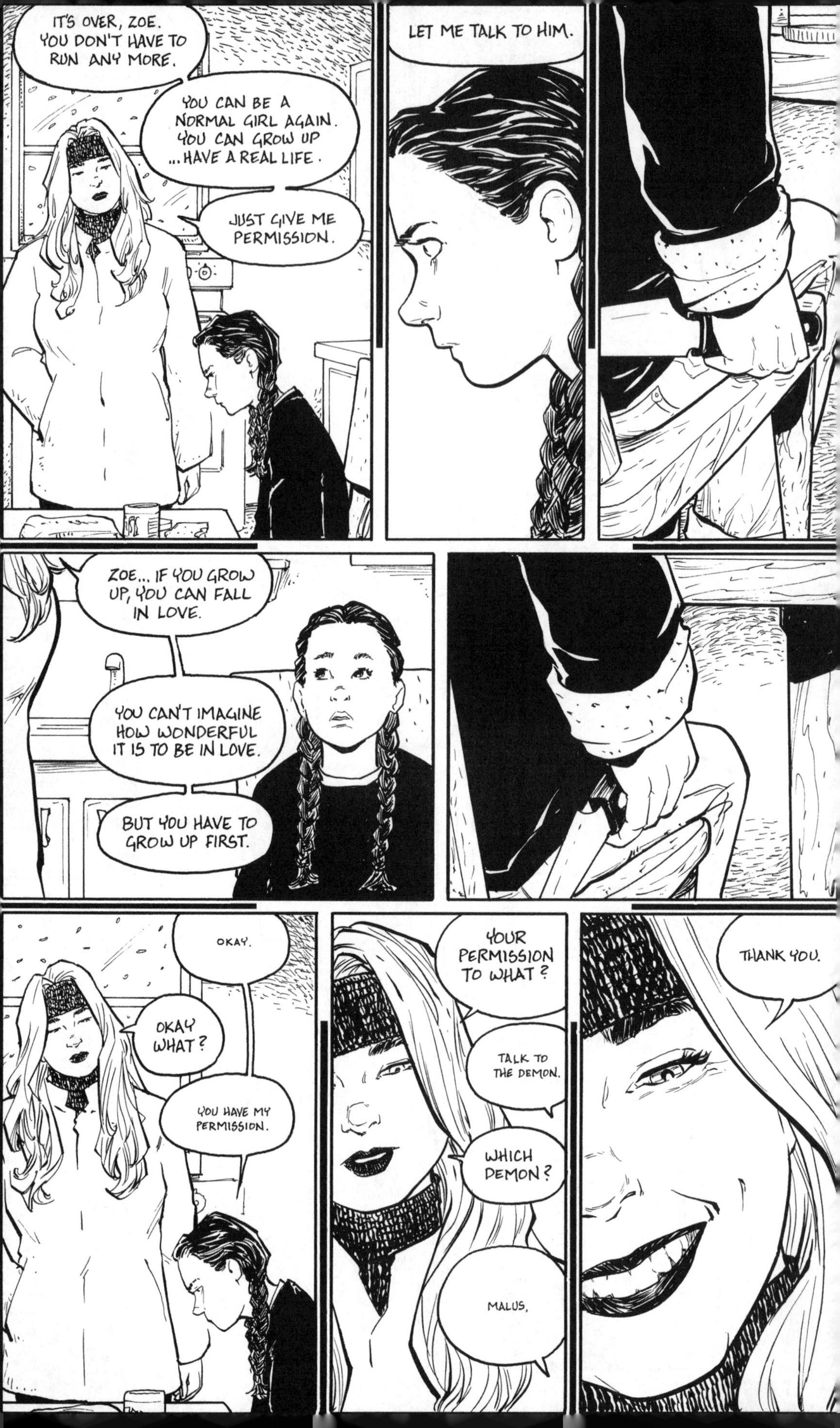
IT'S OVER, ZOE. YOU DON'T HAVE TO RUN ANY MORE.
YOU CAN BE A NORMAL GIRL AGAIN. YOU CAN GROW UP ...HAVE A REAL LIFE.
JUST GIVE ME PERMISSION.
LET ME TALK TO HIM.
ZOE... IF YOU GROW UP, YOU CAN FALL IN LOVE.
YOU CAN'T IMAGINE HOW WONDERFUL IT IS TO BE IN LOVE.
BUT YOU HAVE TO GROW UP FIRST.
OKAY.
OKAY WHAT?
YOU HAVE MY PERMISSION.
YOUR PERMISSION TO WHAT?
TALK TO THE DEMON.
WHICH DEMON?
MALUS,
THANK YOU.

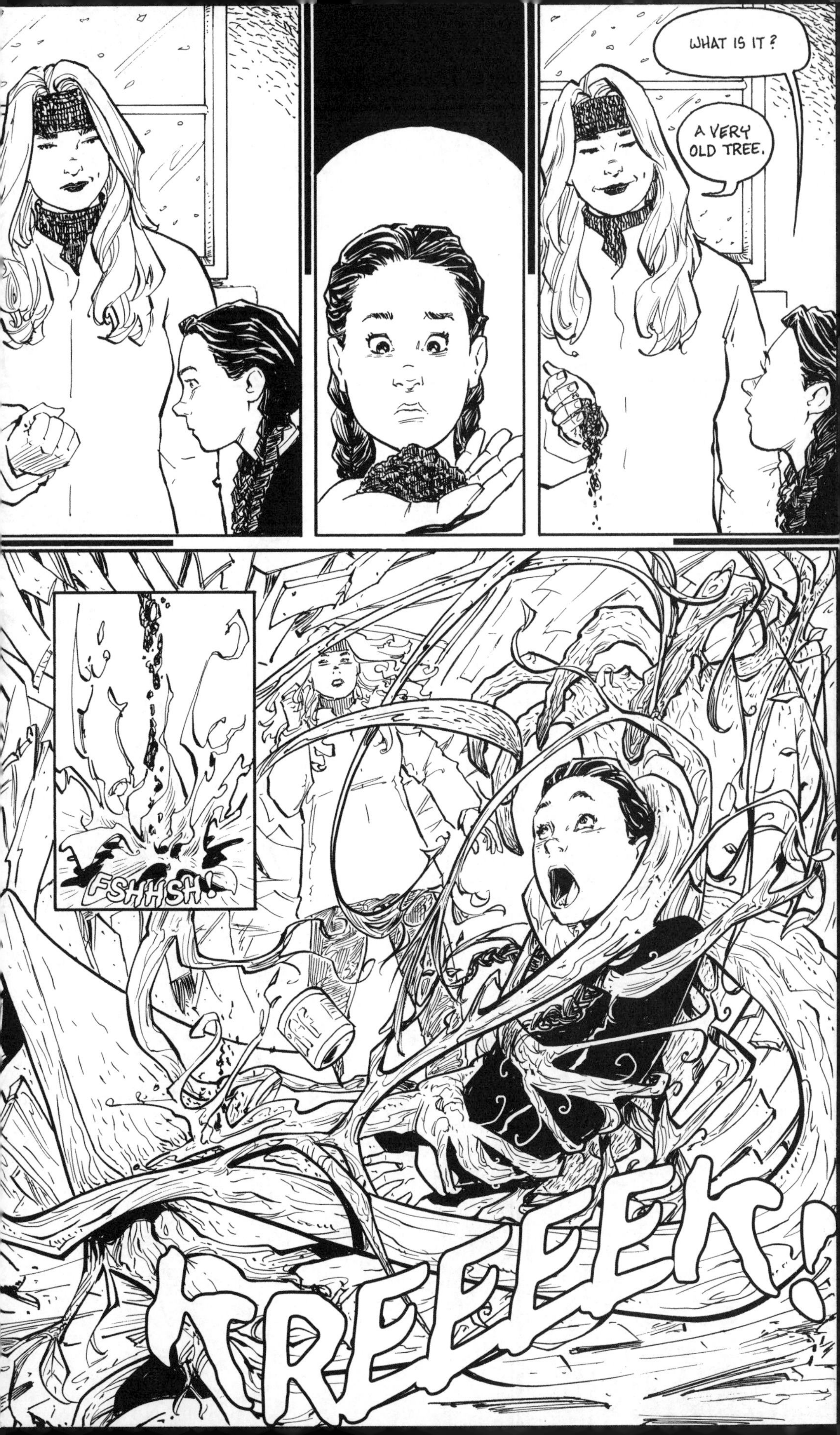
WHAT IS IT?
A VERY OLD TREE.
FSHHSH!
KREEEK!

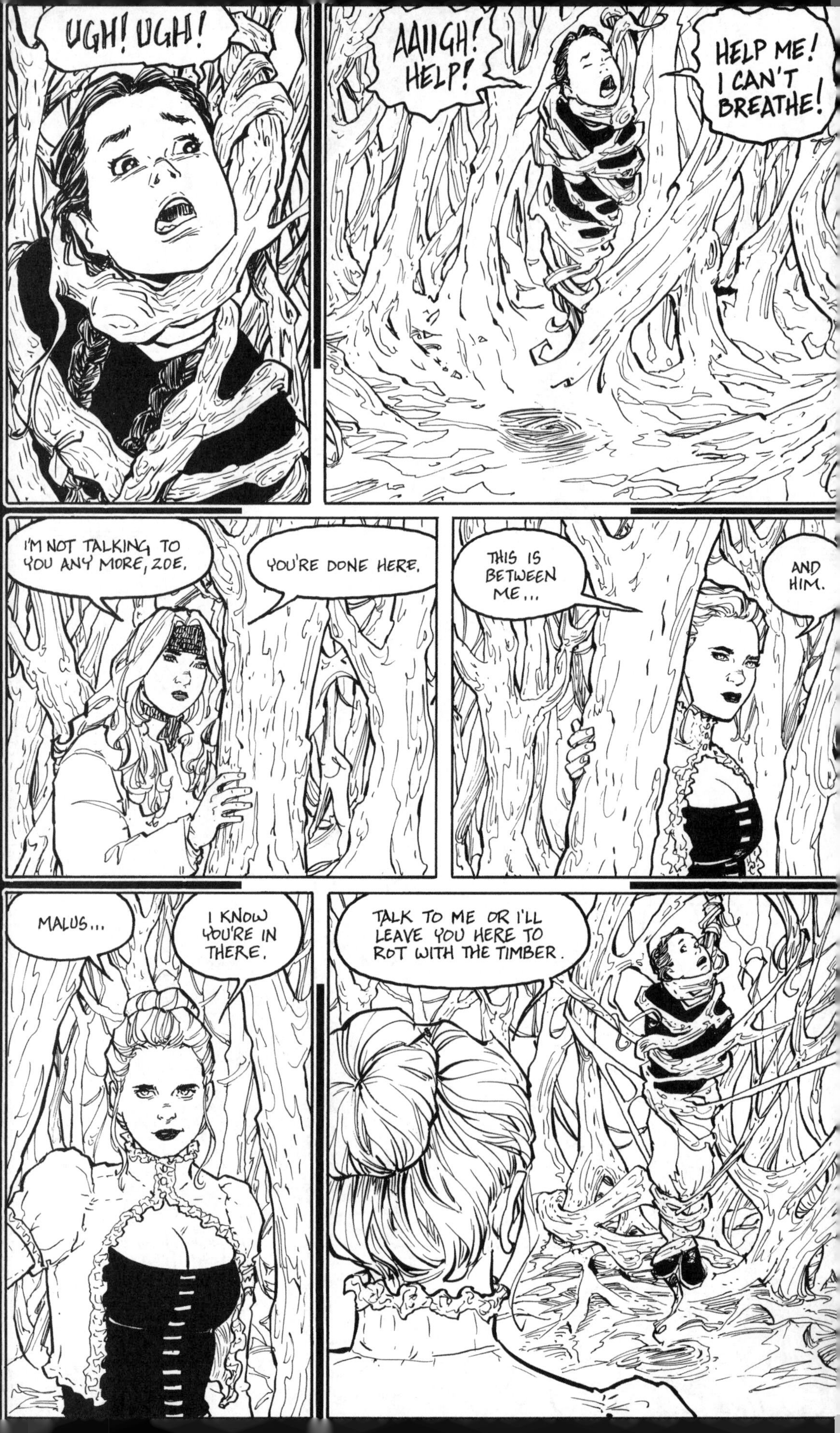
UGH! UGH!
AAIIGH! HELP!
HELP ME! I CAN'T BREATHE!
I'M NOT TALKING TO YOU ANY MORE, ZOE.
YOU'RE DONE HERE.
THIS IS BETWEEN ME...
AND HIM.
MALUS...
I KNOW YOU'RE IN THERE.
TALK TO ME OR I'LL LEAVE YOU HERE TO ROT WITH THE TIMBER.

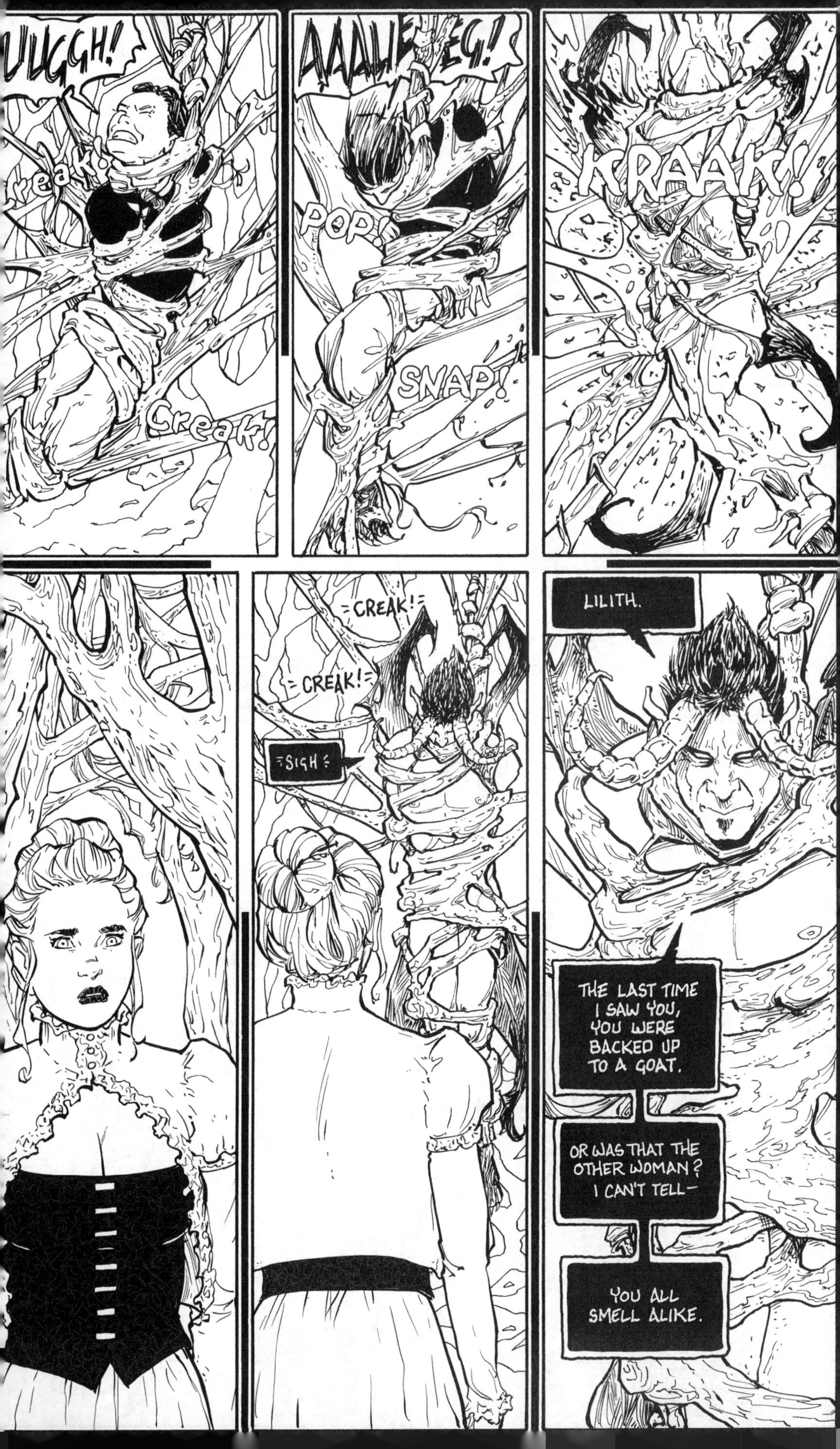
UUGGH!
Creak!
Creak!
AAALIEEEG!
POP!
SNAP!
KRAAK!
=CREAK!=
=CREAK!=
=SIGH=
LILITH.
THE LAST TIME I SAW YOU, YOU WERE BACKED UP TO A GOAT.
OR WAS THAT THE OTHER WOMAN? I CAN'T TELL—
YOU ALL SMELL ALIKE.

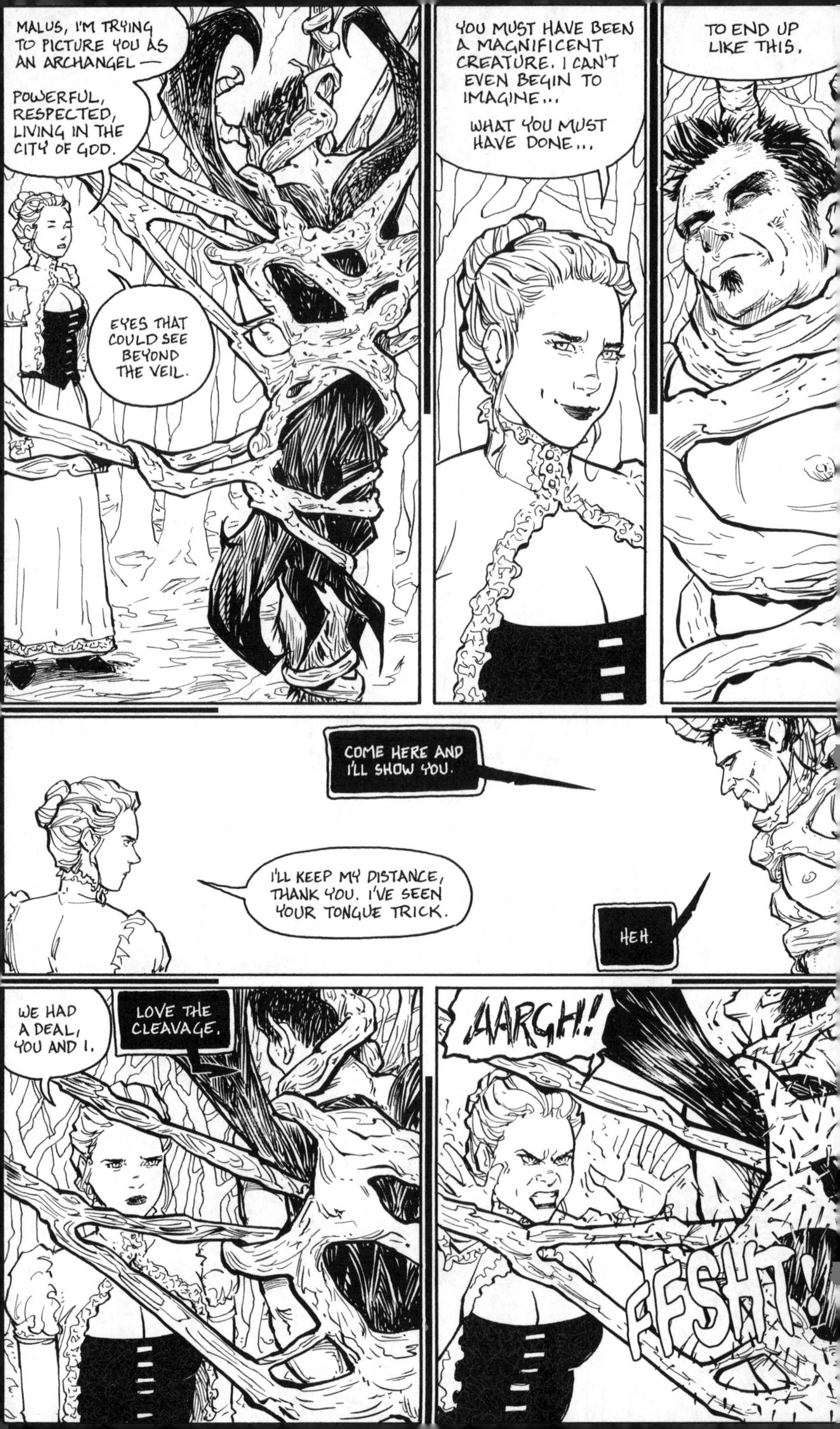
MALUS, I'M TRYING TO PICTURE YOU AS AN ARCHANGEL—
POWERFUL, RESPECTED, LIVING IN THE CITY OF GOD.
EYES THAT COULD SEE BEYOND THE VEIL.
YOU MUST HAVE BEEN A MAGNIFICENT CREATURE. I CAN'T EVEN BEGIN TO IMAGINE...
WHAT YOU MUST HAVE DONE...
TO END UP LIKE THIS.
COME HERE AND I'LL SHOW YOU.
I'LL KEEP MY DISTANCE, THANK YOU. I'VE SEEN YOUR TONGUE TRICK.
HEH.
WE HAD A DEAL, YOU AND I.
LOVE THE CLEAVAGE.
AARGH!
FFSHT!

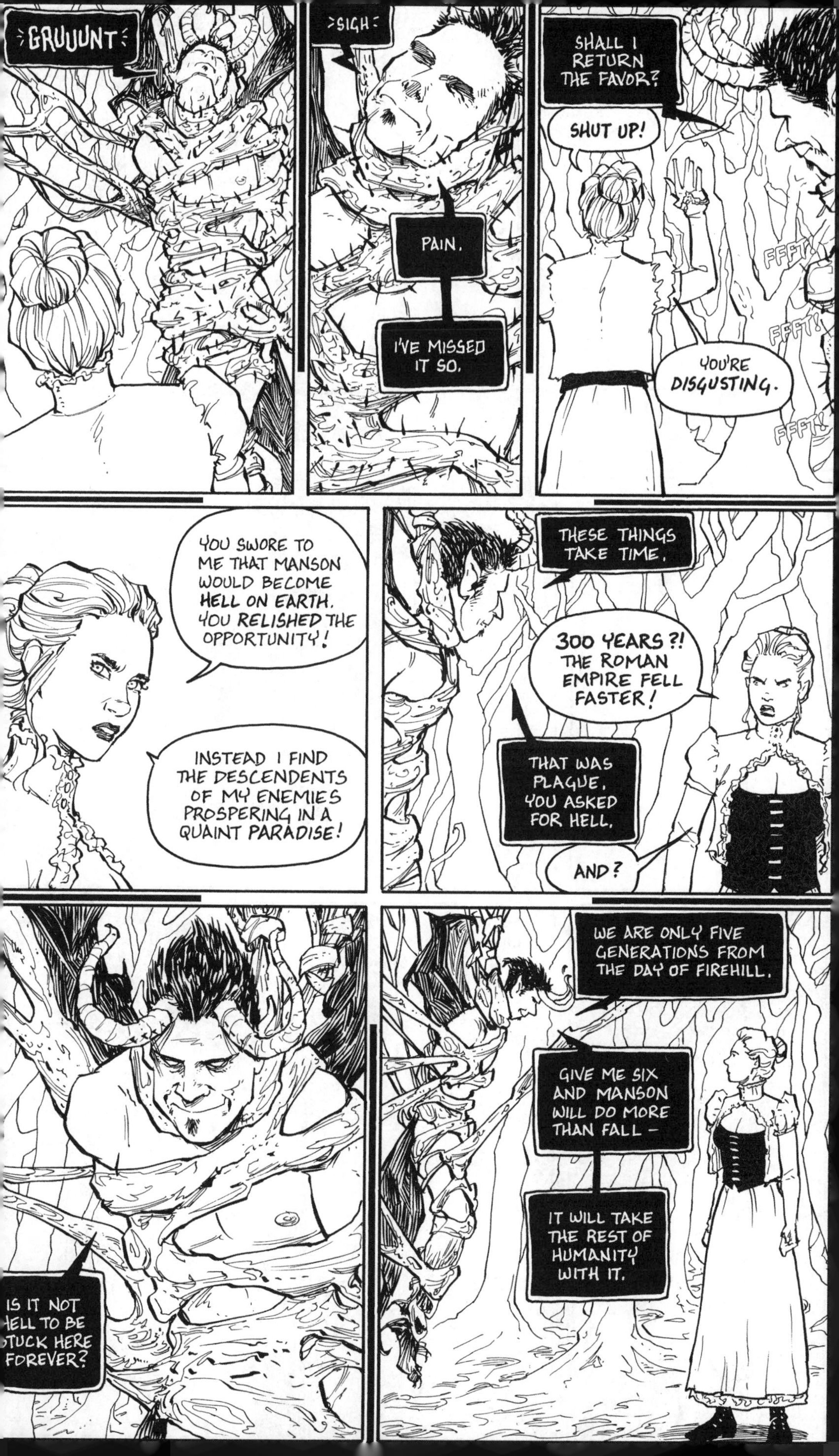
GRUUUNT
SIGH
PAIN.
I'VE MISSED IT SO.
SHALL I RETURN THE FAVOR?
SHUT UP!
FFFT!
FFFT!
YOU'RE DISGUSTING.
FFFT!
YOU SWORE TO ME THAT MANSON WOULD BECOME HELL ON EARTH. YOU RELISHED THE OPPORTUNITY!
INSTEAD I FIND THE DESCENDENTS OF MY ENEMIES PROSPERING IN A QUAINT PARADISE!
THESE THINGS TAKE TIME.
300 YEARS?! THE ROMAN EMPIRE FELL FASTER!
THAT WAS PLAGUE. YOU ASKED FOR HELL.
AND?
IS IT NOT HELL TO BE STUCK HERE FOREVER?
WE ARE ONLY FIVE GENERATIONS FROM THE DAY OF FIREHILL.
GIVE ME SIX AND MANSON WILL DO MORE THAN FALL –
IT WILL TAKE THE REST OF HUMANITY WITH IT.

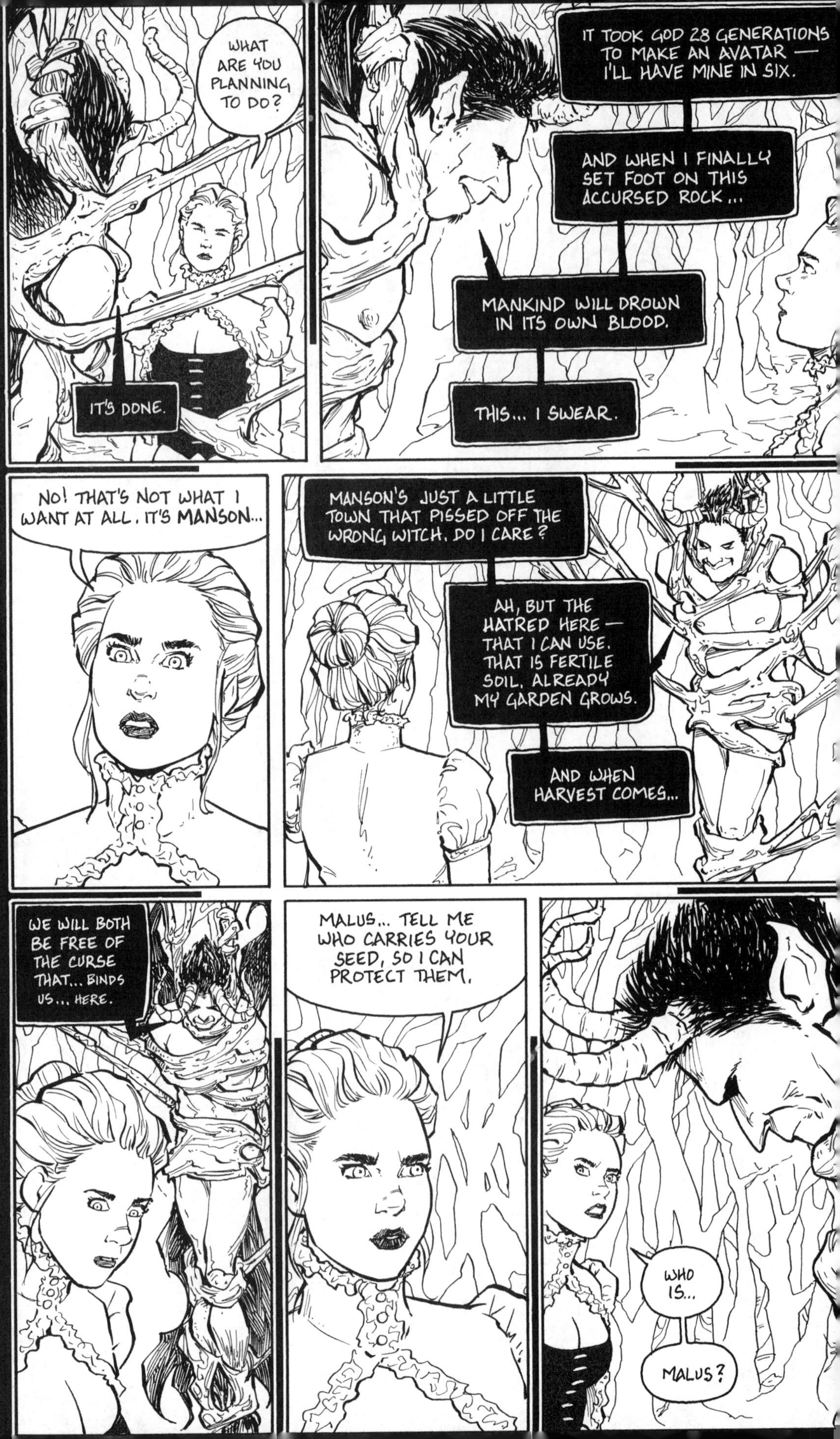
WHAT ARE YOU PLANNING TO DO?
IT'S DONE.
IT TOOK GOD 28 GENERATIONS TO MAKE AN AVATAR — I'LL HAVE MINE IN SIX.
AND WHEN I FINALLY SET FOOT ON THIS ACCURSED ROCK...
MANKIND WILL DROWN IN ITS OWN BLOOD.
THIS... I SWEAR.
NO! THAT'S NOT WHAT I WANT AT ALL. IT'S MANSON...
MANSON'S JUST A LITTLE TOWN THAT PISSED OFF THE WRONG WITCH. DO I CARE?
AH, BUT THE HATRED HERE — THAT I CAN USE. THAT IS FERTILE SOIL. ALREADY MY GARDEN GROWS.
AND WHEN HARVEST COMES...
WE WILL BOTH BE FREE OF THE CURSE THAT... BINDS US... HERE.
MALUS... TELL ME WHO CARRIES YOUR SEED, SO I CAN PROTECT THEM.
WHO IS...
MALUS?

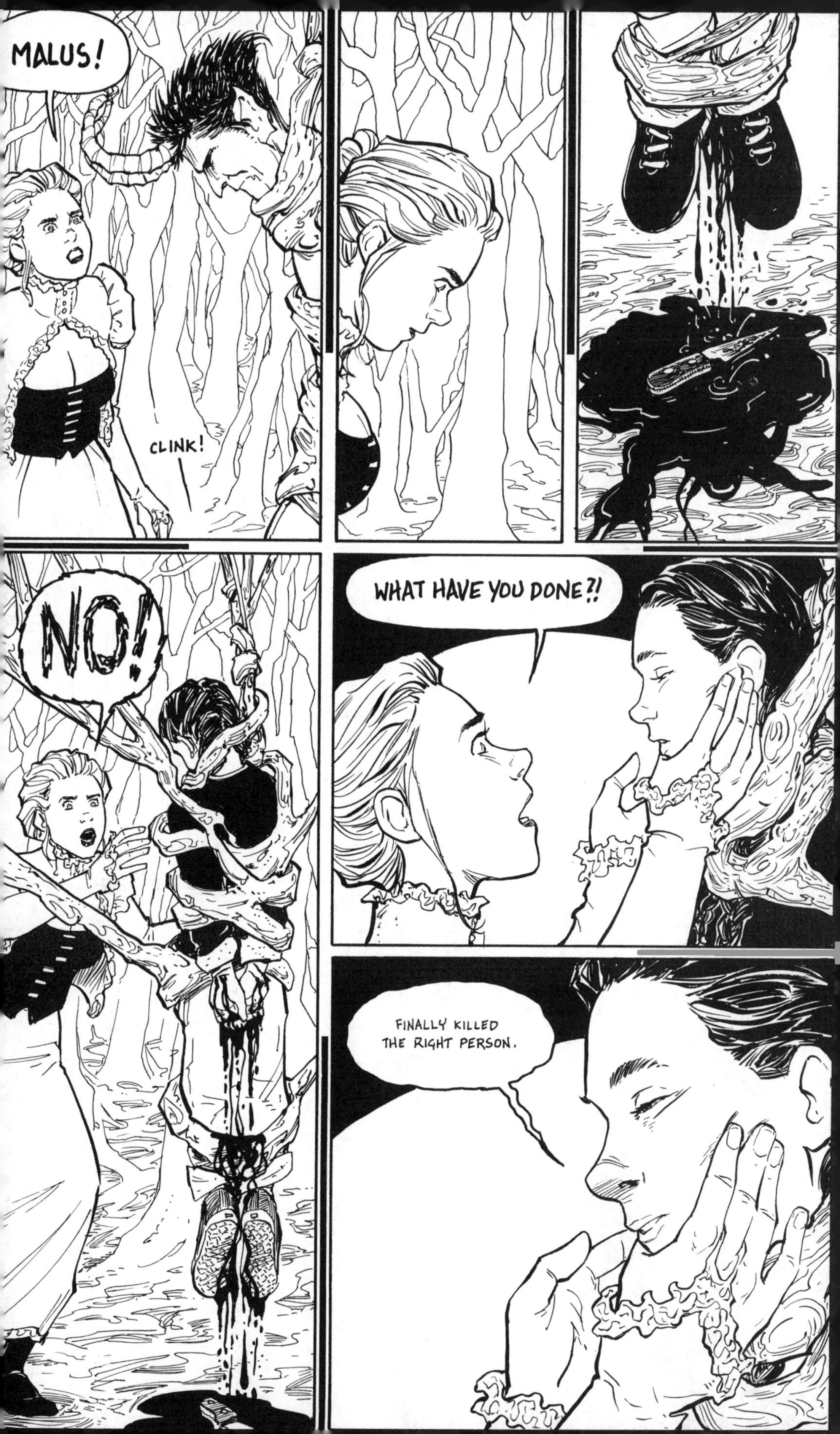
MALUS!
CLINK!
NO!
WHAT HAVE YOU DONE?!
FINALLY KILLED
THE RIGHT PERSON.

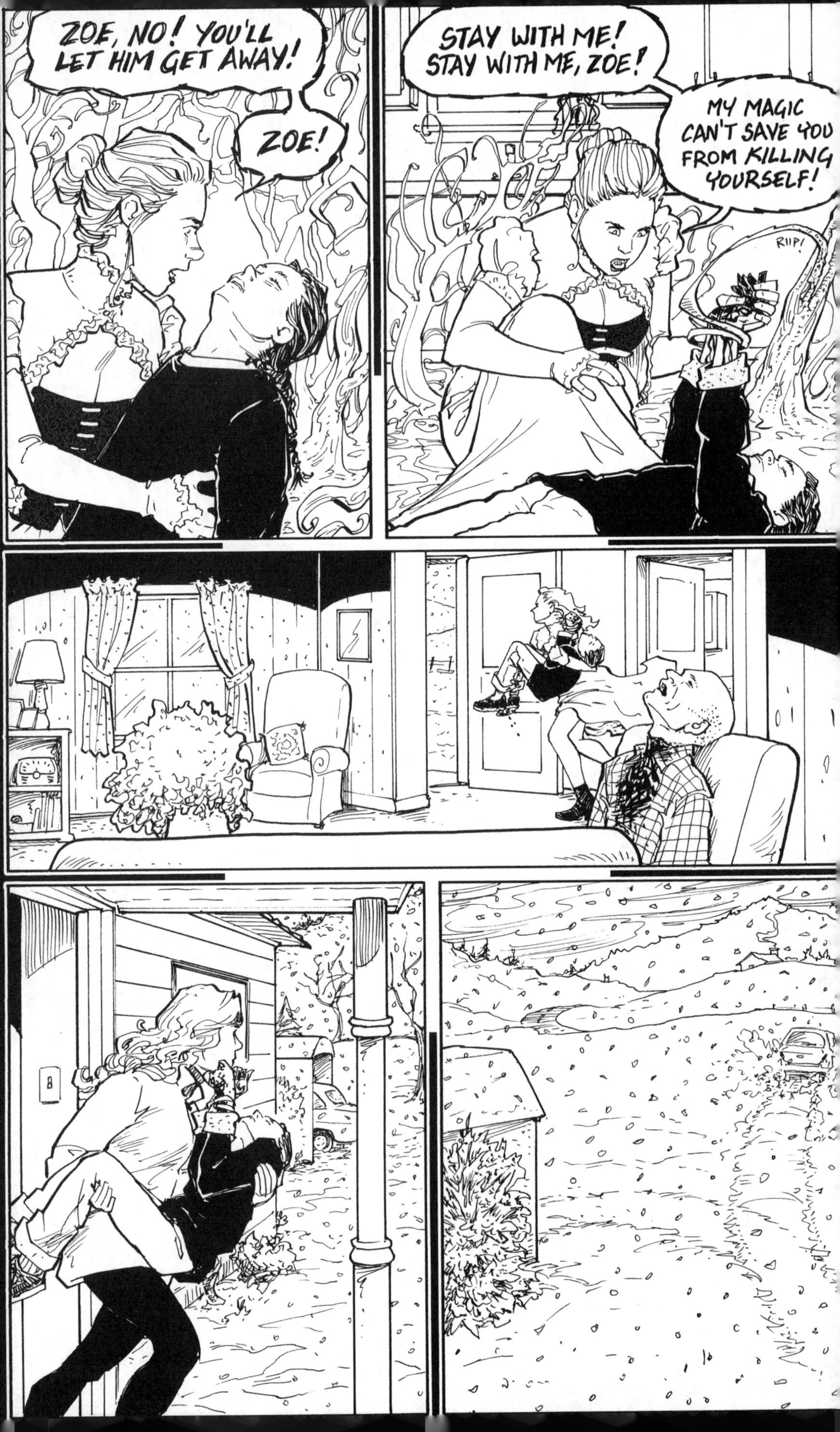
ZOE, NO! YOU'LL LET HIM GET AWAY!
ZOE!
STAY WITH ME! STAY WITH ME, ZOE!
MY MAGIC CAN'T SAVE YOU FROM KILLING YOURSELF!
RIIP!

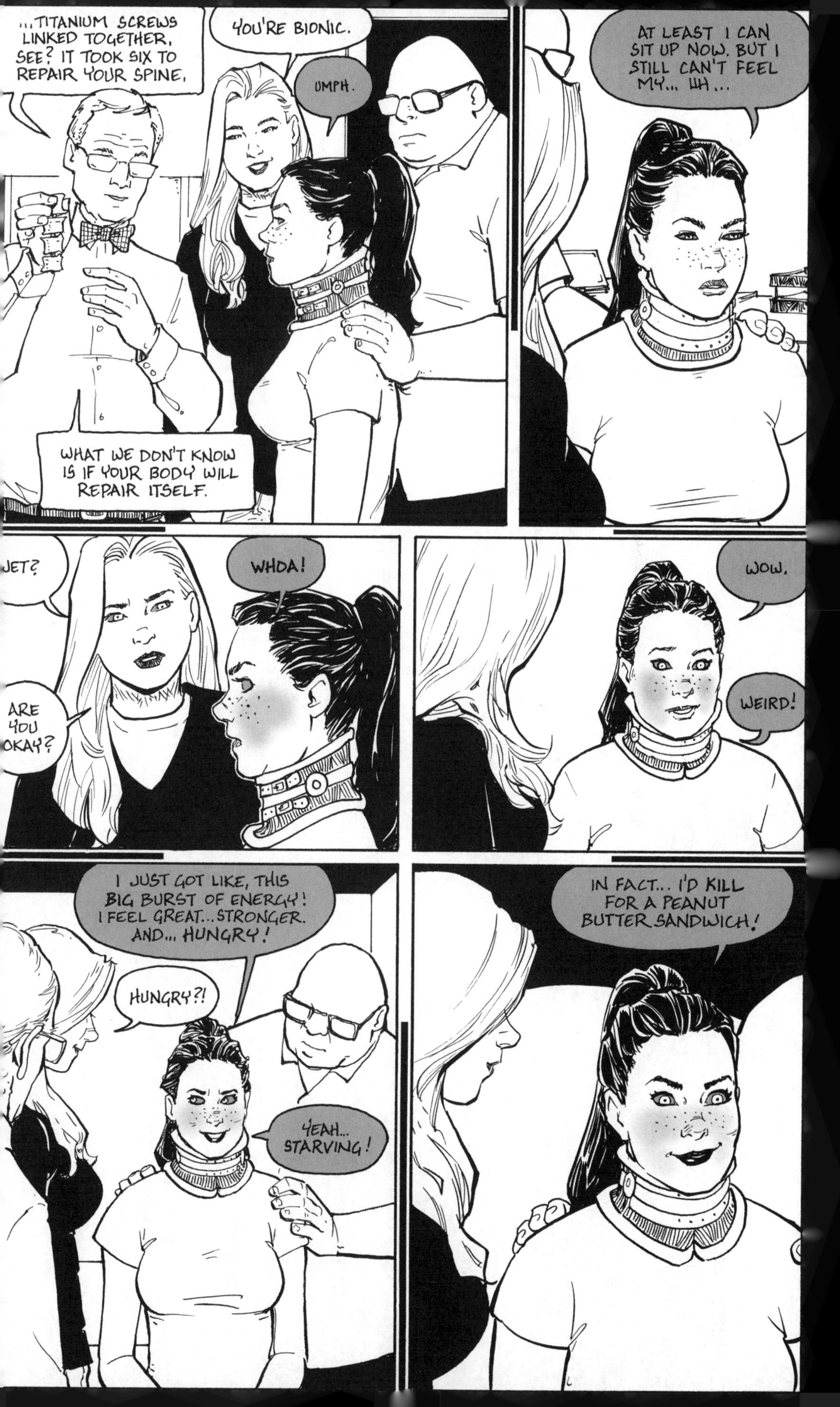
...TITANIUM SCREWS LINKED TOGETHER, SEE? IT TOOK SIX TO REPAIR YOUR SPINE.
YOU'RE BIONIC.
UMPH.
WHAT WE DON'T KNOW IS IF YOUR BODY WILL REPAIR ITSELF.
AT LEAST I CAN SIT UP NOW. BUT I STILL CAN'T FEEL MY... UH...
JET?
WHOA!
ARE YOU OKAY?
WOW.
WEIRD!
I JUST GOT LIKE, THIS BIG BURST OF ENERGY! I FEEL GREAT...STRONGER. AND... HUNGRY!
HUNGRY?!
YEAH... STARVING!
IN FACT... I'D KILL FOR A PEANUT BUTTER SANDWICH!

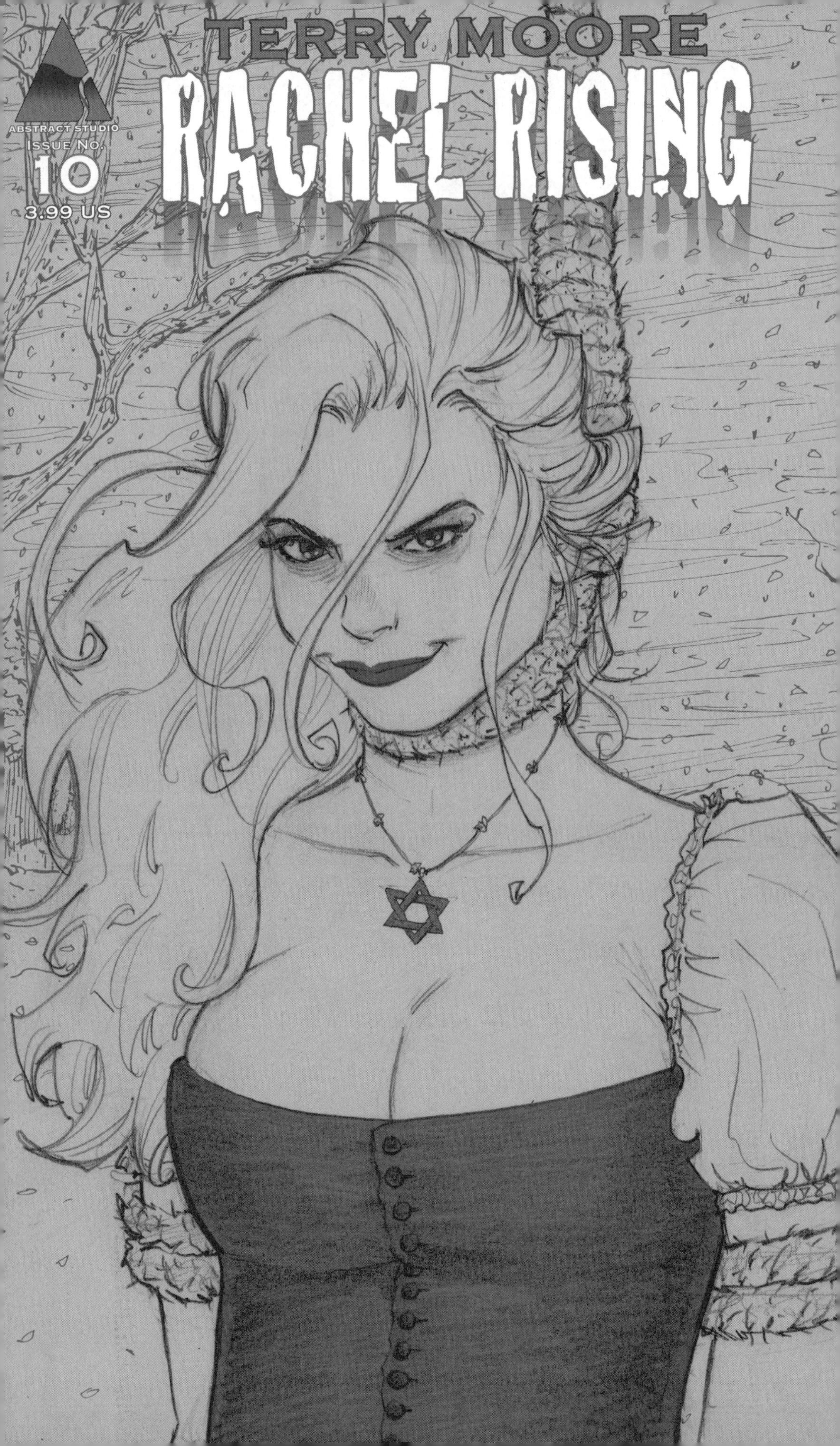
TERRY MOORE
RACHEL RISING
ABSTRACT STUDIO
ISSUE NO.
10
3.99 US

"LILITH WANDERS ABOUT AT NIGHT,
VEXING THE SONS OF MEN AND CAUSING
THEM TO DEFILE THEMSELVES."

—GERSHOM SCHOLEM, THE ZOHAR

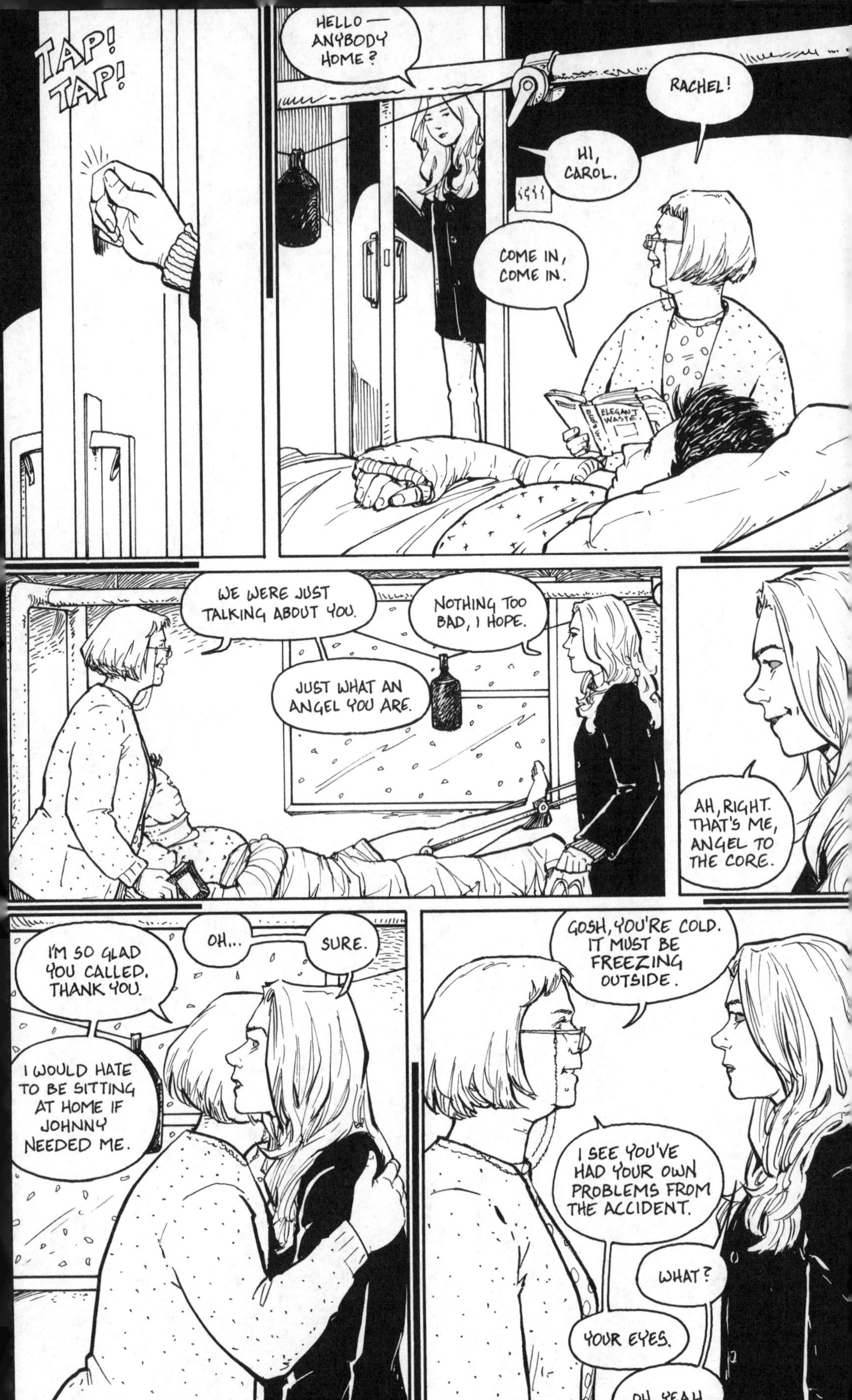
TAP! TAP!
HELLO— ANYBODY HOME?
RACHEL!
HI, CAROL.
COME IN, COME IN.
ELEGANT WASTE
WE WERE JUST TALKING ABOUT YOU.
NOTHING TOO BAD, I HOPE.
JUST WHAT AN ANGEL YOU ARE.
AH, RIGHT. THAT'S ME, ANGEL TO THE CORE.
I'M SO GLAD YOU CALLED. THANK YOU.
OH...
SURE.
I WOULD HATE TO BE SITTING AT HOME IF JOHNNY NEEDED ME.
GOSH, YOU'RE COLD. IT MUST BE FREEZING OUTSIDE.
I SEE YOU'VE HAD YOUR OWN PROBLEMS FROM THE ACCIDENT.
WHAT?
YOUR EYES.
OH, YEAH.

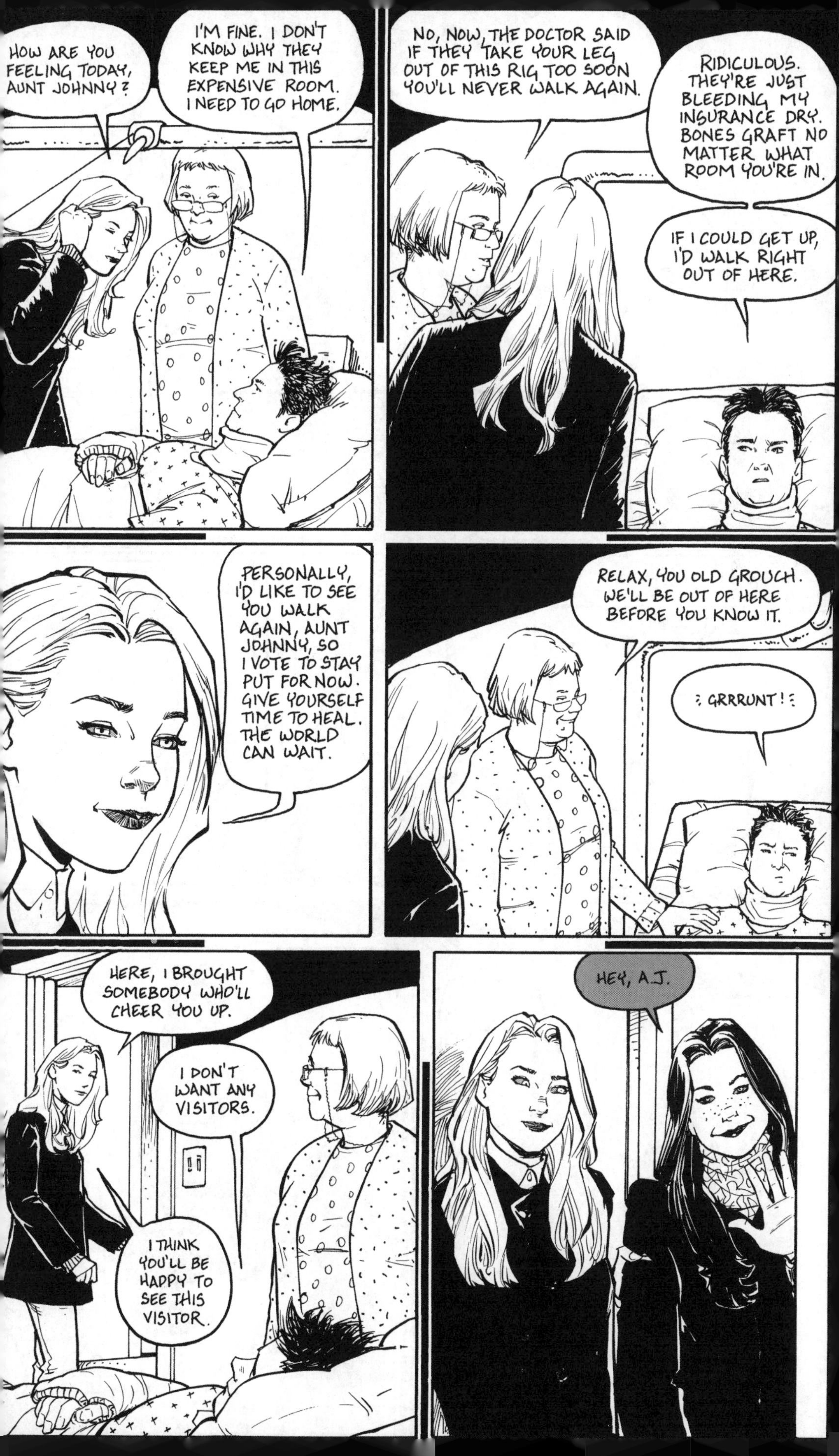
HOW ARE YOU FEELING TODAY, AUNT JOHNNY?
I'M FINE. I DON'T KNOW WHY THEY KEEP ME IN THIS EXPENSIVE ROOM. I NEED TO GO HOME.
NO, NOW, THE DOCTOR SAID IF THEY TAKE YOUR LEG OUT OF THIS RIG TOO SOON YOU'LL NEVER WALK AGAIN.
RIDICULOUS. THEY'RE JUST BLEEDING MY INSURANCE DRY. BONES GRAFT NO MATTER WHAT ROOM YOU'RE IN.
IF I COULD GET UP, I'D WALK RIGHT OUT OF HERE.
PERSONALLY, I'D LIKE TO SEE YOU WALK AGAIN, AUNT JOHNNY, SO I VOTE TO STAY PUT FOR NOW. GIVE YOURSELF TIME TO HEAL. THE WORLD CAN WAIT.
RELAX, YOU OLD GROUCH. WE'LL BE OUT OF HERE BEFORE YOU KNOW IT.
GRRRUNT!
HERE, I BROUGHT SOMEBODY WHO'LL CHEER YOU UP.
I DON'T WANT ANY VISITORS.
I THINK YOU'LL BE HAPPY TO SEE THIS VISITOR.
HEY, A.J.

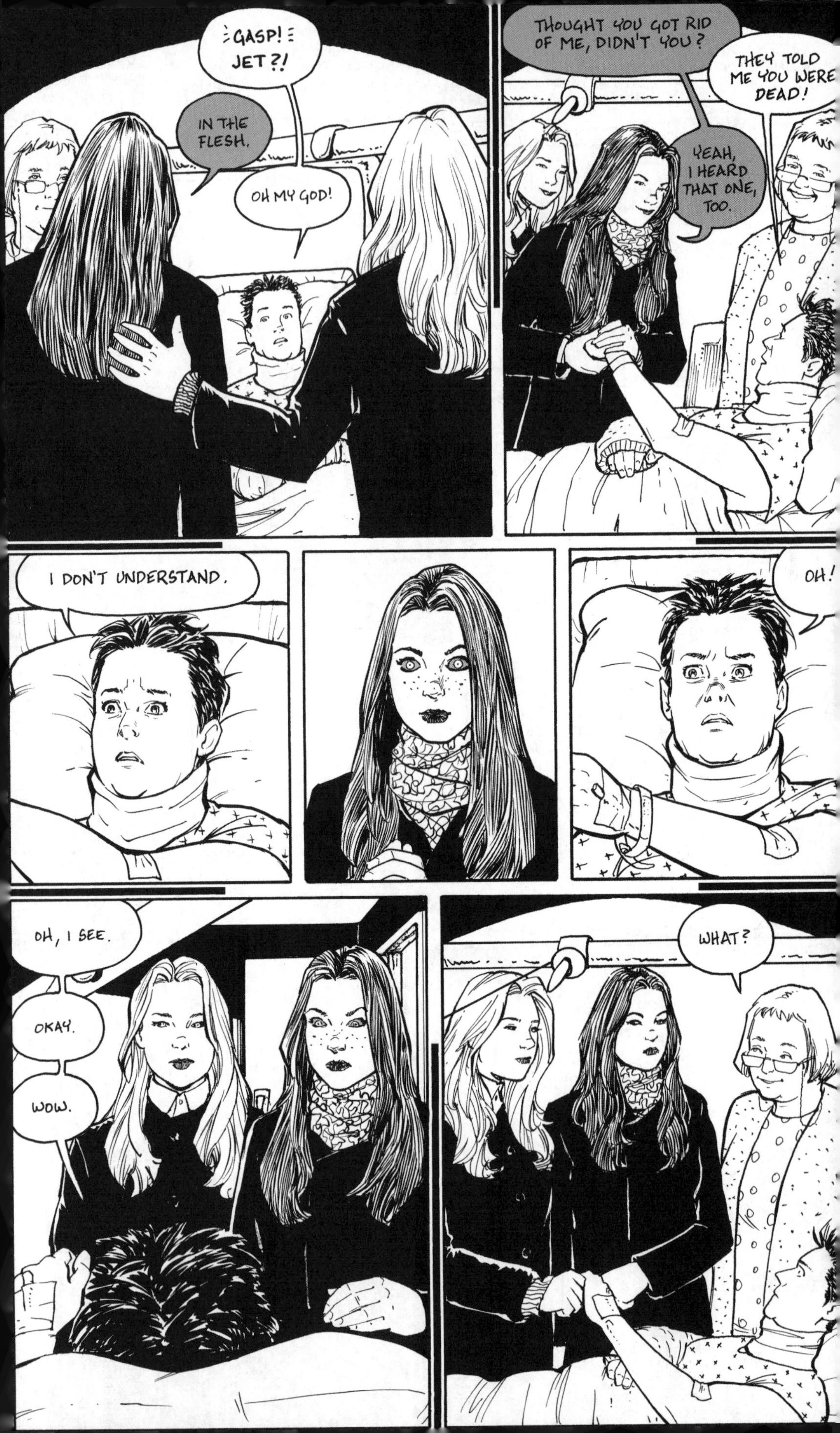

GASP! JET?!
IN THE FLESH.
OH MY GOD!
THOUGHT YOU GOT RID OF ME, DIDN'T YOU?
THEY TOLD ME YOU WERE DEAD!
YEAH, I HEARD THAT ONE, TOO.
I DON'T UNDERSTAND.
OH!
OH, I SEE.
OKAY.
WOW.
WHAT?

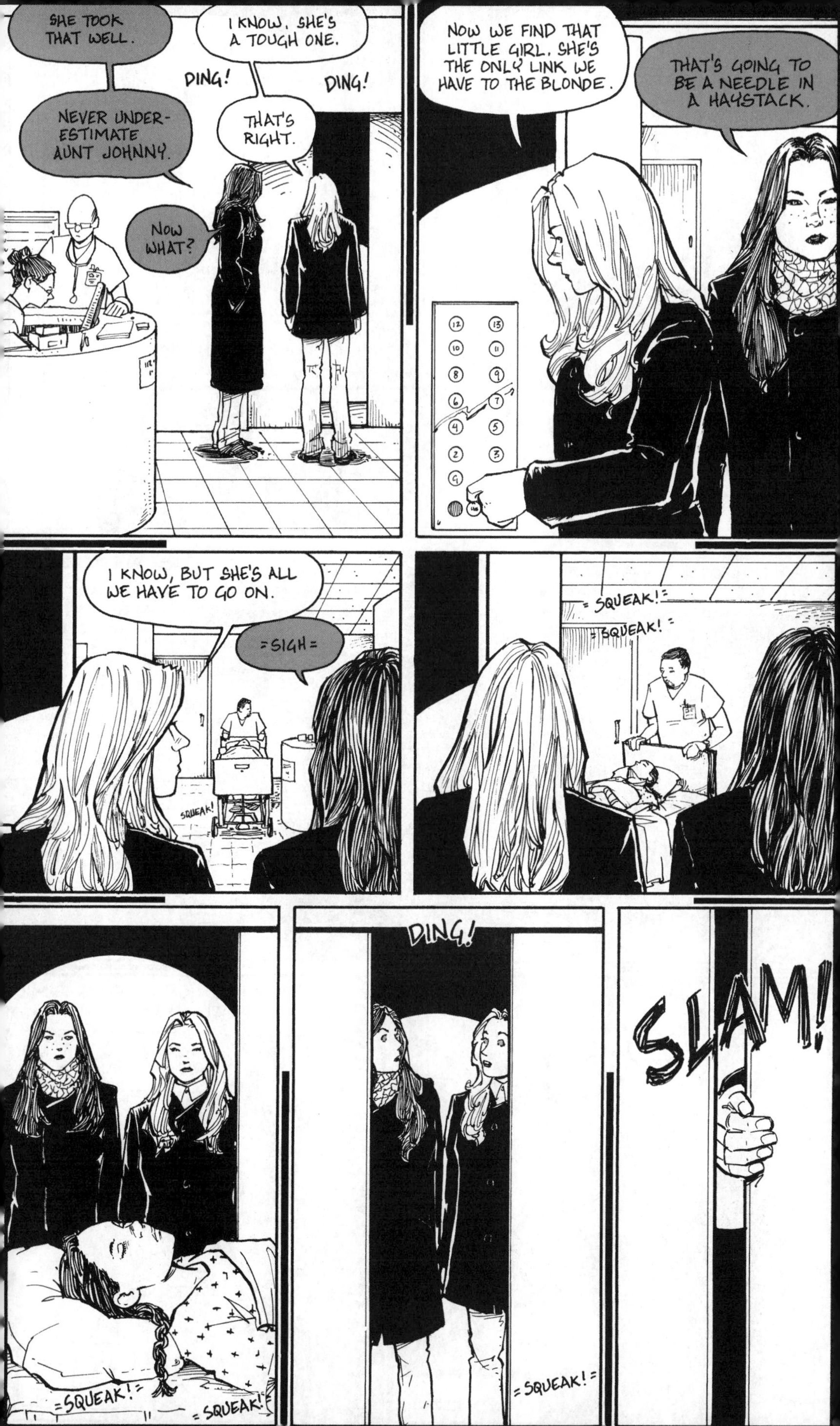
SHE TOOK THAT WELL.
I KNOW. SHE'S A TOUGH ONE.
DING!
DING!
NEVER UNDER-ESTIMATE AUNT JOHNNY.
THAT'S RIGHT.
NOW WHAT?
NOW WE FIND THAT LITTLE GIRL. SHE'S THE ONLY LINK WE HAVE TO THE BLONDE.
THAT'S GOING TO BE A NEEDLE IN A HAYSTACK.
I KNOW, BUT SHE'S ALL WE HAVE TO GO ON.
=SIGH=
SQUEAK!
=SQUEAK!=
=SQUEAK!=
=SQUEAK!=
=SQUEAK!
DING!
=SQUEAK!=
SLAM!

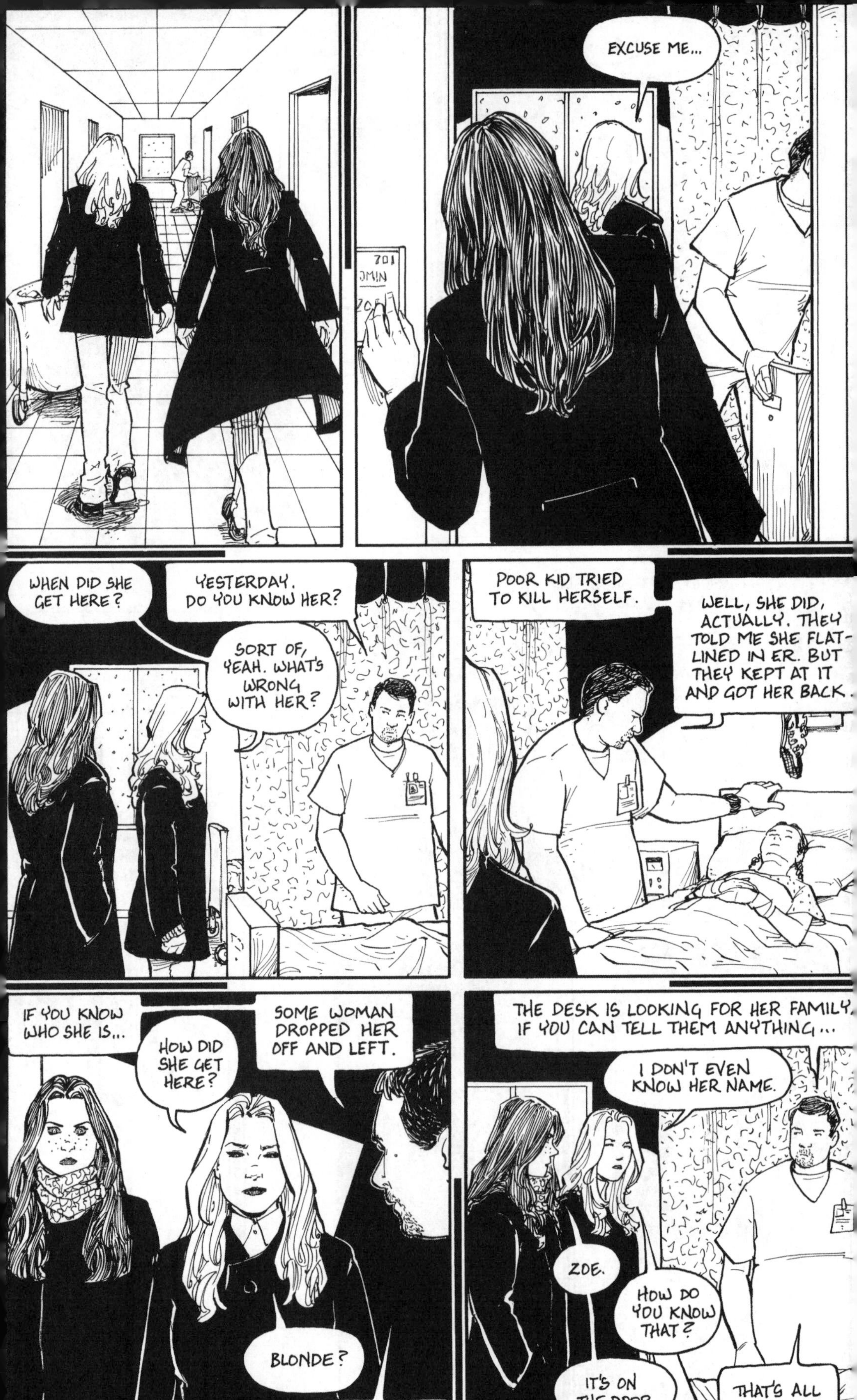
EXCUSE ME...
WHEN DID SHE GET HERE?
YESTERDAY. DO YOU KNOW HER?
SORT OF, YEAH. WHAT'S WRONG WITH HER?
POOR KID TRIED TO KILL HERSELF.
WELL, SHE DID, ACTUALLY. THEY TOLD ME SHE FLAT-LINED IN ER. BUT THEY KEPT AT IT AND GOT HER BACK.
IF YOU KNOW WHO SHE IS...
HOW DID SHE GET HERE?
SOME WOMAN DROPPED HER OFF AND LEFT.
BLONDE?
I DON'T KNOW.
THE DESK IS LOOKING FOR HER FAMILY. IF YOU CAN TELL THEM ANYTHING...
I DON'T EVEN KNOW HER NAME.
ZOE.
HOW DO YOU KNOW THAT?
IT'S ON THE DOOR.
THAT'S ALL WE HAVE.

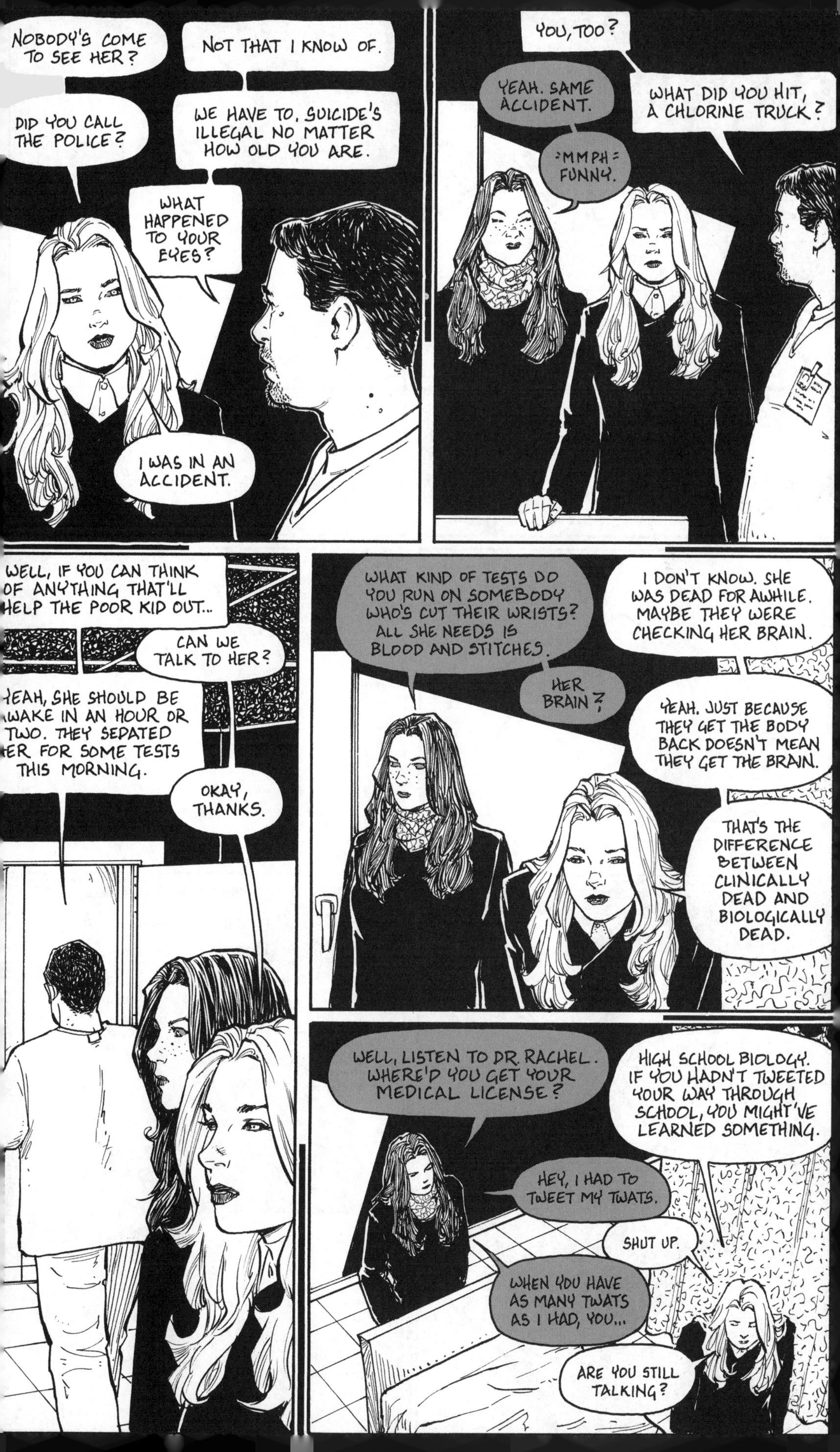
NOBODY'S COME TO SEE HER?
NOT THAT I KNOW OF.
DID YOU CALL THE POLICE?
WE HAVE TO. SUICIDE'S ILLEGAL NO MATTER HOW OLD YOU ARE.
WHAT HAPPENED TO YOUR EYES?
I WAS IN AN ACCIDENT.
YOU, TOO?
YEAH. SAME ACCIDENT.
WHAT DID YOU HIT, A CHLORINE TRUCK?
=MMPH= FUNNY.
WELL, IF YOU CAN THINK OF ANYTHING THAT'LL HELP THE POOR KID OUT...
CAN WE TALK TO HER?
YEAH, SHE SHOULD BE AWAKE IN AN HOUR OR TWO. THEY SEDATED HER FOR SOME TESTS THIS MORNING.
OKAY, THANKS.
WHAT KIND OF TESTS DO YOU RUN ON SOMEBODY WHO'S CUT THEIR WRISTS? ALL SHE NEEDS IS BLOOD AND STITCHES.
I DON'T KNOW. SHE WAS DEAD FOR AWHILE. MAYBE THEY WERE CHECKING HER BRAIN.
HER BRAIN?
YEAH. JUST BECAUSE THEY GET THE BODY BACK DOESN'T MEAN THEY GET THE BRAIN.
THAT'S THE DIFFERENCE BETWEEN CLINICALLY DEAD AND BIOLOGICALLY DEAD.
WELL, LISTEN TO DR. RACHEL. WHERE'D YOU GET YOUR MEDICAL LICENSE?
HIGH SCHOOL BIOLOGY. IF YOU HADN'T TWEETED YOUR WAY THROUGH SCHOOL, YOU MIGHT'VE LEARNED SOMETHING.
HEY, I HAD TO TWEET MY TWATS.
SHUT UP.
WHEN YOU HAVE AS MANY TWATS AS I HAD, YOU...
ARE YOU STILL TALKING?

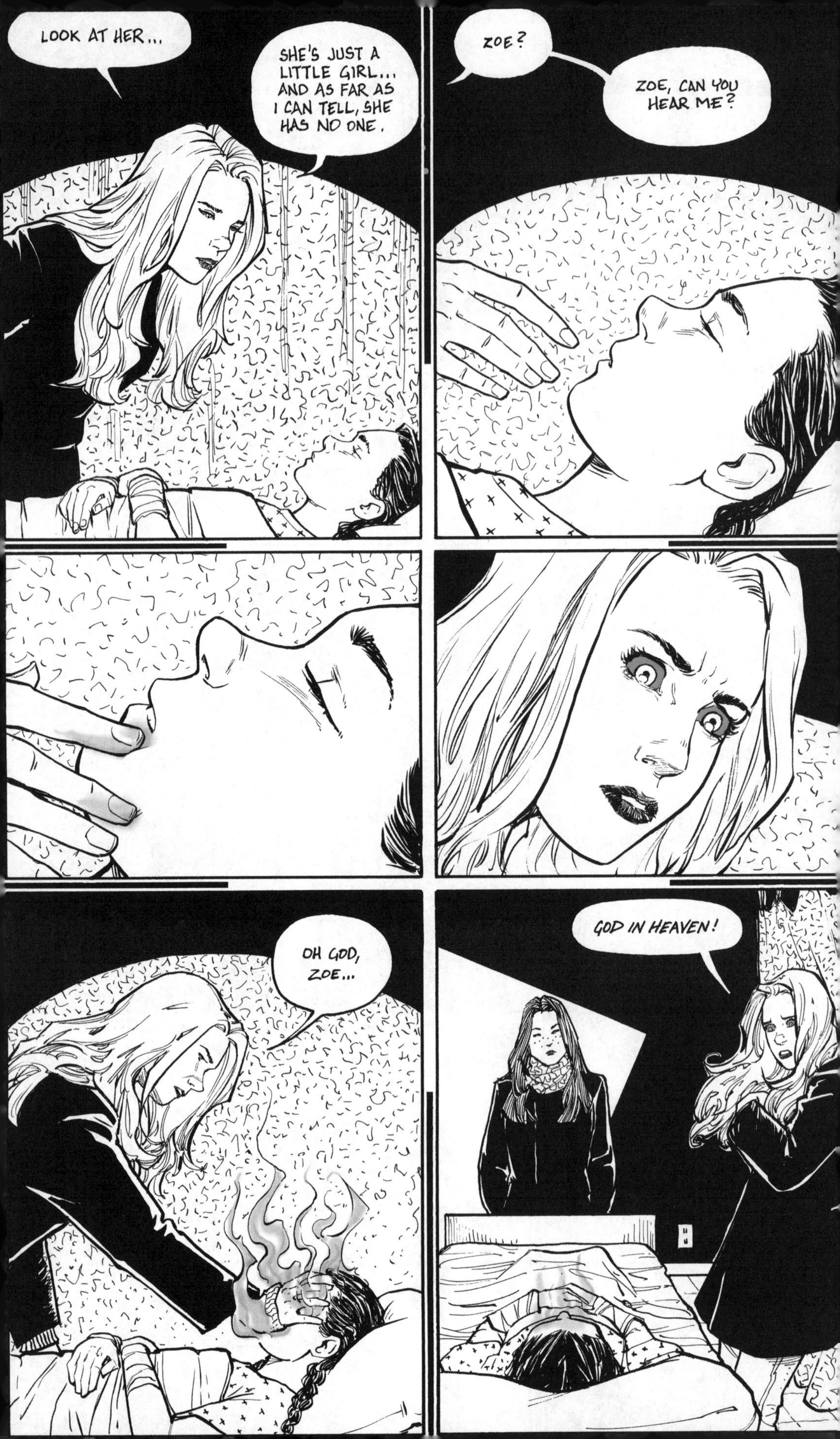
LOOK AT HER...
SHE'S JUST A LITTLE GIRL... AND AS FAR AS I CAN TELL, SHE HAS NO ONE.
ZOE?
ZOE, CAN YOU HEAR ME?
OH GOD, ZOE...
GOD IN HEAVEN!

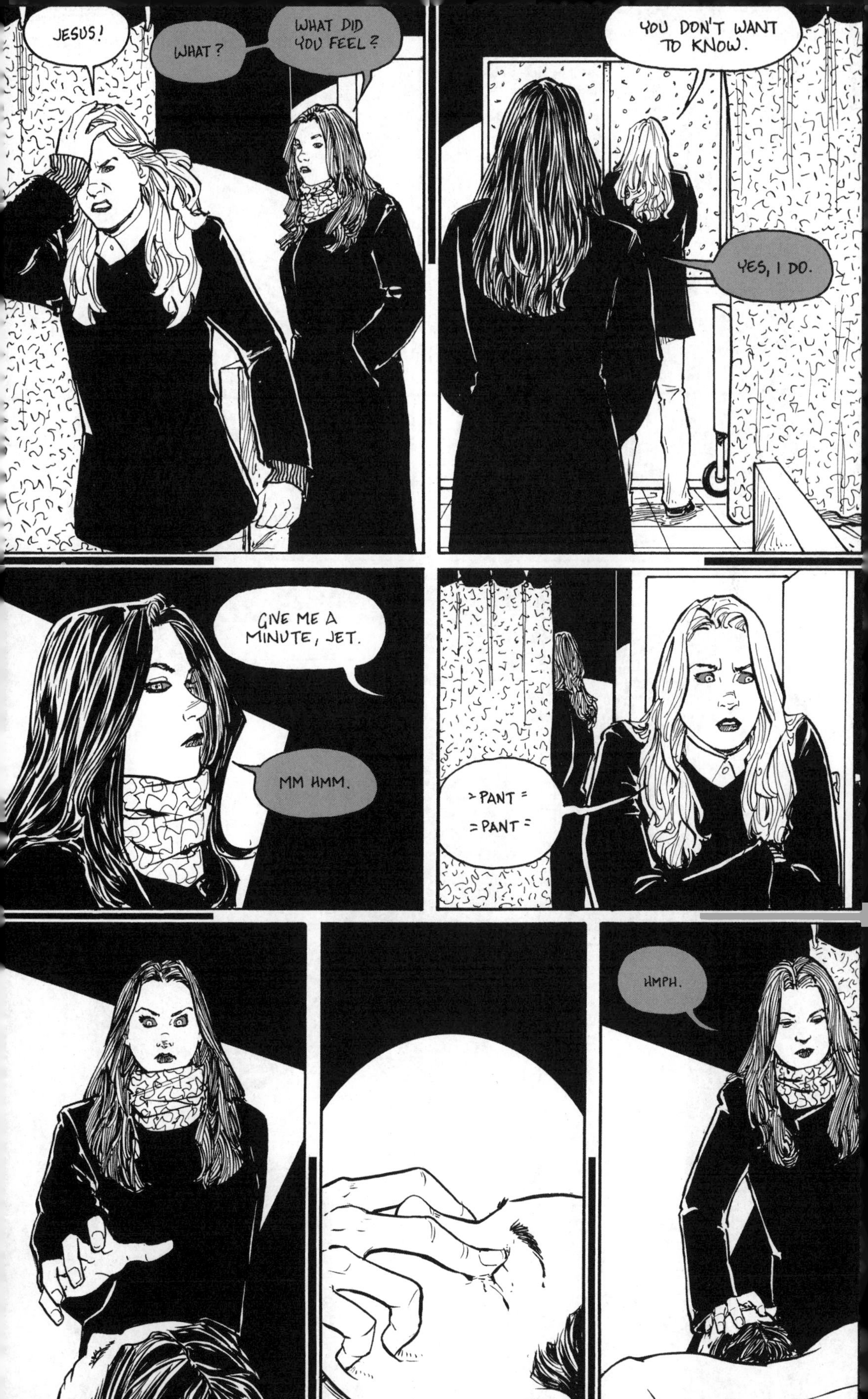
JESUS!
WHAT?
WHAT DID YOU FEEL?
YOU DON'T WANT TO KNOW.
YES, I DO.
GIVE ME A MINUTE, JET.
MM HMM.
=PANT=
=PANT=
HMPH.

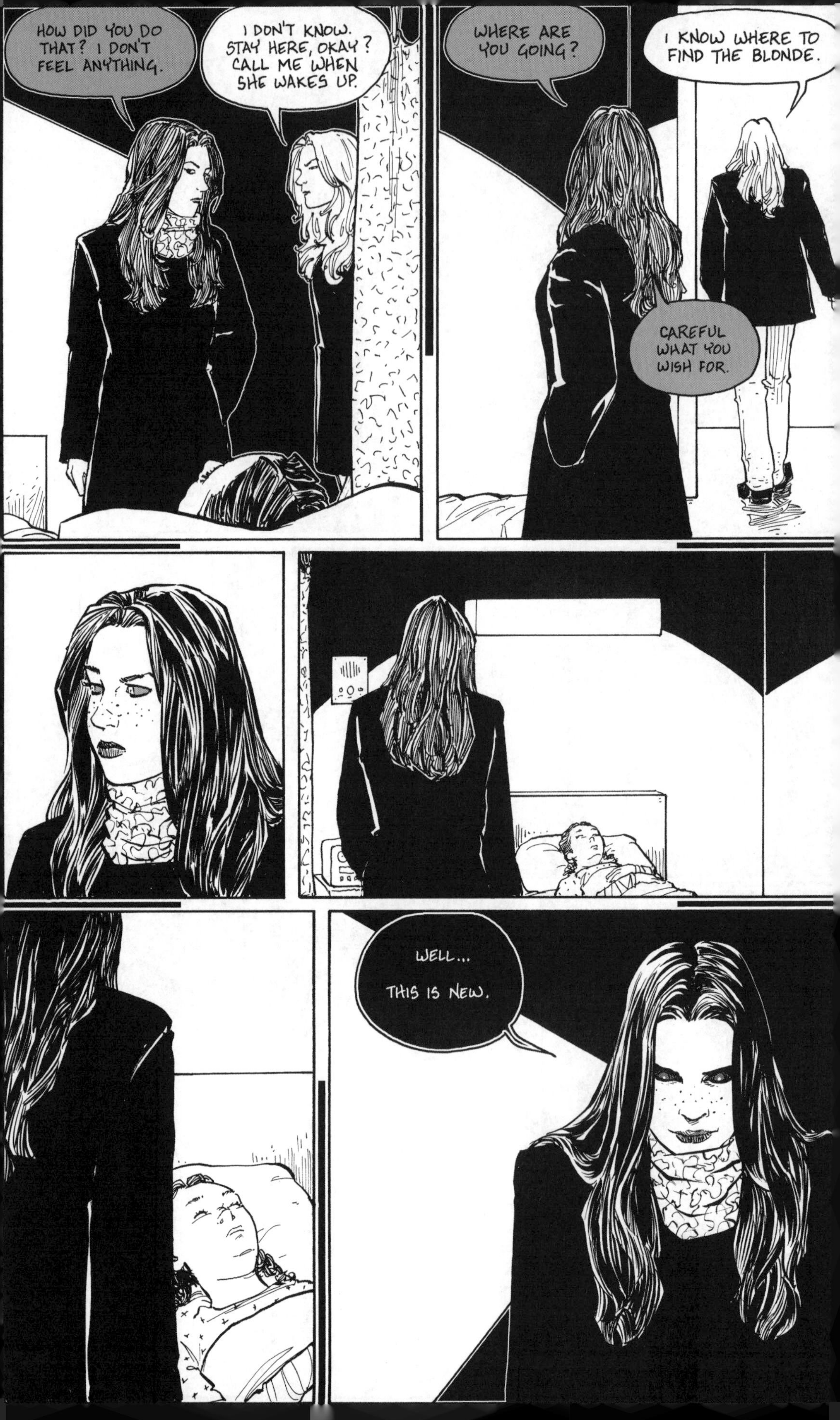
HOW DID YOU DO THAT? I DON'T FEEL ANYTHING.
I DON'T KNOW. STAY HERE, OKAY? CALL ME WHEN SHE WAKES UP.
WHERE ARE YOU GOING?
I KNOW WHERE TO FIND THE BLONDE.
CAREFUL WHAT YOU WISH FOR.
WELL...
THIS IS NEW.

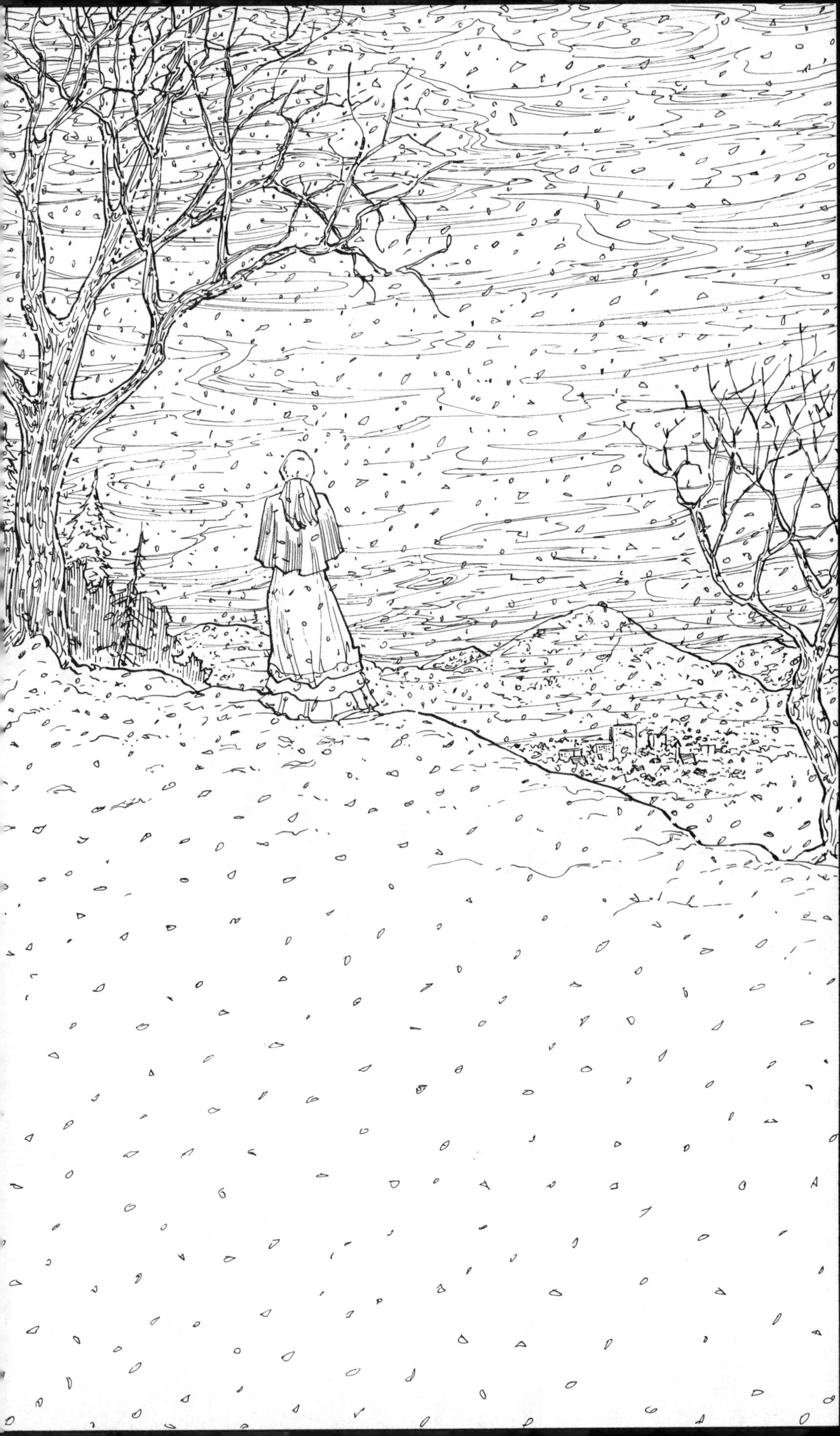

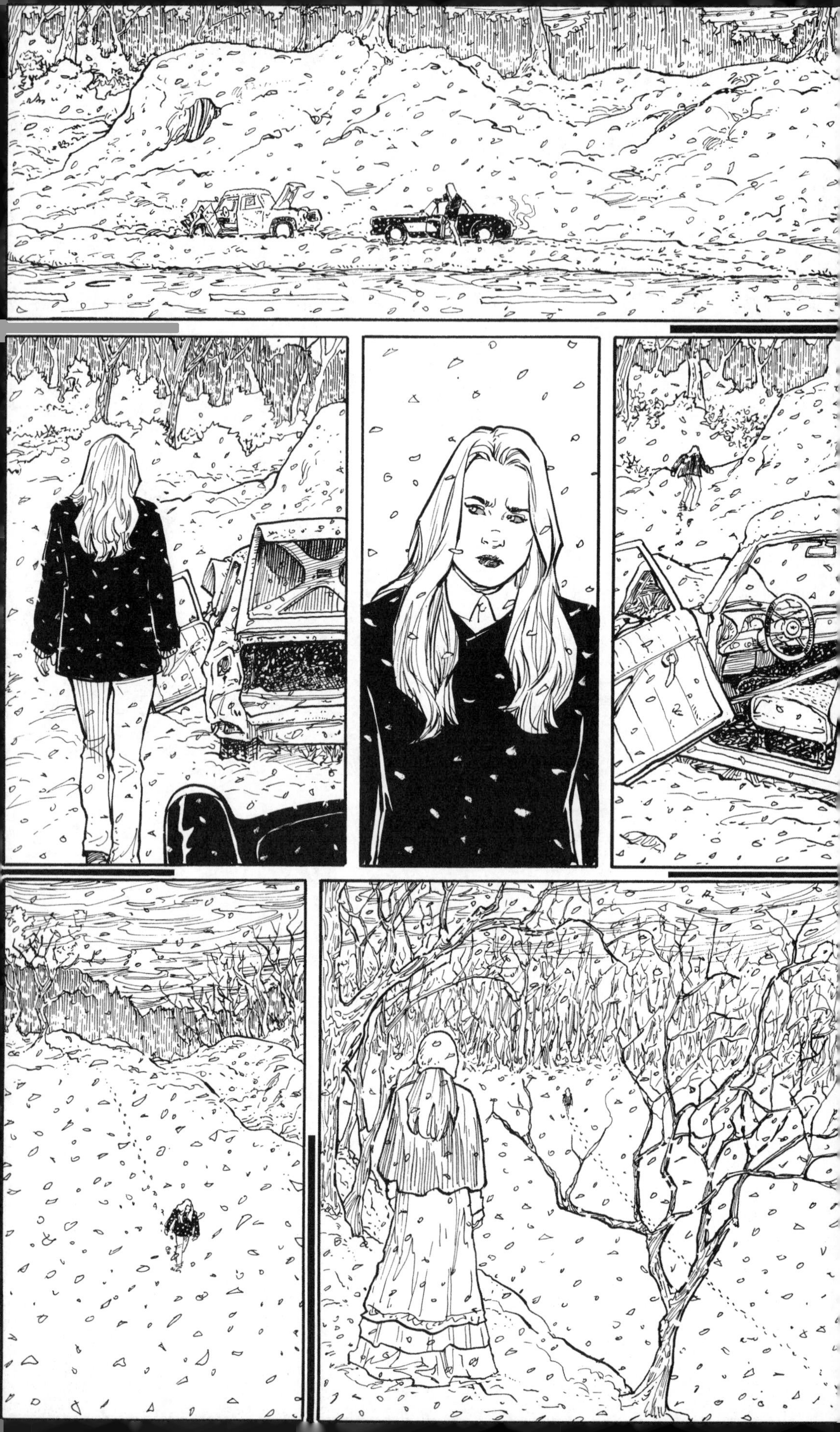

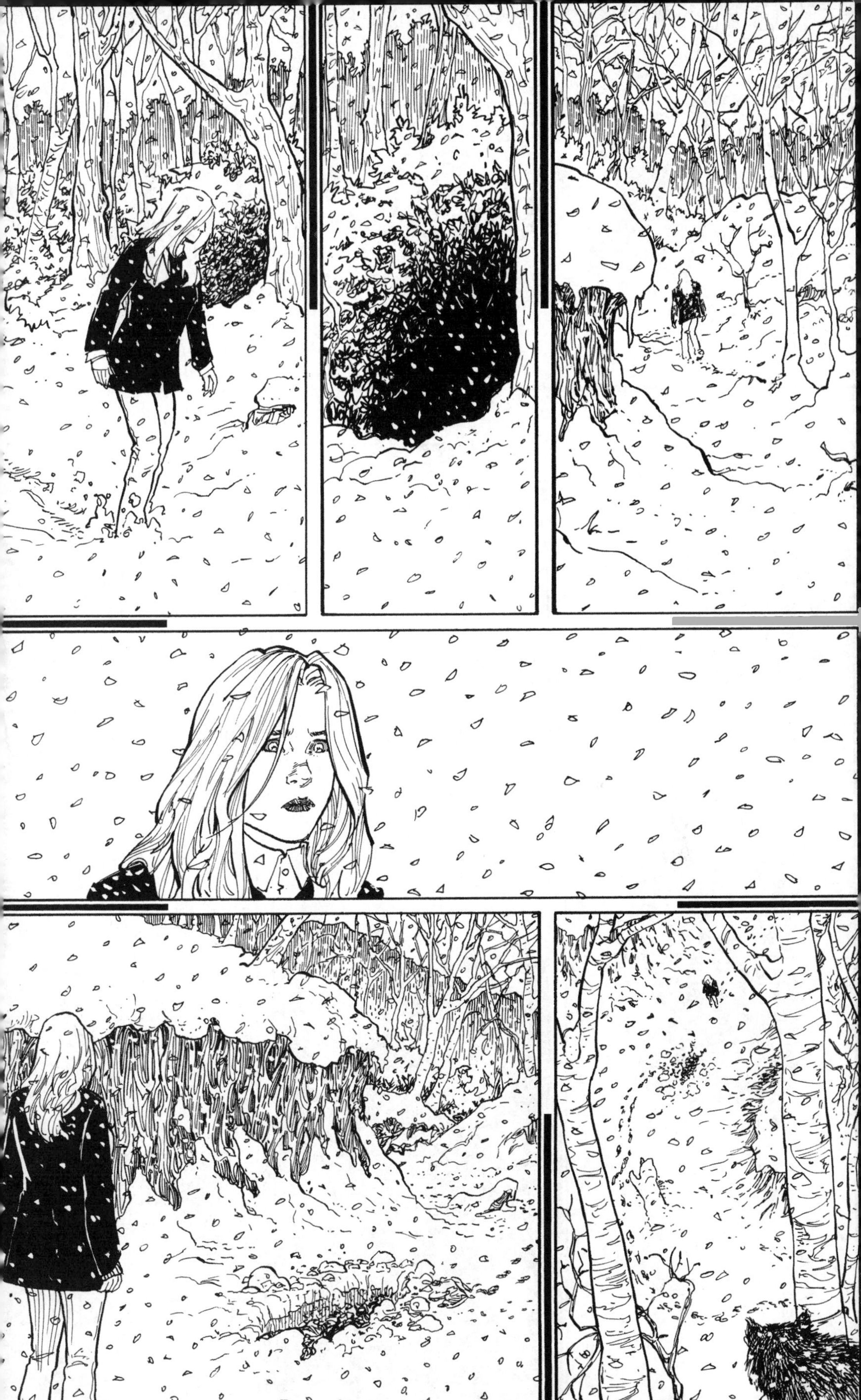

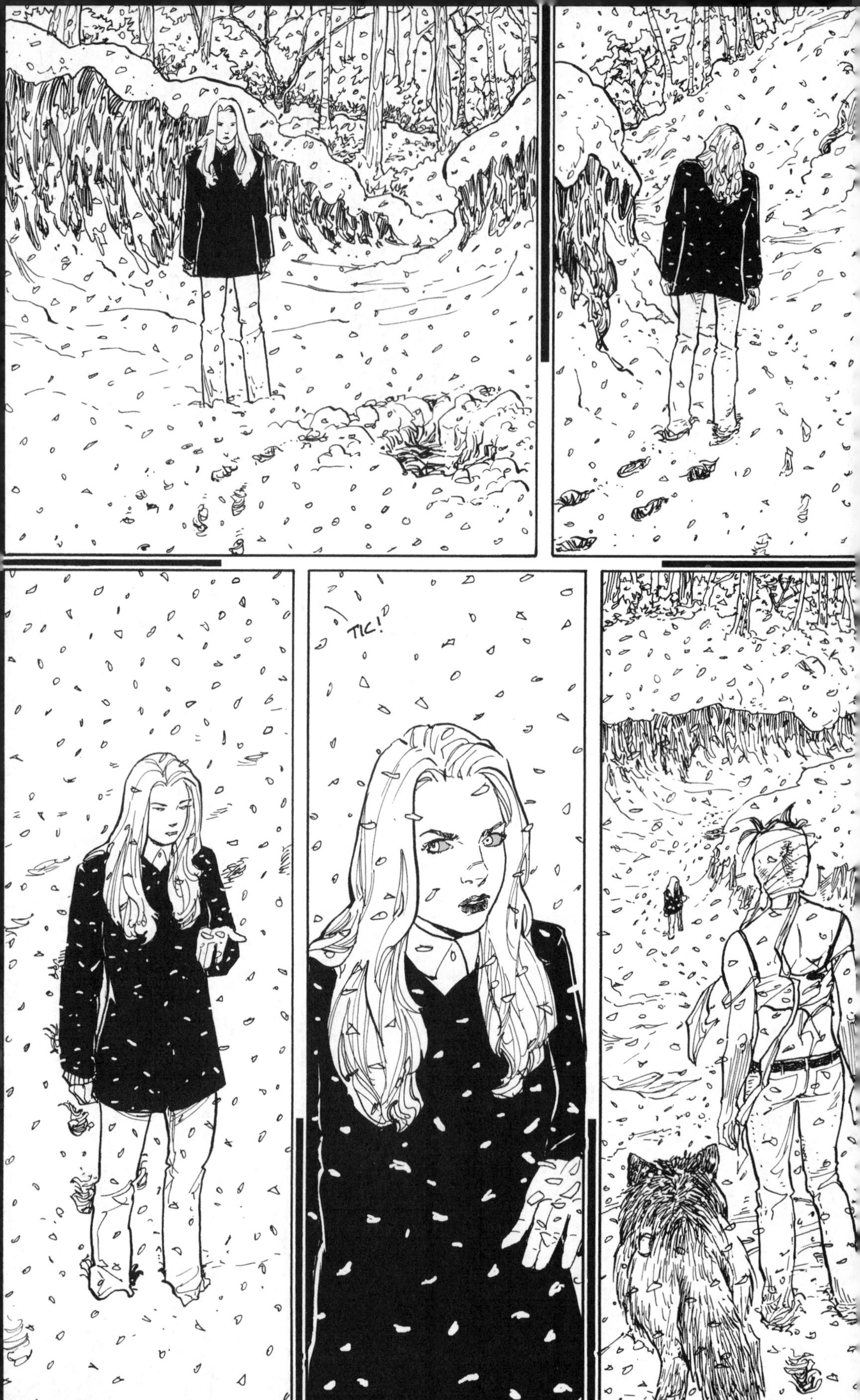
TIC!

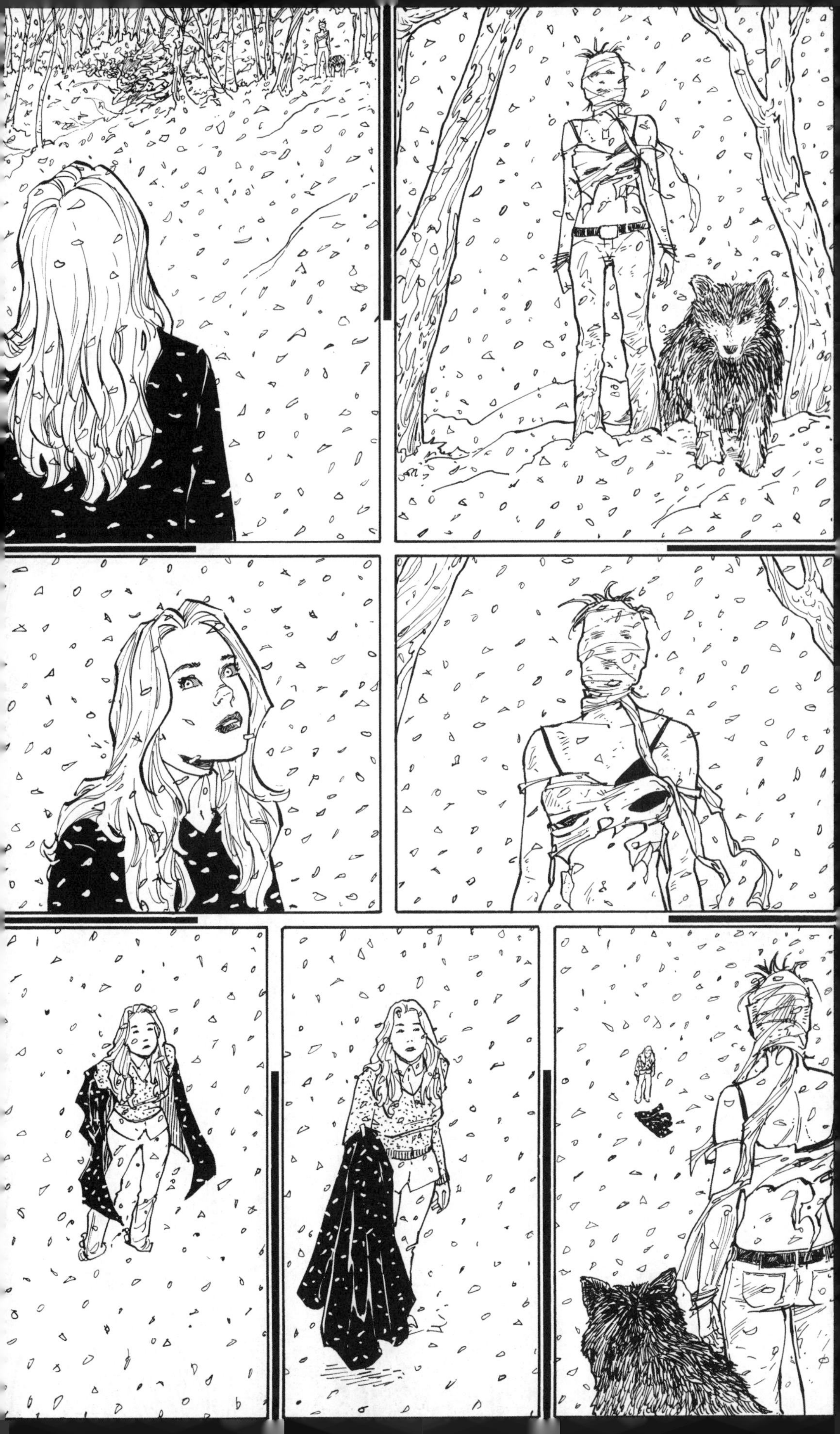

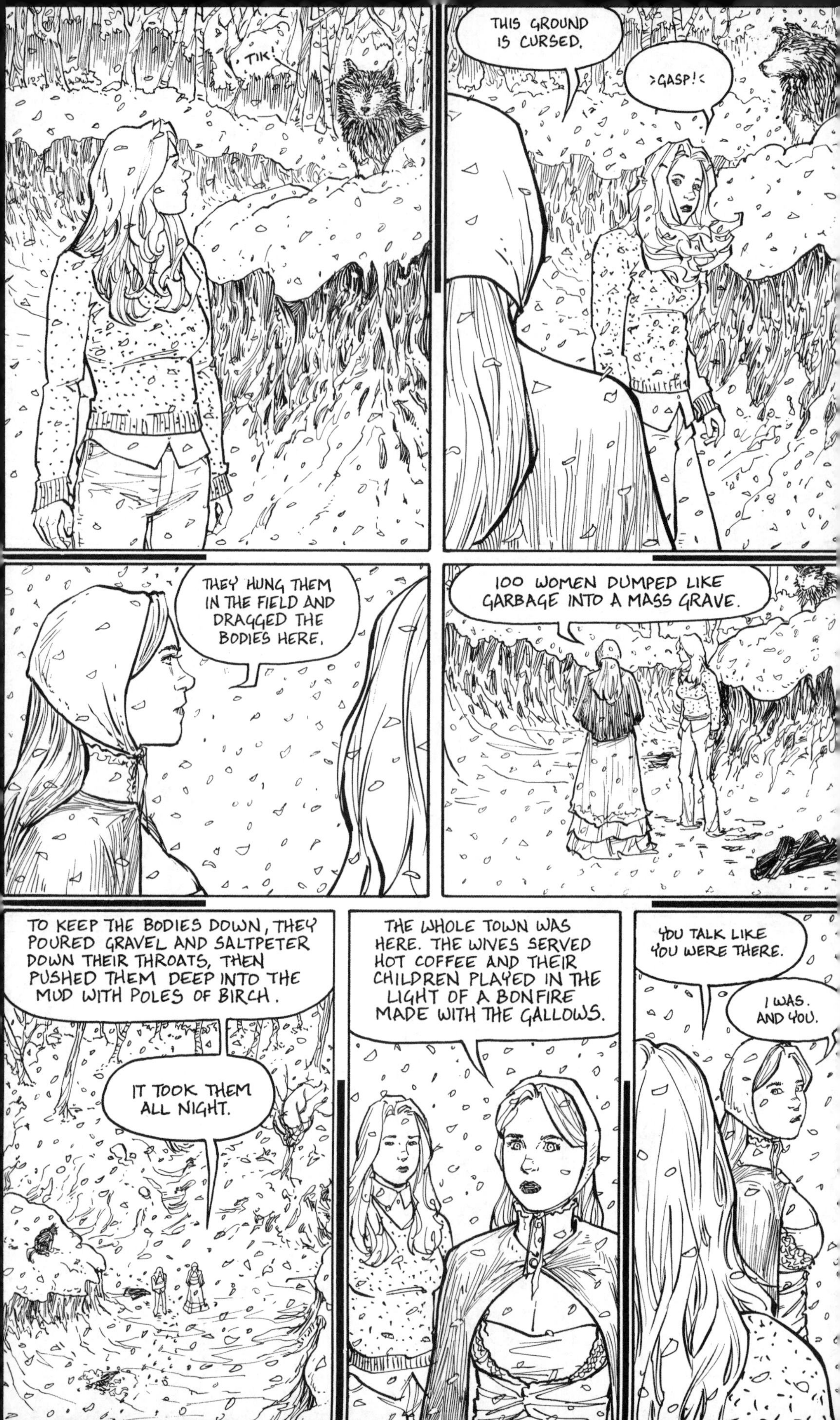
TIK!
THIS GROUND IS CURSED.
>GASP!<
THEY HUNG THEM IN THE FIELD AND DRAGGED THE BODIES HERE.
100 WOMEN DUMPED LIKE GARBAGE INTO A MASS GRAVE.
TO KEEP THE BODIES DOWN, THEY POURED GRAVEL AND SALTPETER DOWN THEIR THROATS, THEN PUSHED THEM DEEP INTO THE MUD WITH POLES OF BIRCH.
IT TOOK THEM ALL NIGHT.
THE WHOLE TOWN WAS HERE. THE WIVES SERVED HOT COFFEE AND THEIR CHILDREN PLAYED IN THE LIGHT OF A BONFIRE MADE WITH THE GALLOWS.
YOU TALK LIKE YOU WERE THERE.
I WAS. AND YOU.

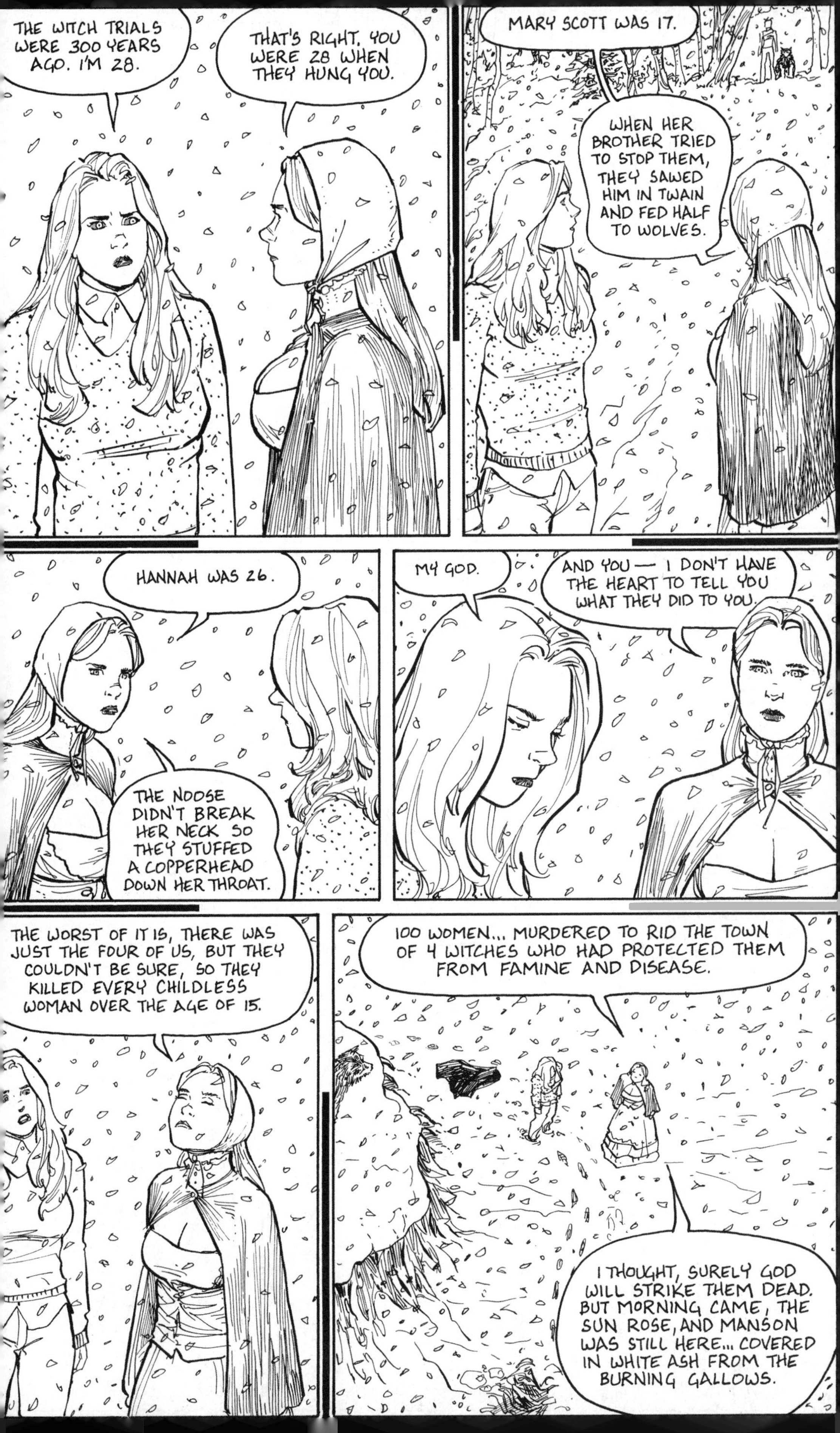
THE WITCH TRIALS WERE 300 YEARS AGO. I'M 28.
THAT'S RIGHT. YOU WERE 28 WHEN THEY HUNG YOU.
MARY SCOTT WAS 17.
WHEN HER BROTHER TRIED TO STOP THEM, THEY SAWED HIM IN TWAIN AND FED HALF TO WOLVES.
HANNAH WAS 26.
THE NOOSE DIDN'T BREAK HER NECK SO THEY STUFFED A COPPERHEAD DOWN HER THROAT.
MY GOD.
AND YOU — I DON'T HAVE THE HEART TO TELL YOU WHAT THEY DID TO YOU.
THE WORST OF IT IS, THERE WAS JUST THE FOUR OF US, BUT THEY COULDN'T BE SURE, SO THEY KILLED EVERY CHILDLESS WOMAN OVER THE AGE OF 15.
100 WOMEN... MURDERED TO RID THE TOWN OF 4 WITCHES WHO HAD PROTECTED THEM FROM FAMINE AND DISEASE.
I THOUGHT, SURELY GOD WILL STRIKE THEM DEAD. BUT MORNING CAME, THE SUN ROSE, AND MANSON WAS STILL HERE... COVERED IN WHITE ASH FROM THE BURNING GALLOWS.

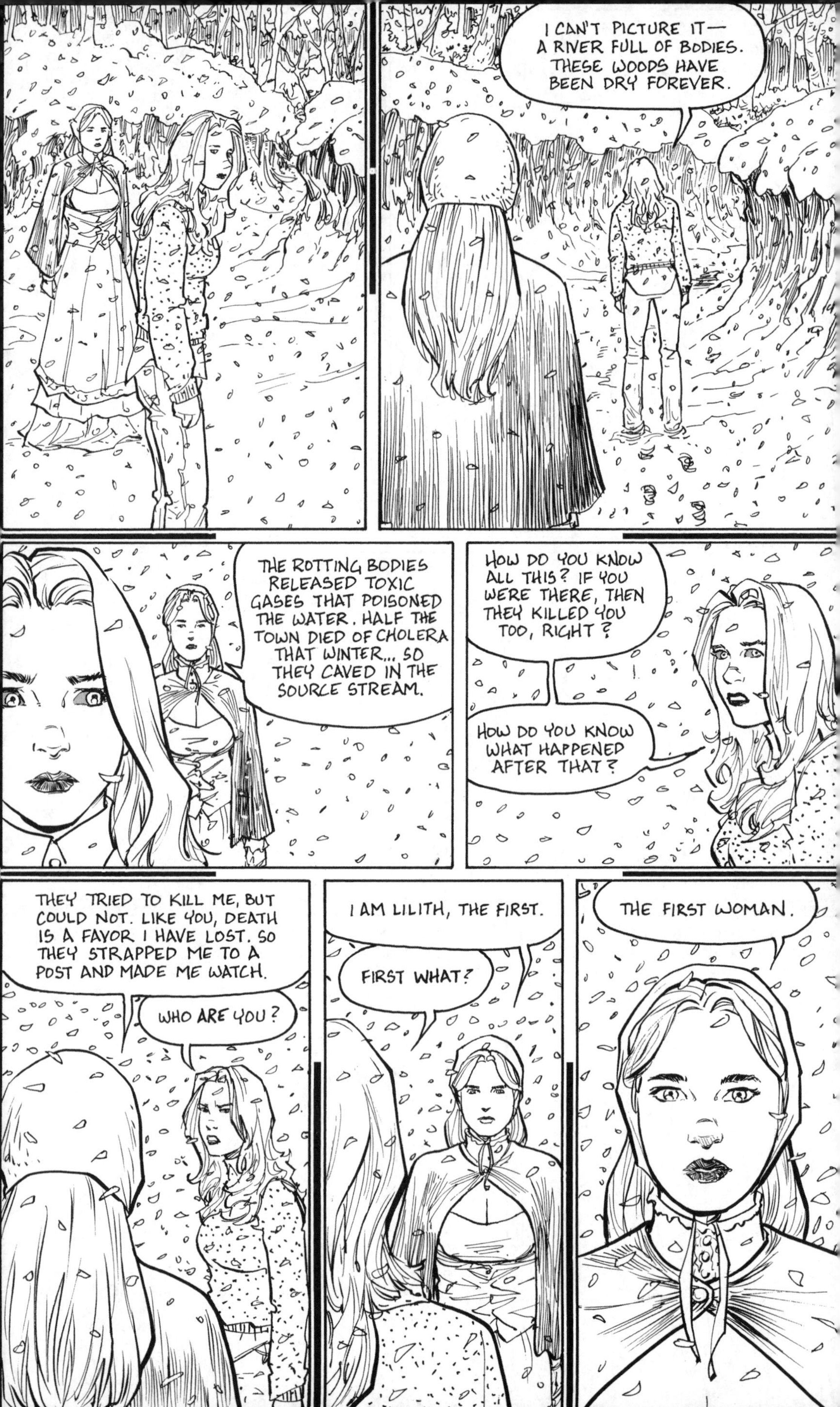
I CAN'T PICTURE IT— A RIVER FULL OF BODIES. THESE WOODS HAVE BEEN DRY FOREVER.
THE ROTTING BODIES RELEASED TOXIC GASES THAT POISONED THE WATER. HALF THE TOWN DIED OF CHOLERA THAT WINTER... SO THEY CAVED IN THE SOURCE STREAM.
HOW DO YOU KNOW ALL THIS? IF YOU WERE THERE, THEN THEY KILLED YOU TOO, RIGHT?
HOW DO YOU KNOW WHAT HAPPENED AFTER THAT?
THEY TRIED TO KILL ME, BUT COULD NOT. LIKE YOU, DEATH IS A FAVOR I HAVE LOST. SO THEY STRAPPED ME TO A POST AND MADE ME WATCH.
WHO ARE YOU?
I AM LILITH, THE FIRST.
FIRST WHAT?
THE FIRST WOMAN.

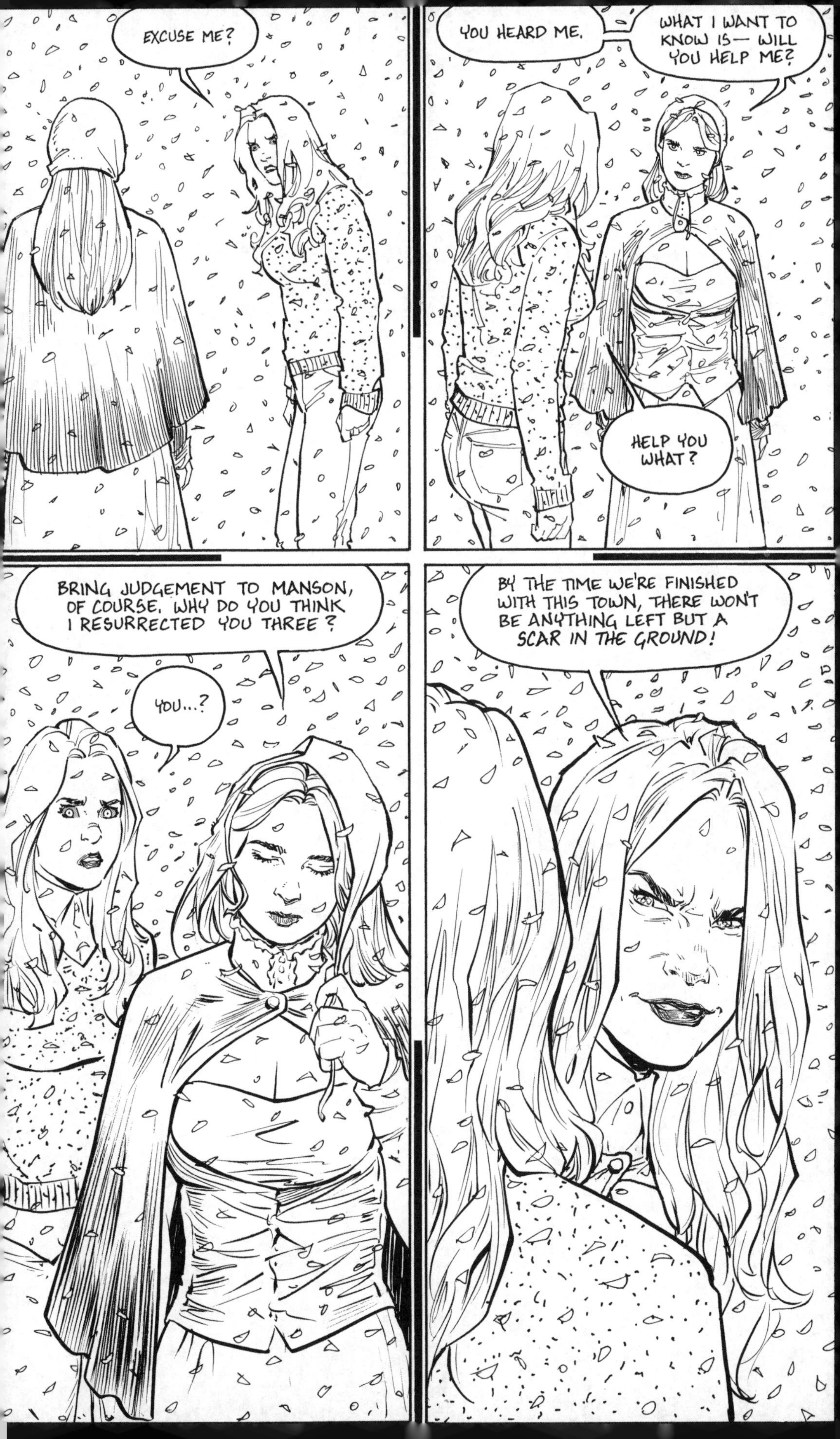
EXCUSE ME?
YOU HEARD ME.
WHAT I WANT TO KNOW IS— WILL YOU HELP ME?
HELP YOU WHAT?
BRING JUDGEMENT TO MANSON, OF COURSE. WHY DO YOU THINK I RESURRECTED YOU THREE?
YOU...?
BY THE TIME WE'RE FINISHED WITH THIS TOWN, THERE WON'T BE ANYTHING LEFT BUT A SCAR IN THE GROUND!

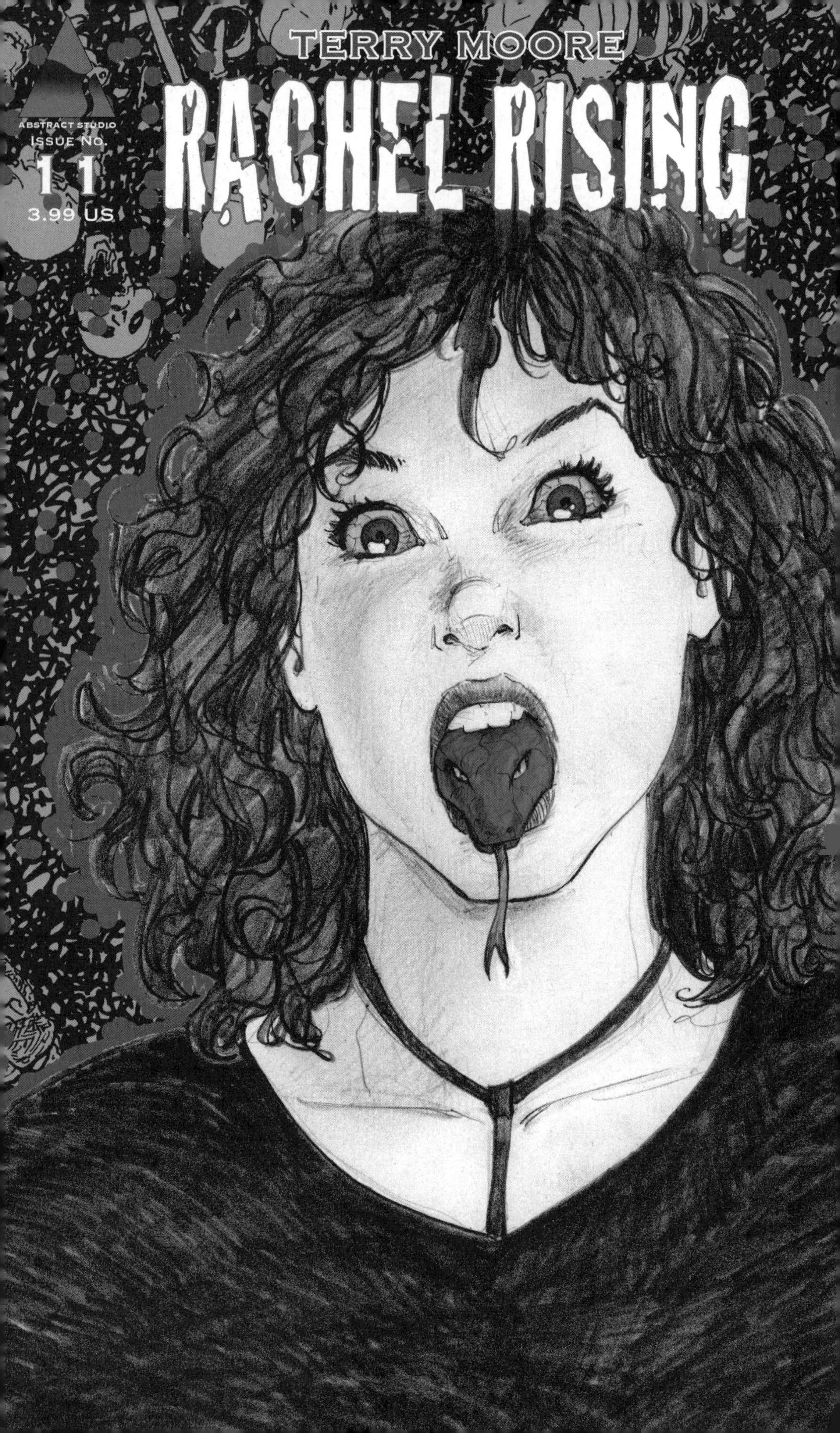

TERRY MOORE
RACHEL RISING
ABSTRACT STUDIO
ISSUE No.
11
3.99 US

"LET MY ENEMIES DEVOUR EACH OTHER."
—SALVADOR DALI

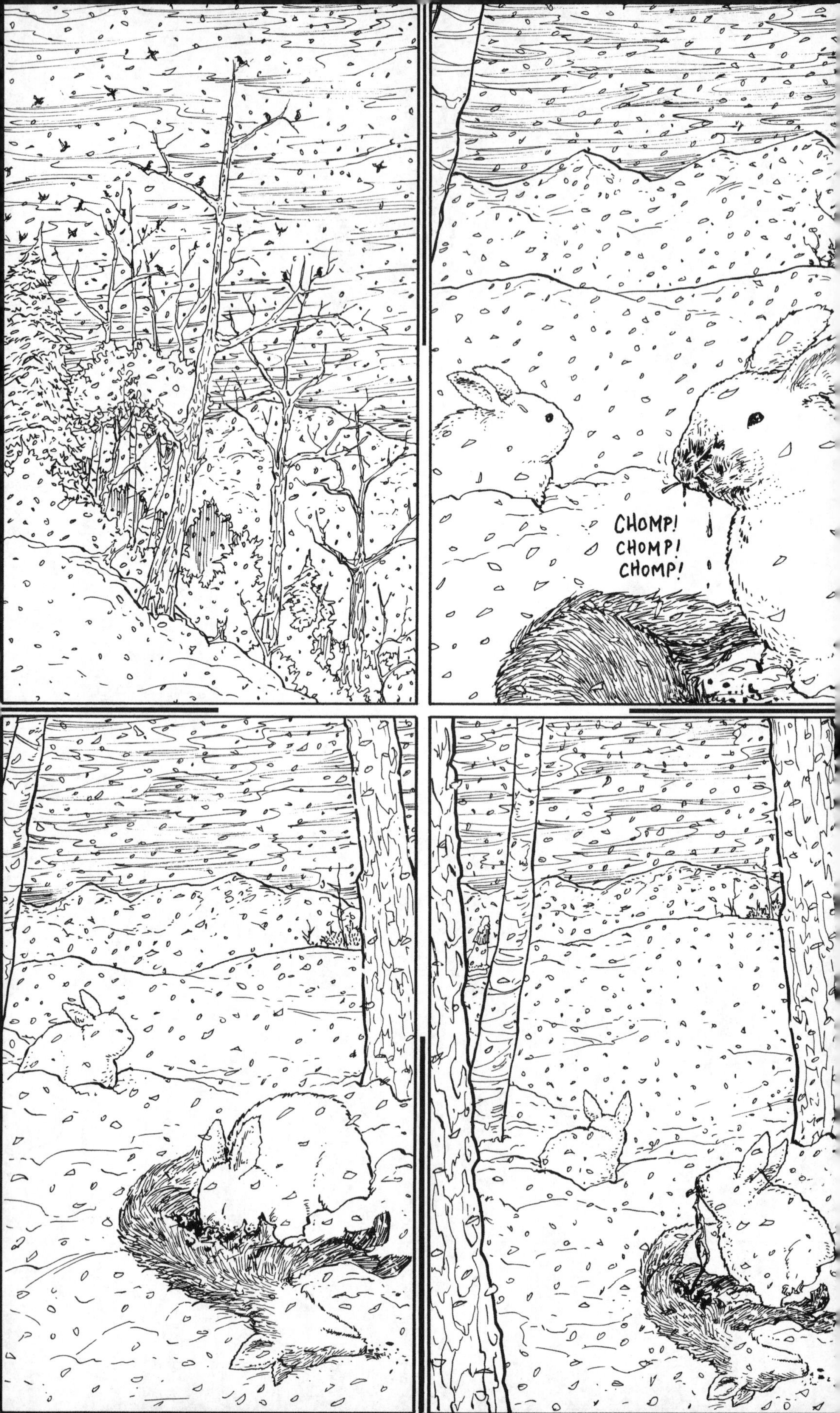
CHOMP!
CHOMP!
CHOMP!

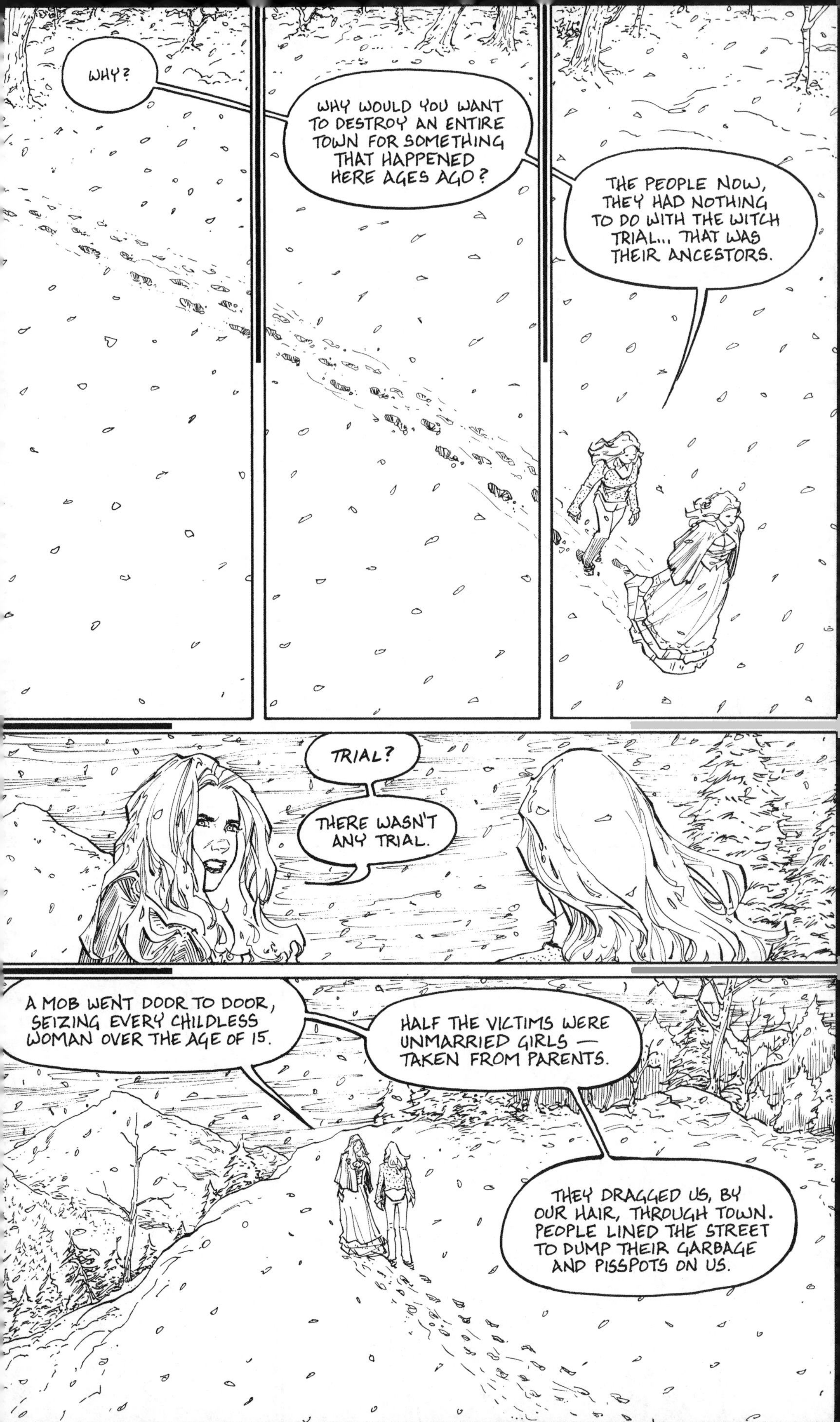
WHY?
WHY WOULD YOU WANT TO DESTROY AN ENTIRE TOWN FOR SOMETHING THAT HAPPENED HERE AGES AGO?
THE PEOPLE NOW, THEY HAD NOTHING TO DO WITH THE WITCH TRIAL... THAT WAS THEIR ANCESTORS.
TRIAL?
THERE WASN'T ANY TRIAL.
A MOB WENT DOOR TO DOOR, SEIZING EVERY CHILDLESS WOMAN OVER THE AGE OF 15.
HALF THE VICTIMS WERE UNMARRIED GIRLS — TAKEN FROM PARENTS.
THEY DRAGGED US, BY OUR HAIR, THROUGH TOWN. PEOPLE LINED THE STREET TO DUMP THEIR GARBAGE AND PISSPOTS ON US.

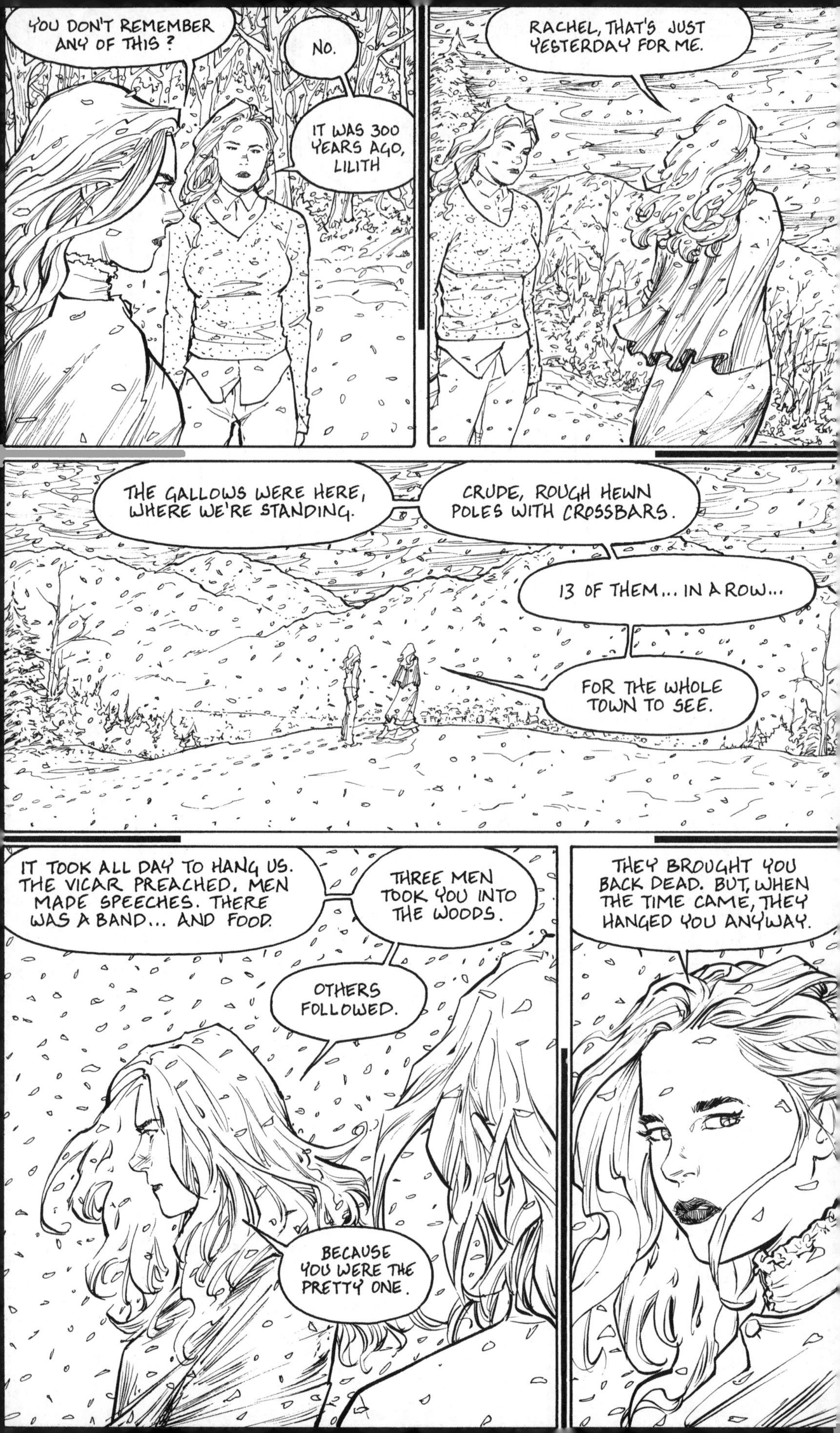

YOU DON'T REMEMBER ANY OF THIS ?
NO.
IT WAS 300 YEARS AGO, LILITH
RACHEL, THAT'S JUST YESTERDAY FOR ME.
THE GALLOWS WERE HERE, WHERE WE'RE STANDING.
CRUDE, ROUGH HEWN POLES WITH CROSSBARS.
13 OF THEM... IN A ROW...
FOR THE WHOLE TOWN TO SEE.
IT TOOK ALL DAY TO HANG US. THE VICAR PREACHED. MEN MADE SPEECHES. THERE WAS A BAND... AND FOOD.
THREE MEN TOOK YOU INTO THE WOODS.
OTHERS FOLLOWED.
BECAUSE YOU WERE THE PRETTY ONE.
THEY BROUGHT YOU BACK DEAD. BUT, WHEN THE TIME CAME, THEY HANGED YOU ANYWAY.

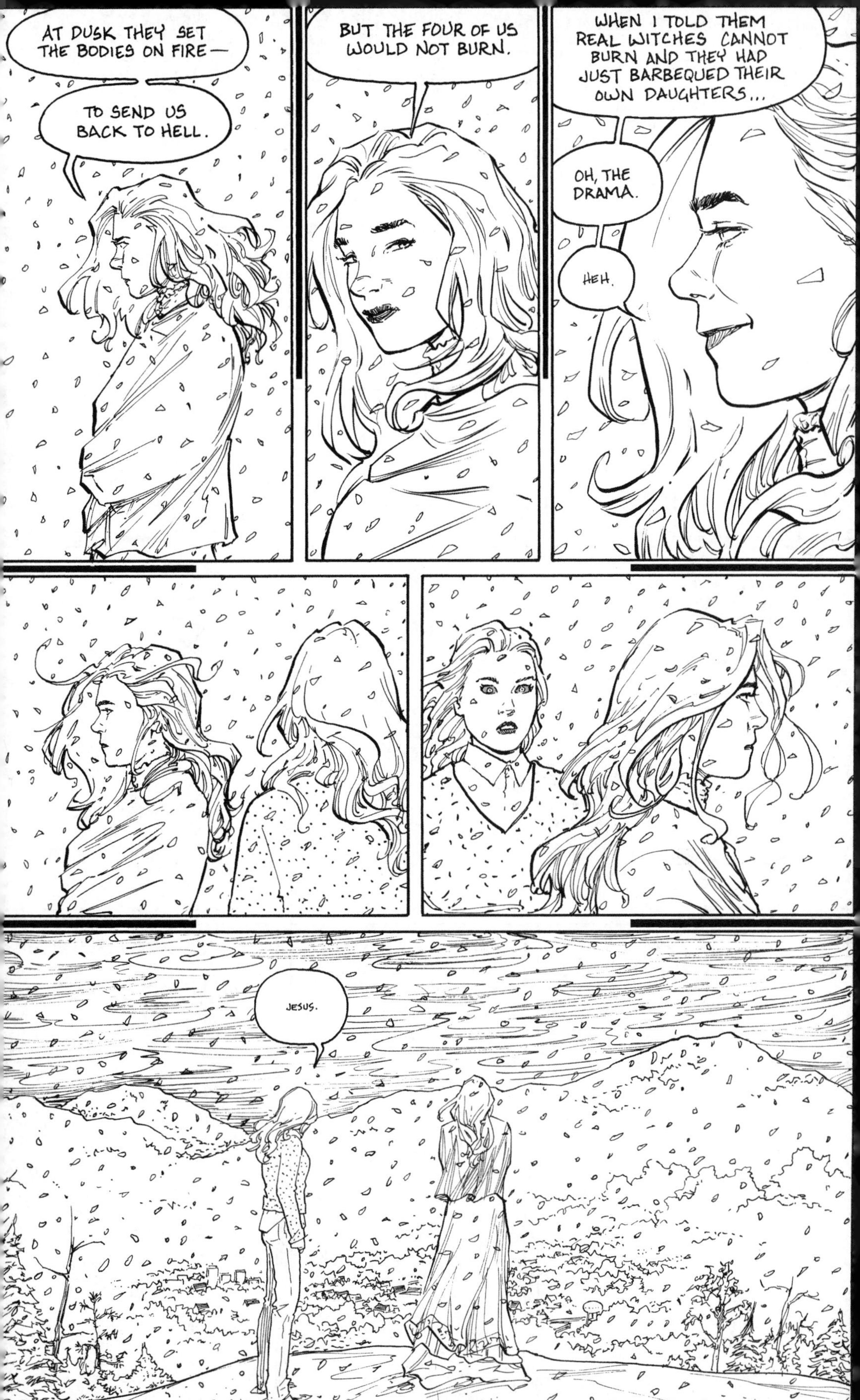
AT DUSK THEY SET THE BODIES ON FIRE—
TO SEND US BACK TO HELL.
BUT THE FOUR OF US WOULD NOT BURN.
WHEN I TOLD THEM REAL WITCHES CANNOT BURN AND THEY HAD JUST BARBEQUED THEIR OWN DAUGHTERS...
OH, THE DRAMA.
HEH.
JESUS.

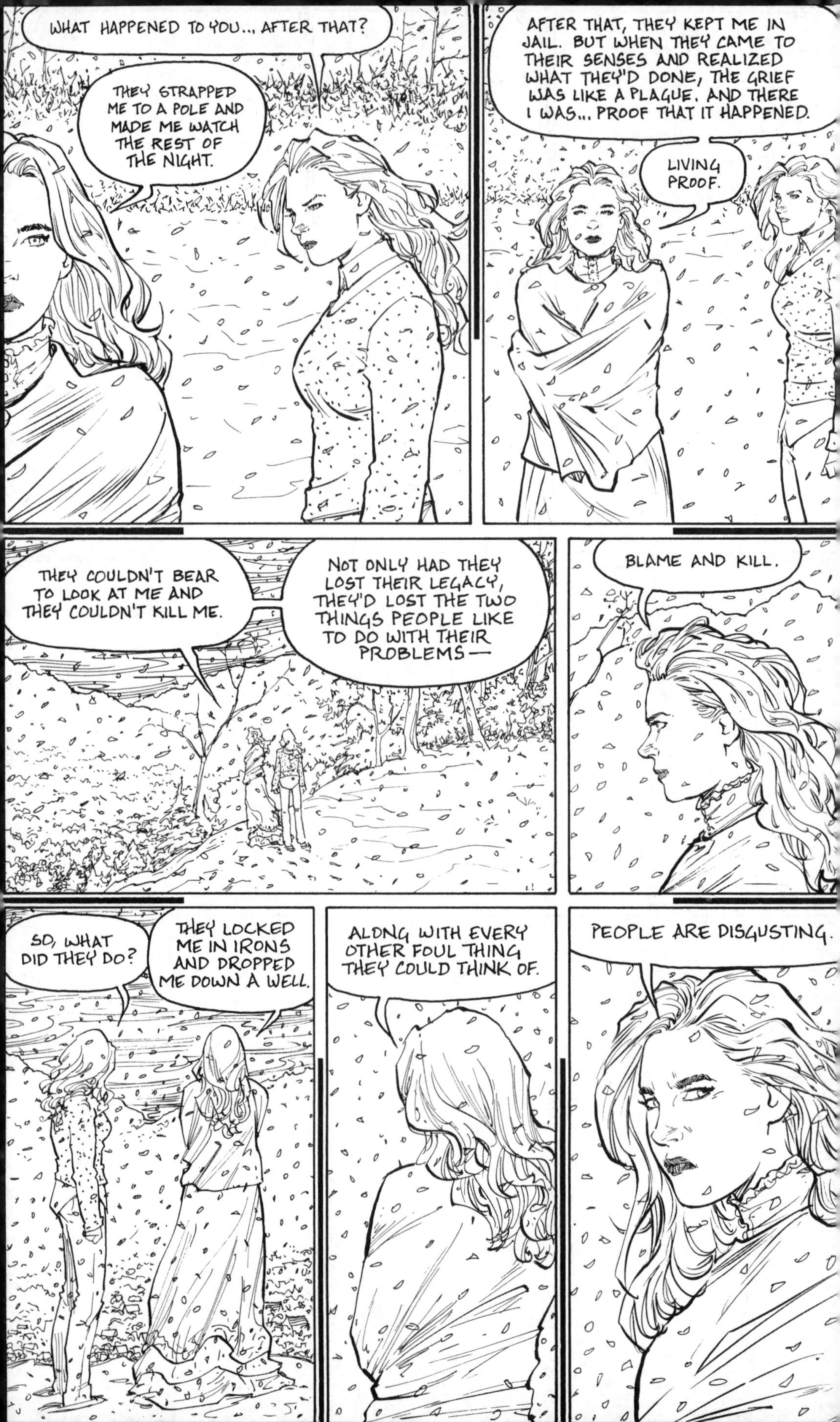

WHAT HAPPENED TO YOU... AFTER THAT?
THEY STRAPPED ME TO A POLE AND MADE ME WATCH THE REST OF THE NIGHT.
AFTER THAT, THEY KEPT ME IN JAIL. BUT WHEN THEY CAME TO THEIR SENSES AND REALIZED WHAT THEY'D DONE, THE GRIEF WAS LIKE A PLAGUE. AND THERE I WAS... PROOF THAT IT HAPPENED.
LIVING PROOF.
THEY COULDN'T BEAR TO LOOK AT ME AND THEY COULDN'T KILL ME.
NOT ONLY HAD THEY LOST THEIR LEGACY, THEY'D LOST THE TWO THINGS PEOPLE LIKE TO DO WITH THEIR PROBLEMS—
BLAME AND KILL.
SO, WHAT DID THEY DO?
THEY LOCKED ME IN IRONS AND DROPPED ME DOWN A WELL.
ALONG WITH EVERY OTHER FOUL THING THEY COULD THINK OF.
PEOPLE ARE DISGUSTING.

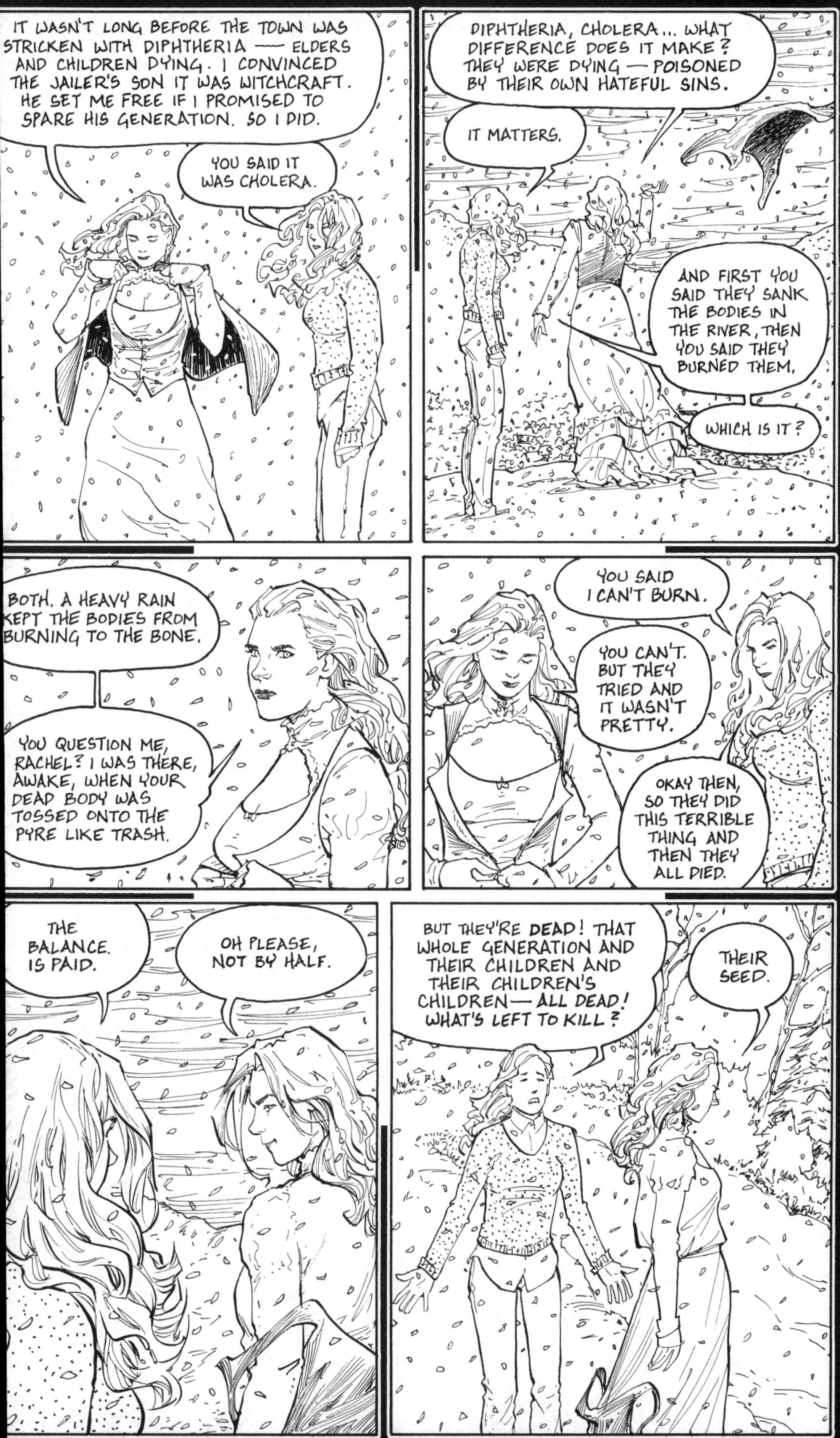

IT WASN'T LONG BEFORE THE TOWN WAS STRICKEN WITH DIPHTHERIA — ELDERS AND CHILDREN DYING. I CONVINCED THE JAILER'S SON IT WAS WITCHCRAFT. HE SET ME FREE IF I PROMISED TO SPARE HIS GENERATION. SO I DID.
YOU SAID IT WAS CHOLERA.
DIPHTHERIA, CHOLERA... WHAT DIFFERENCE DOES IT MAKE? THEY WERE DYING — POISONED BY THEIR OWN HATEFUL SINS.
IT MATTERS.
AND FIRST YOU SAID THEY SANK THE BODIES IN THE RIVER, THEN YOU SAID THEY BURNED THEM.
WHICH IS IT?
BOTH. A HEAVY RAIN KEPT THE BODIES FROM BURNING TO THE BONE.
YOU QUESTION ME, RACHEL? I WAS THERE, AWAKE, WHEN YOUR DEAD BODY WAS TOSSED ONTO THE PYRE LIKE TRASH.
YOU SAID I CAN'T BURN.
YOU CAN'T. BUT THEY TRIED AND IT WASN'T PRETTY.
OKAY THEN, SO THEY DID THIS TERRIBLE THING AND THEN THEY ALL DIED.
THE BALANCE IS PAID.
OH PLEASE, NOT BY HALF.
BUT THEY'RE DEAD! THAT WHOLE GENERATION AND THEIR CHILDREN AND THEIR CHILDREN'S CHILDREN — ALL DEAD! WHAT'S LEFT TO KILL?
THEIR SEED.

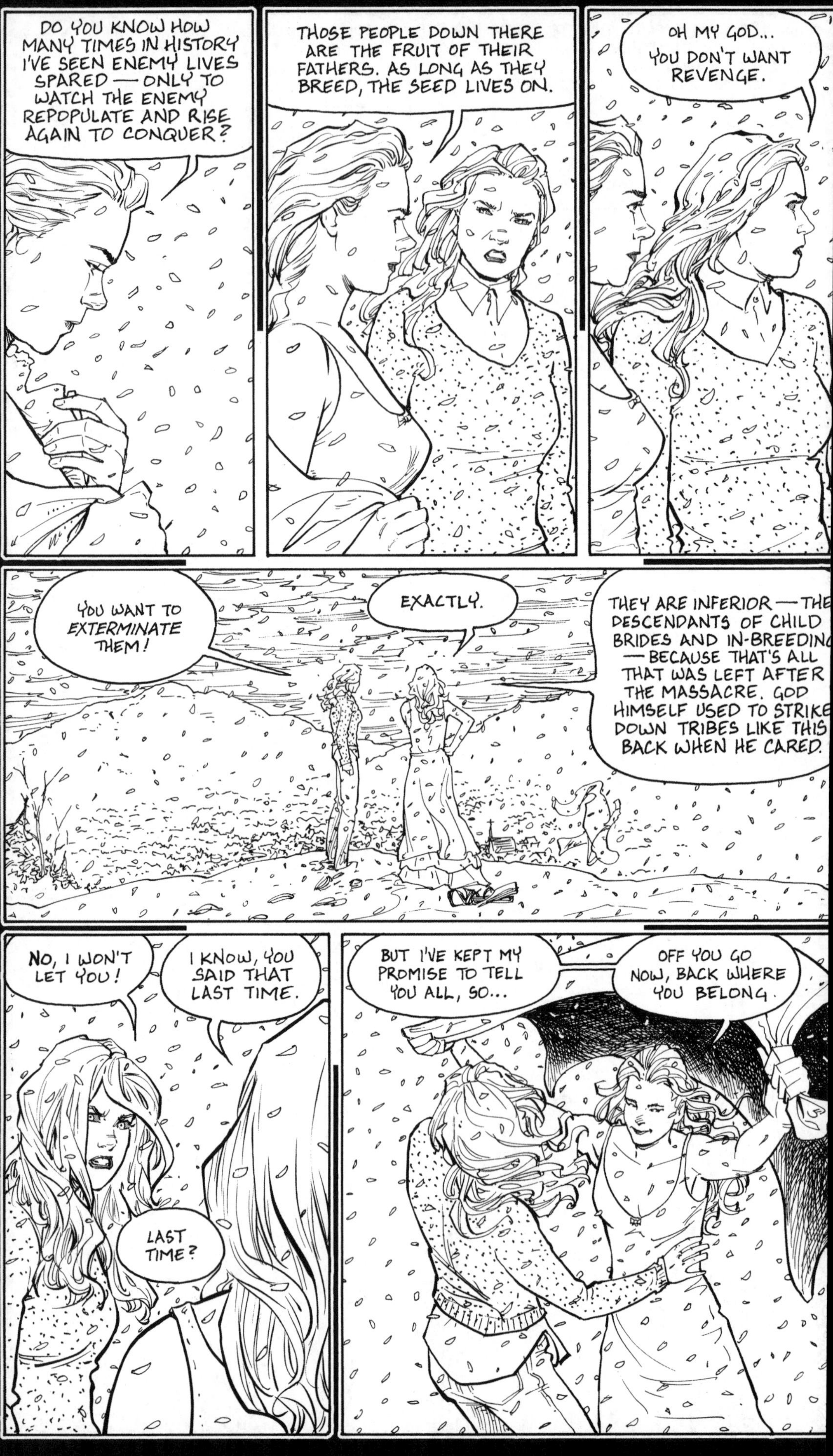

DO YOU KNOW HOW MANY TIMES IN HISTORY I'VE SEEN ENEMY LIVES SPARED — ONLY TO WATCH THE ENEMY REPOPULATE AND RISE AGAIN TO CONQUER?
THOSE PEOPLE DOWN THERE ARE THE FRUIT OF THEIR FATHERS. AS LONG AS THEY BREED, THE SEED LIVES ON.
OH MY GOD... YOU DON'T WANT REVENGE.
YOU WANT TO *EXTERMINATE* THEM!
EXACTLY.
THEY ARE INFERIOR — THE DESCENDANTS OF CHILD BRIDES AND IN-BREEDING — BECAUSE THAT'S ALL THAT WAS LEFT AFTER THE MASSACRE. GOD HIMSELF USED TO STRIKE DOWN TRIBES LIKE THIS BACK WHEN HE CARED.
NO, I WON'T LET YOU!
I KNOW, YOU SAID THAT LAST TIME.
LAST TIME?
BUT I'VE KEPT MY PROMISE TO TELL YOU ALL, SO...
OFF YOU GO NOW, BACK WHERE YOU BELONG.

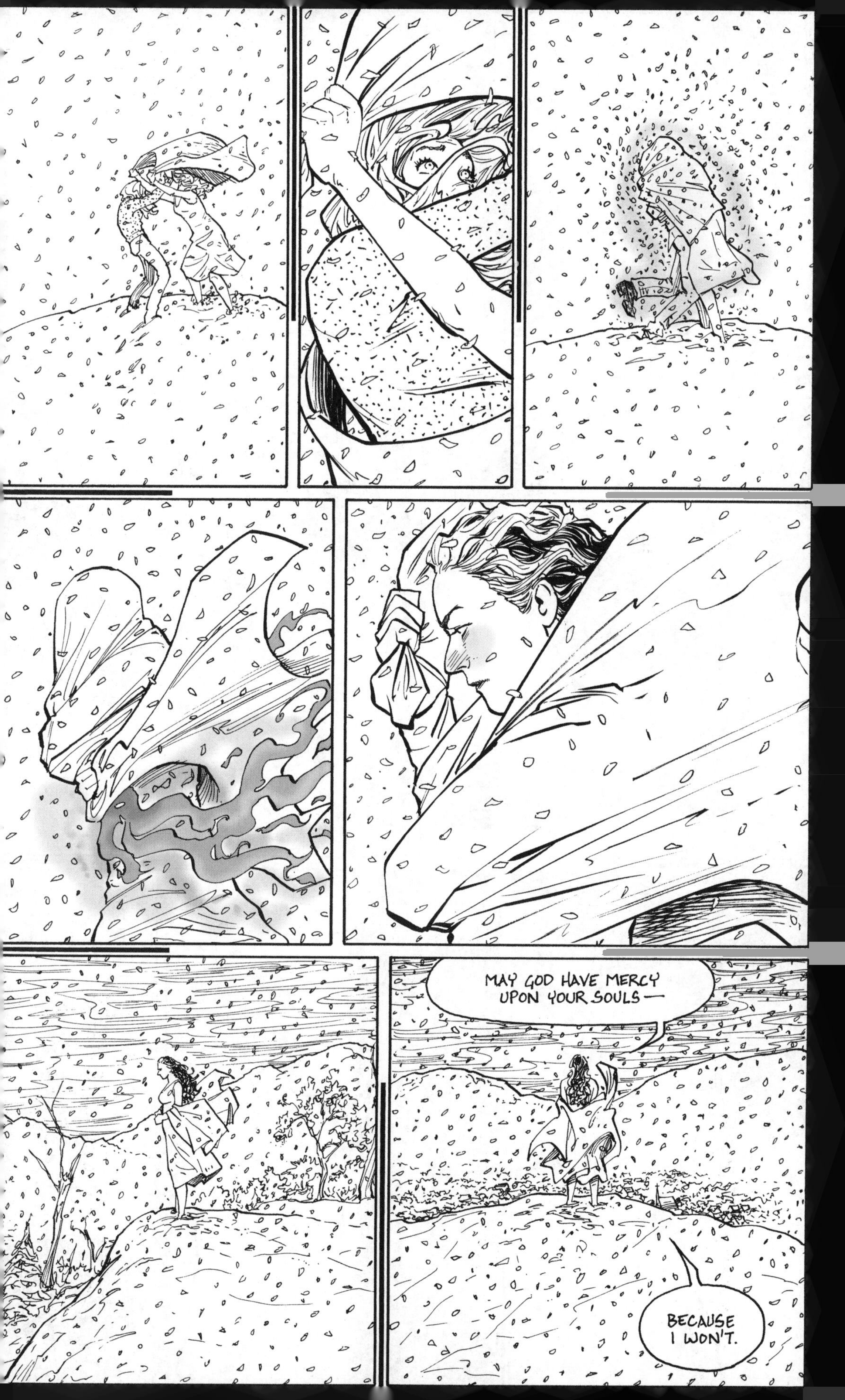
MAY GOD HAVE MERCY UPON YOUR SOULS—
BECAUSE I WON'T.

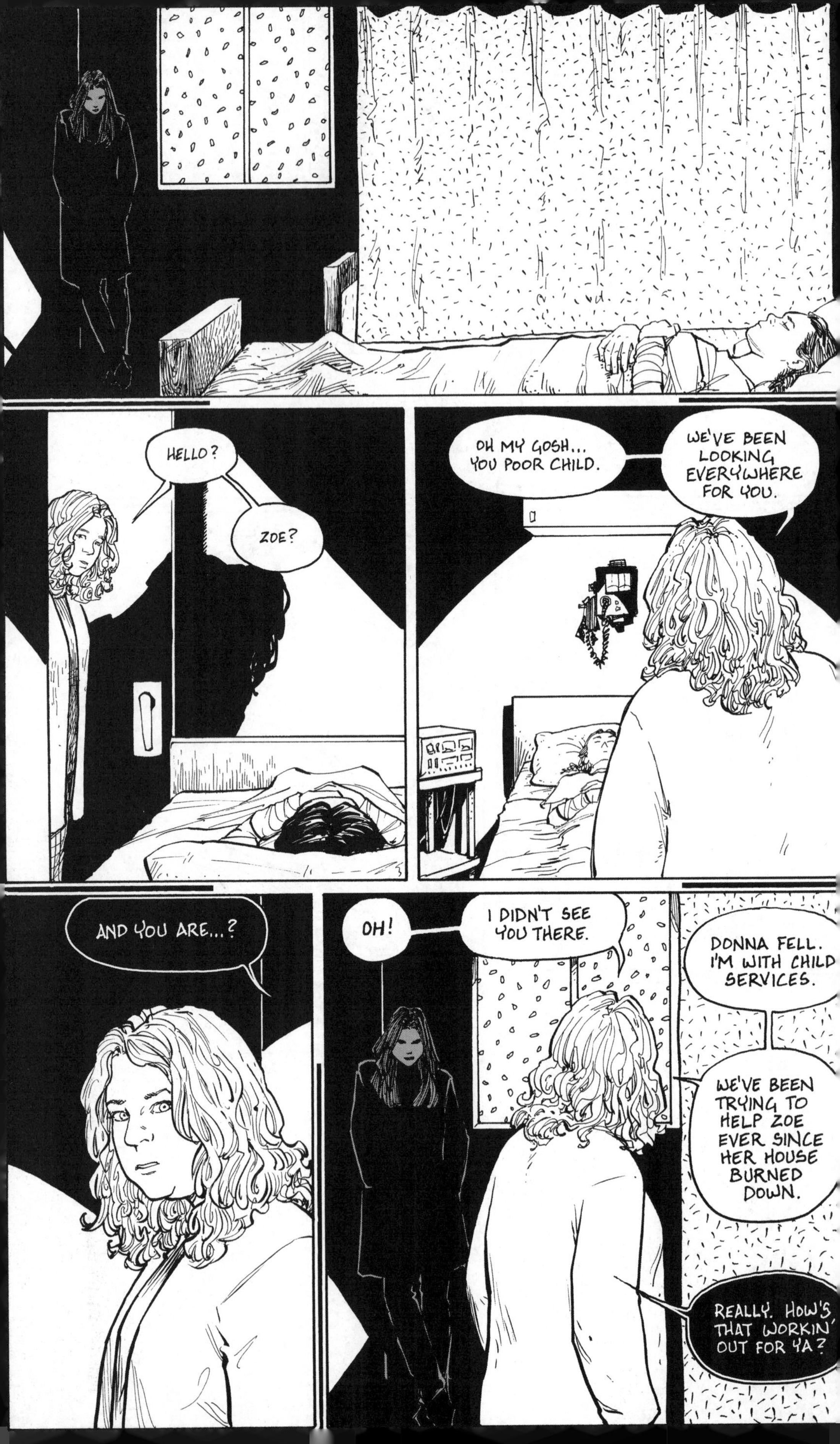
HELLO?
ZOE?
OH MY GOSH... YOU POOR CHILD.
WE'VE BEEN LOOKING EVERYWHERE FOR YOU.
AND YOU ARE...?
OH!
I DIDN'T SEE YOU THERE.
DONNA FELL. I'M WITH CHILD SERVICES.
WE'VE BEEN TRYING TO HELP ZOE EVER SINCE HER HOUSE BURNED DOWN.
REALLY. HOW'S THAT WORKIN' OUT FOR YA?

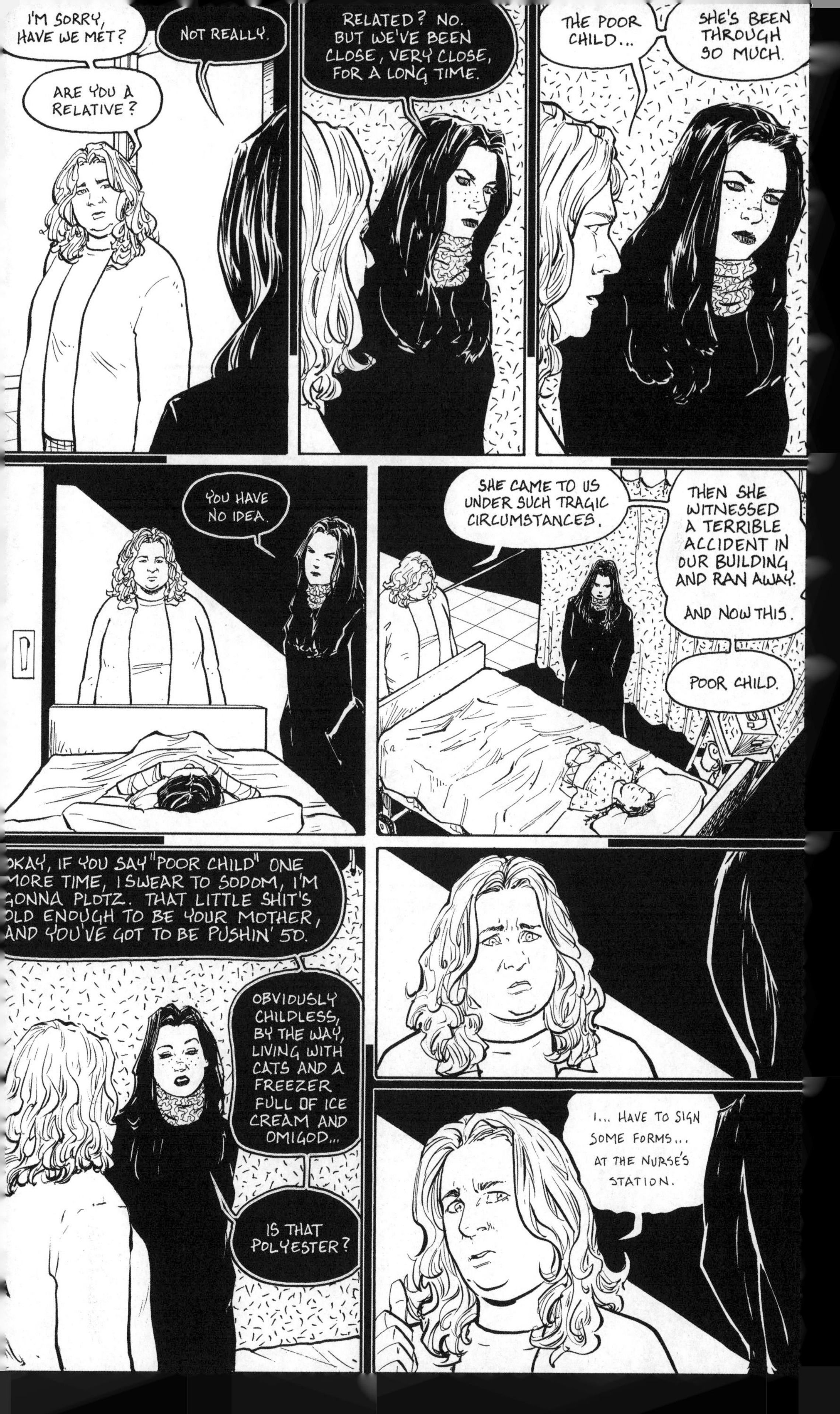
I'M SORRY, HAVE WE MET?
NOT REALLY.
ARE YOU A RELATIVE?
RELATED? NO. BUT WE'VE BEEN CLOSE, VERY CLOSE, FOR A LONG TIME.
THE POOR CHILD...
SHE'S BEEN THROUGH SO MUCH.
YOU HAVE NO IDEA.
SHE CAME TO US UNDER SUCH TRAGIC CIRCUMSTANCES.
THEN SHE WITNESSED A TERRIBLE ACCIDENT IN OUR BUILDING AND RAN AWAY.
AND NOW THIS.
POOR CHILD.
OKAY, IF YOU SAY "POOR CHILD" ONE MORE TIME, I SWEAR TO SODOM, I'M GONNA PLOTZ. THAT LITTLE SHIT'S OLD ENOUGH TO BE YOUR MOTHER, AND YOU'VE GOT TO BE PUSHIN' 50.
OBVIOUSLY CHILDLESS, BY THE WAY, LIVING WITH CATS AND A FREEZER FULL OF ICE CREAM AND OMIGOD...
IS THAT POLYESTER?
I... HAVE TO SIGN SOME FORMS... AT THE NURSE'S STATION.

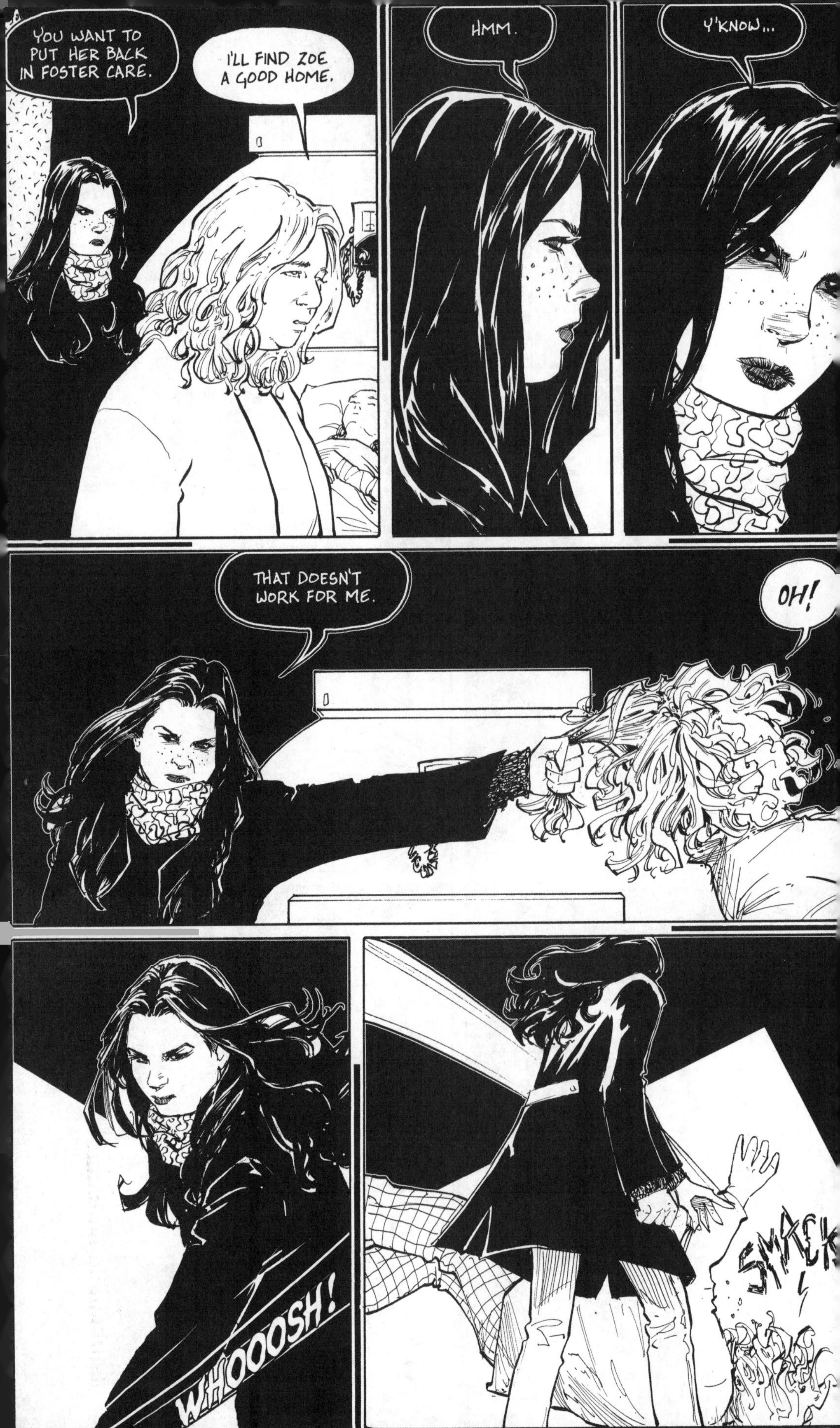
YOU WANT TO PUT HER BACK IN FOSTER CARE.
I'LL FIND ZOE A GOOD HOME.
HMM.
Y'KNOW...
THAT DOESN'T WORK FOR ME.
OH!
WHOOOSH!
SMACK!

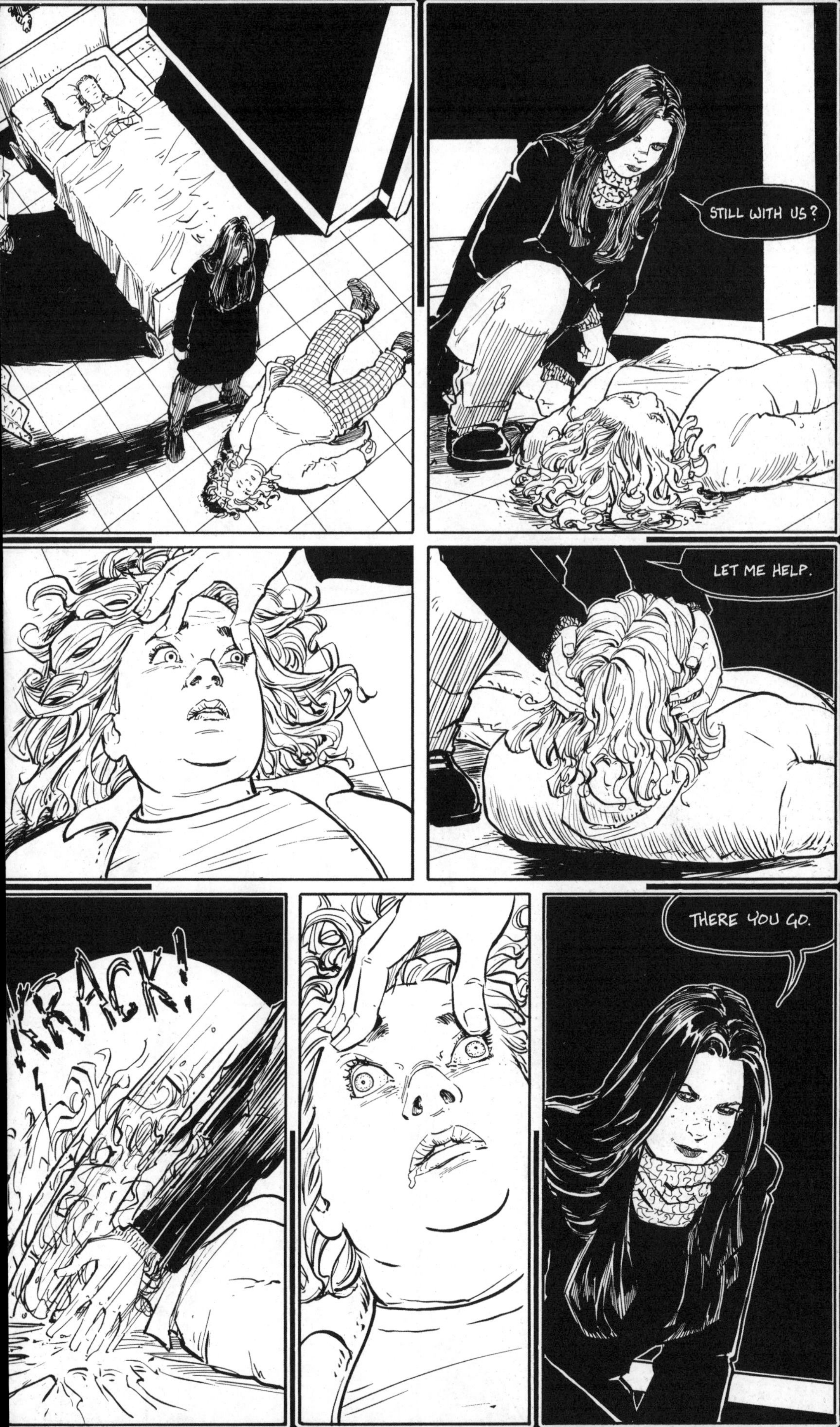
STILL WITH US?
LET ME HELP.
KRACK!
THERE YOU GO.

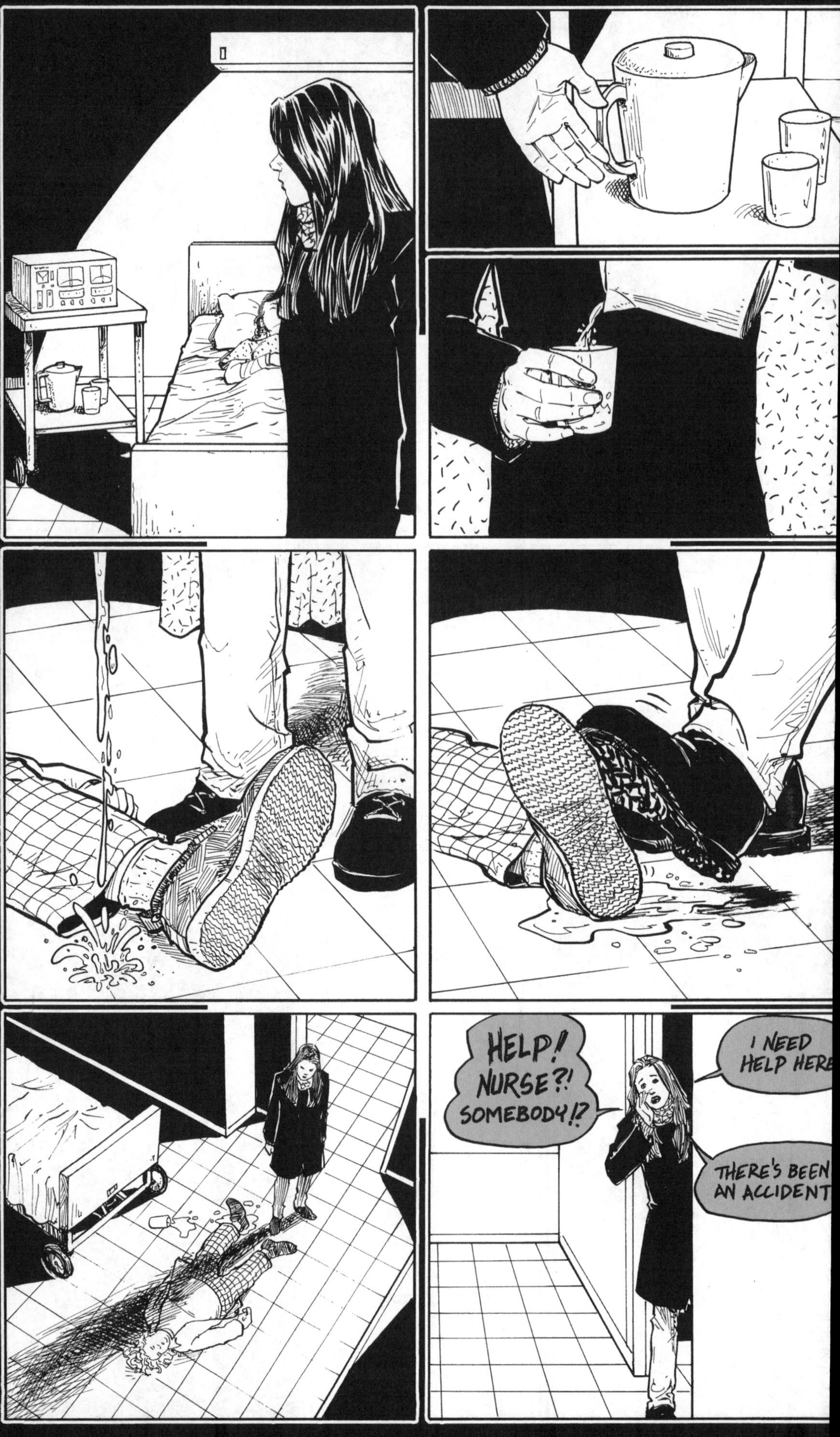
HELP! NURSE?! SOMEBODY!?
I NEED HELP HERE
THERE'S BEEN AN ACCIDENT

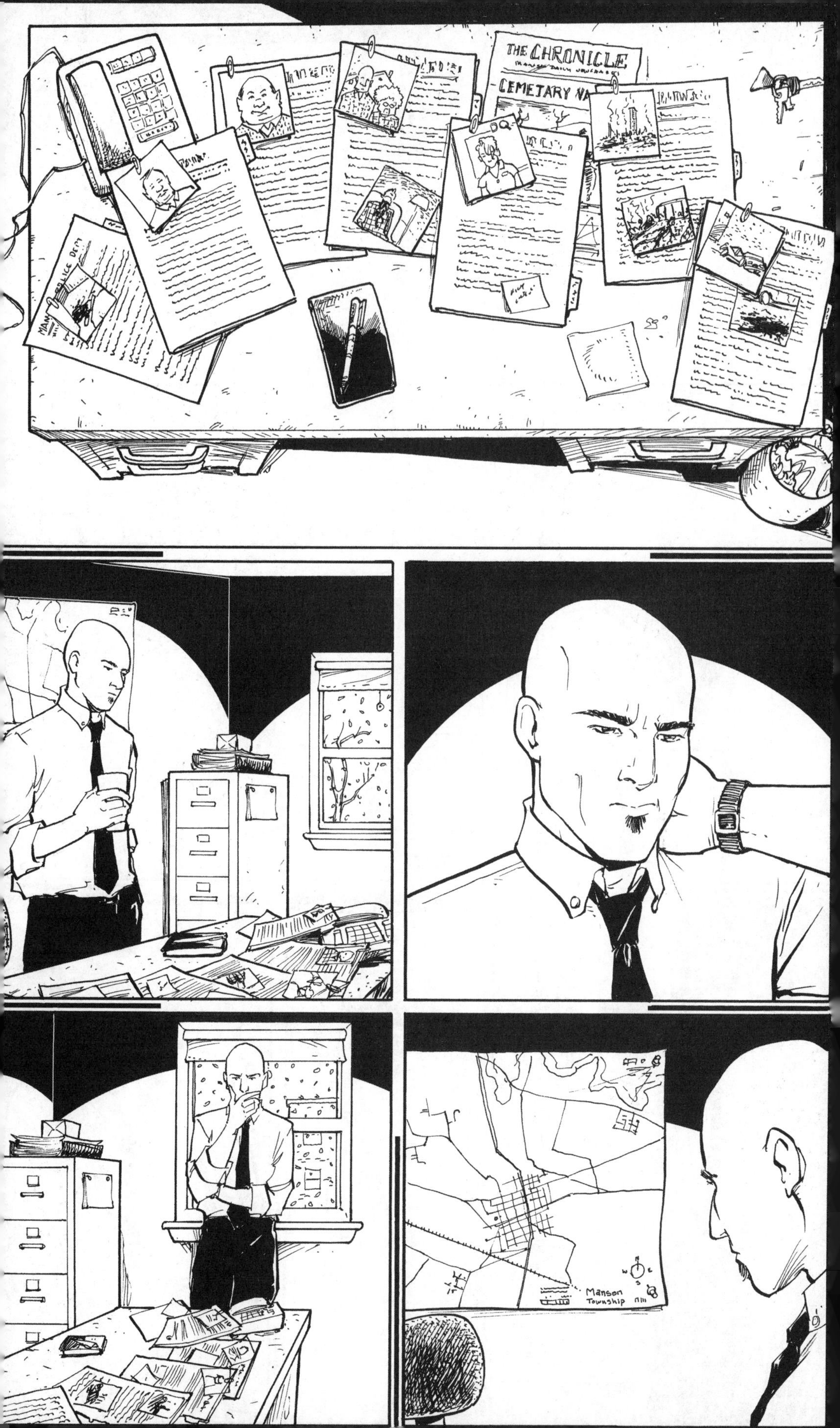
THE CHRONICLE
CEMETARY NA
Manson
Township

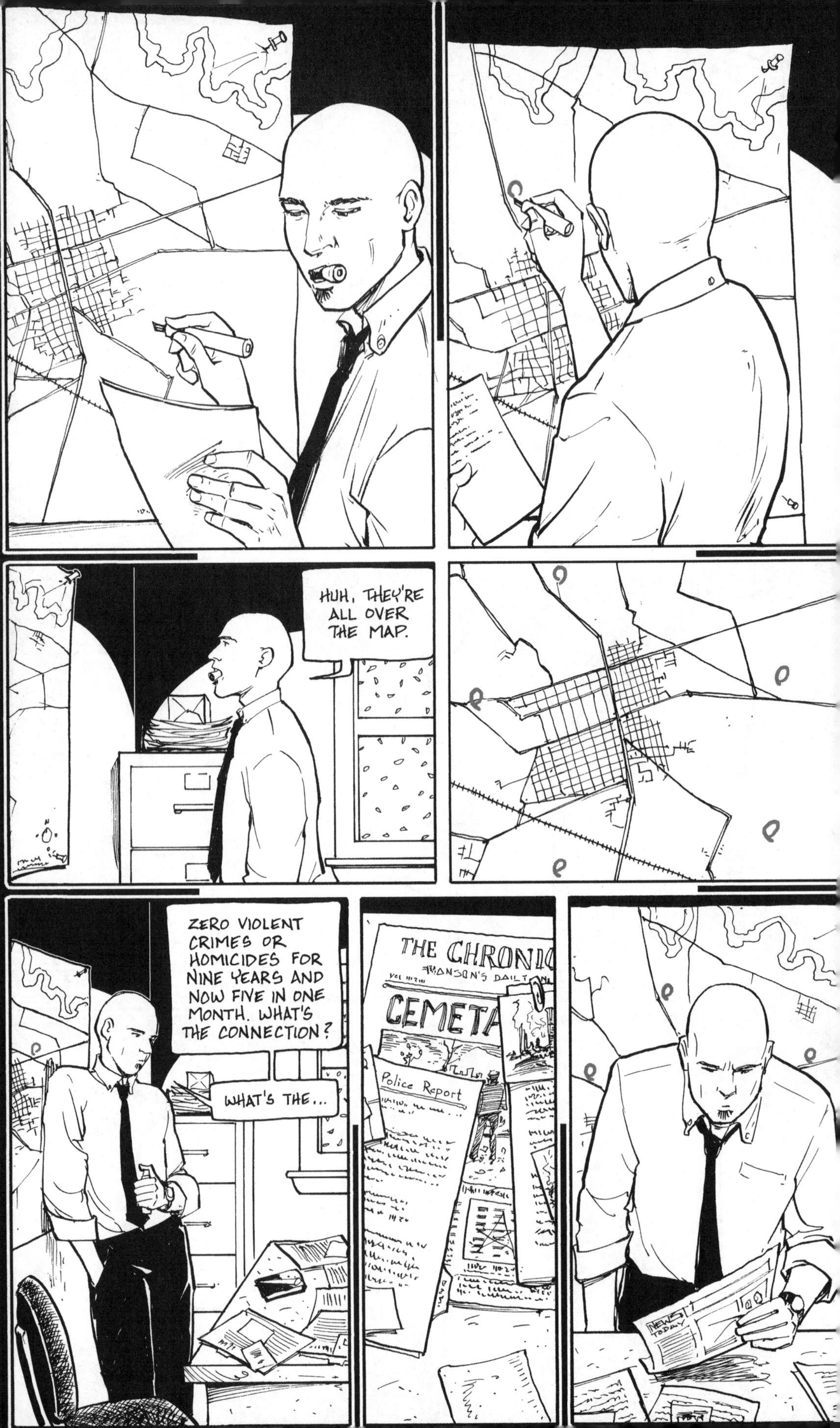
HUH, THEY'RE ALL OVER THE MAP.
ZERO VIOLENT CRIMES OR HOMICIDES FOR NINE YEARS AND NOW FIVE IN ONE MONTH. WHAT'S THE CONNECTION?
WHAT'S THE...
THE CHRONIC
CEMETA
Police Report
NEWS TODAY

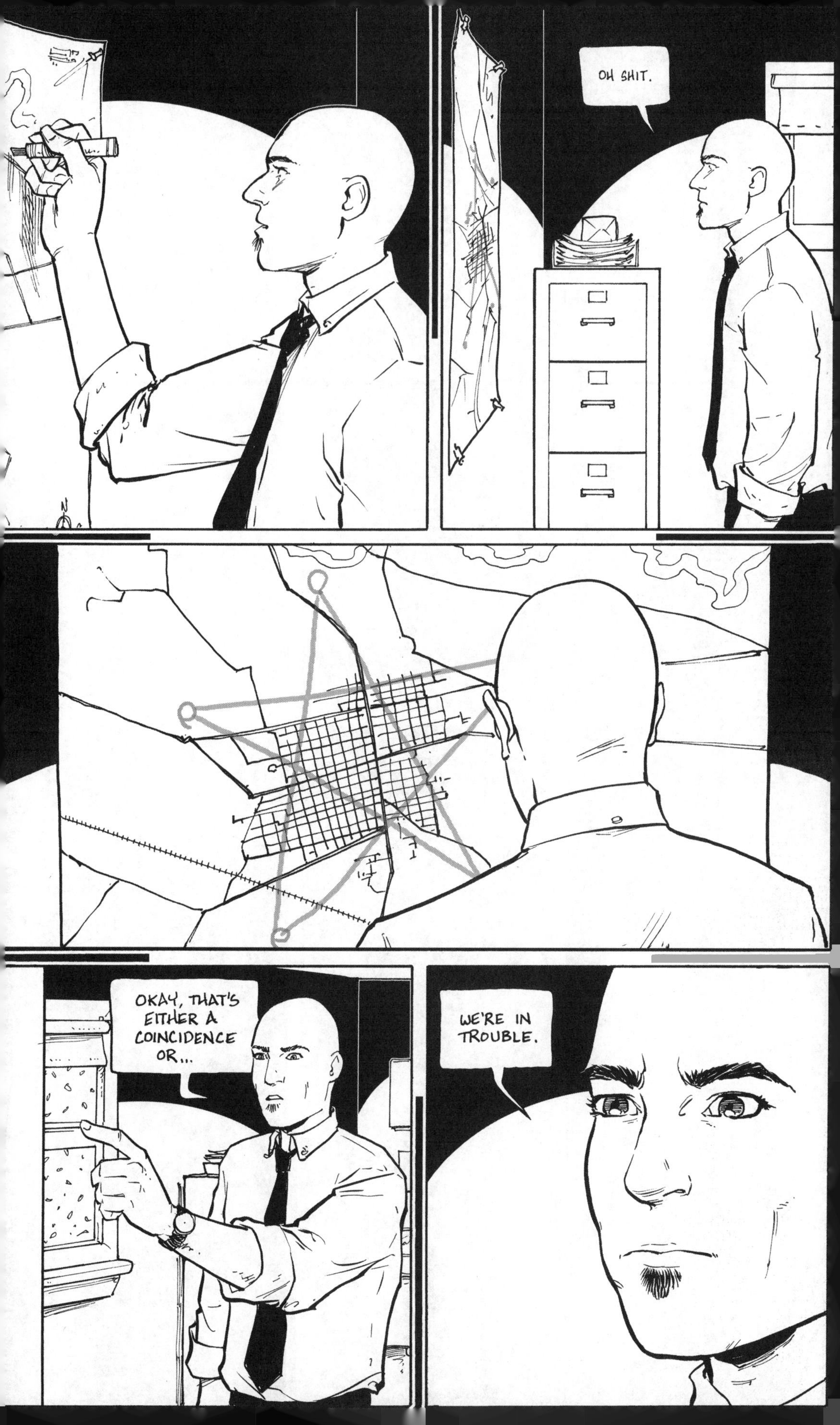
OH SHIT.
OKAY, THAT'S EITHER A COINCIDENCE OR...
WE'RE IN TROUBLE.

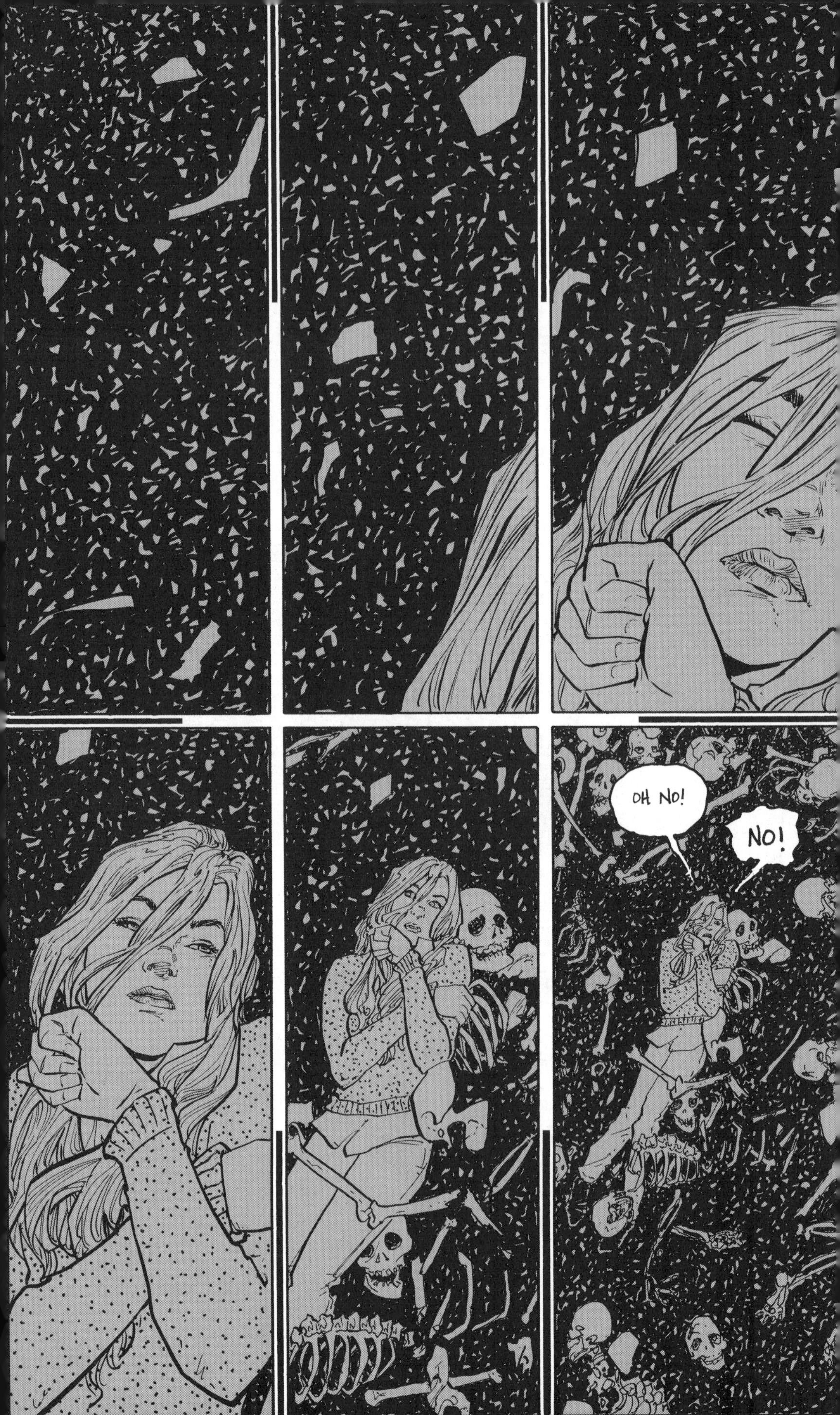
OH NO!
NO!

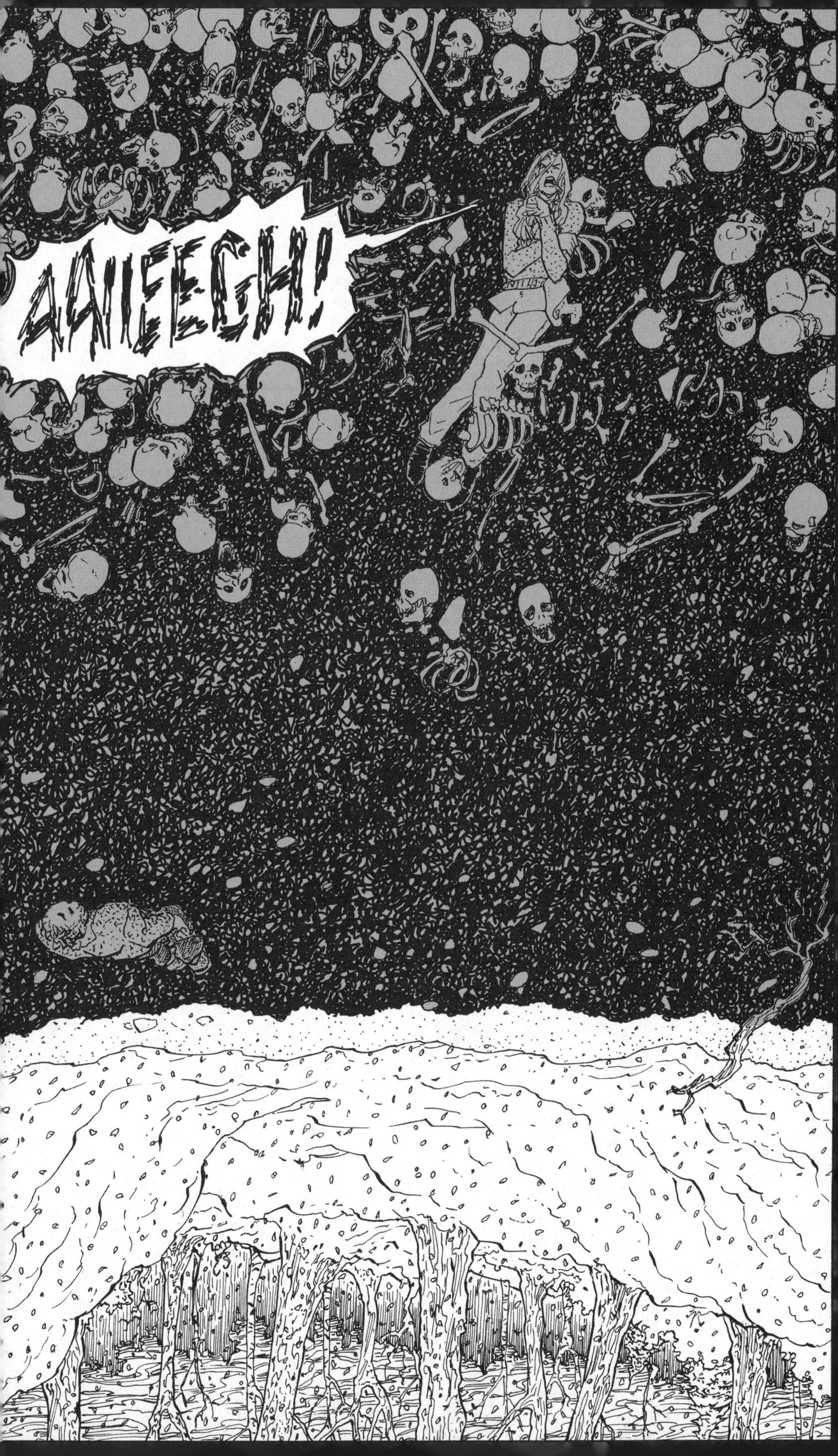
AAIIEEGH!

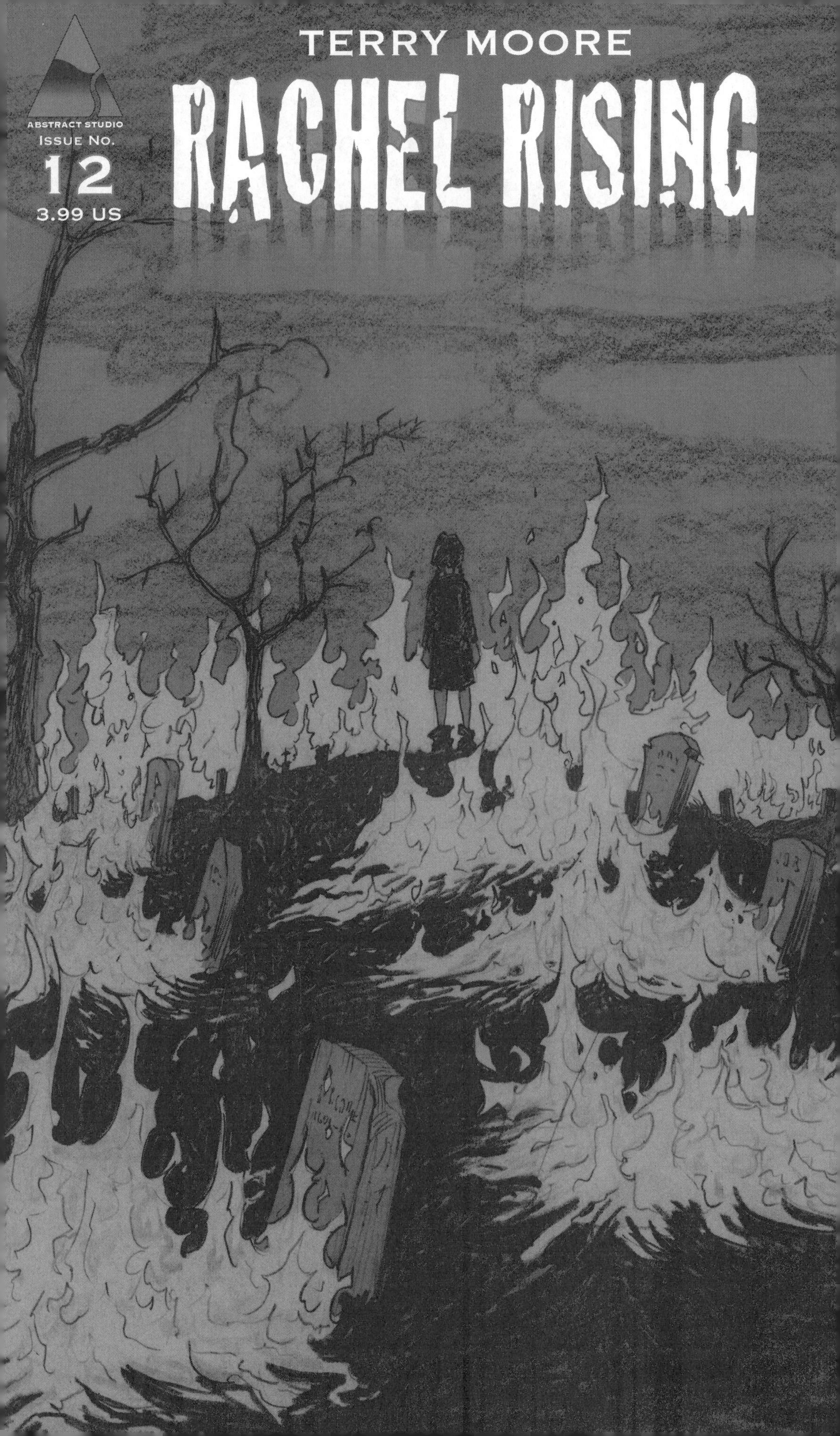
ABSTRACT STUDIO
Issue No.
12
3.99 US
TERRY MOORE
RACHEL RISING

"YOU NEVER REALISE DEATH UNTIL YOU REALISE LOVE."
—KATHARINE BUTLER HATHAWAY

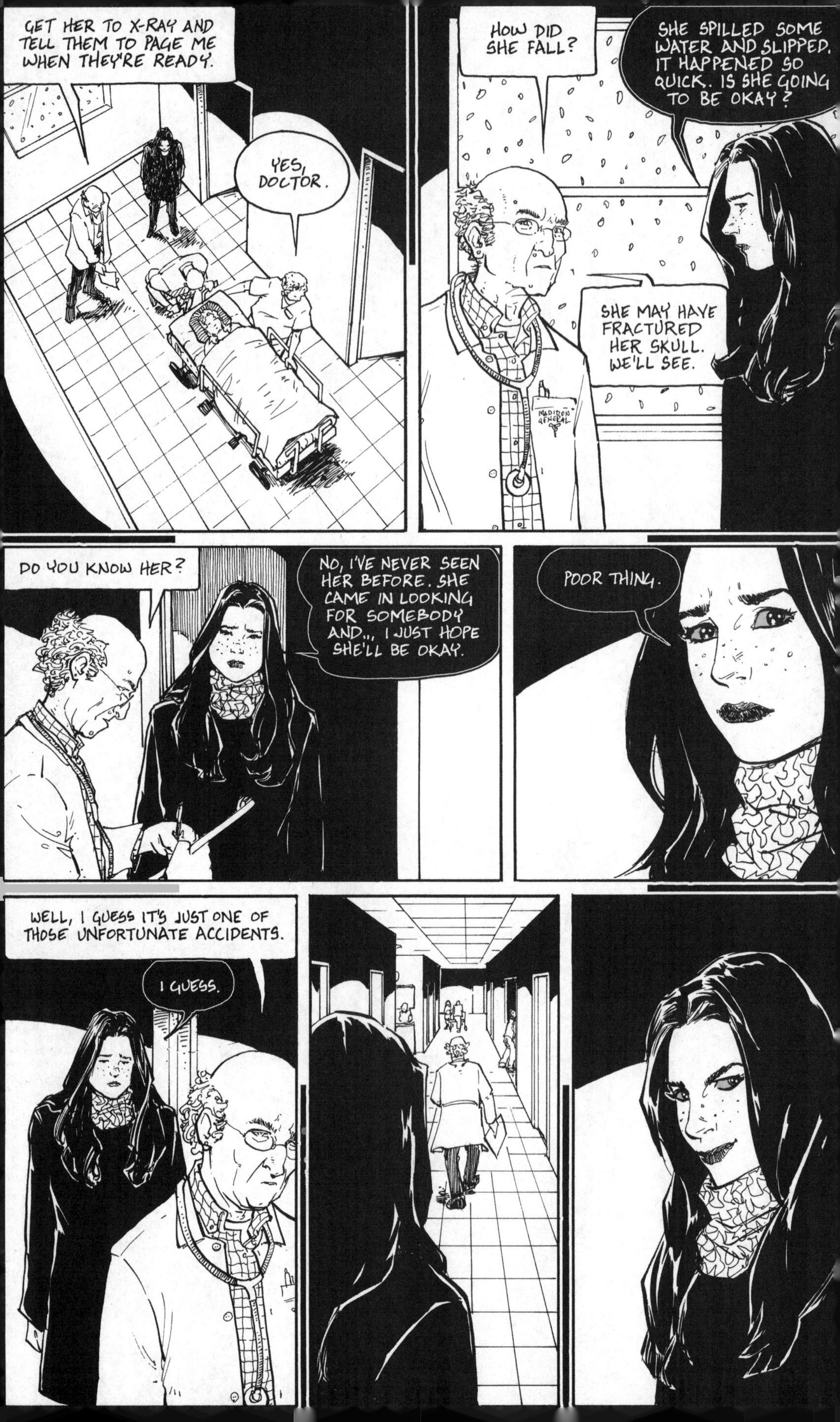
GET HER TO X-RAY AND TELL THEM TO PAGE ME WHEN THEY'RE READY.
YES, DOCTOR.
HOW DID SHE FALL?
SHE SPILLED SOME WATER AND SLIPPED. IT HAPPENED SO QUICK. IS SHE GOING TO BE OKAY?
SHE MAY HAVE FRACTURED HER SKULL. WE'LL SEE.
MADISON GENERAL
DO YOU KNOW HER?
NO, I'VE NEVER SEEN HER BEFORE. SHE CAME IN LOOKING FOR SOMEBODY AND... I JUST HOPE SHE'LL BE OKAY.
POOR THING.
WELL, I GUESS IT'S JUST ONE OF THOSE UNFORTUNATE ACCIDENTS.
I GUESS.

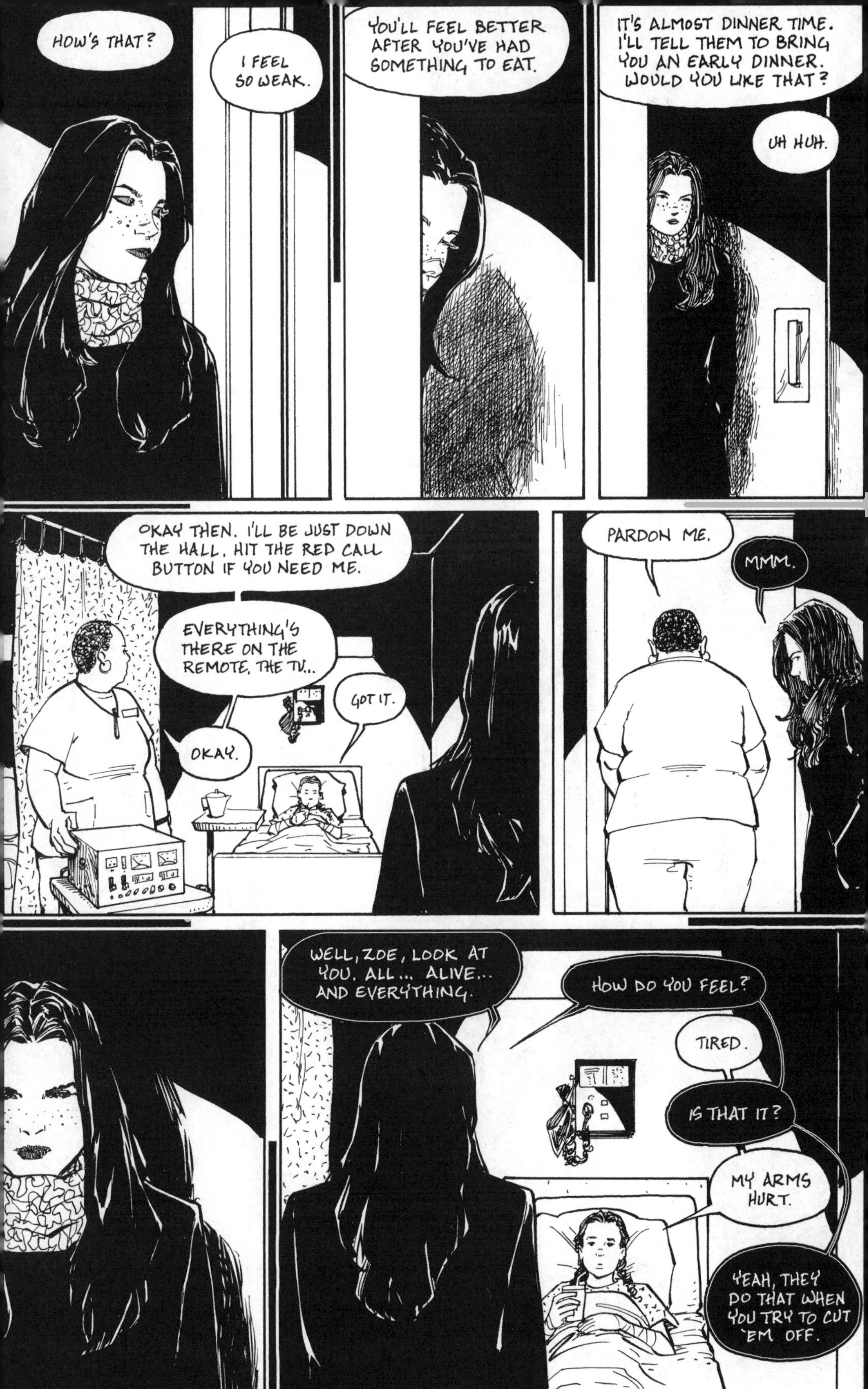

HOW'S THAT?
I FEEL SO WEAK.
YOU'LL FEEL BETTER AFTER YOU'VE HAD SOMETHING TO EAT.
IT'S ALMOST DINNER TIME. I'LL TELL THEM TO BRING YOU AN EARLY DINNER. WOULD YOU LIKE THAT?
UH HUH.
OKAY THEN. I'LL BE JUST DOWN THE HALL. HIT THE RED CALL BUTTON IF YOU NEED ME.
EVERYTHING'S THERE ON THE REMOTE, THE TV...
OKAY.
GOT IT.
PARDON ME.
MMM.
WELL, ZOE, LOOK AT YOU. ALL... ALIVE... AND EVERYTHING.
HOW DO YOU FEEL?
TIRED.
IS THAT IT?
MY ARMS HURT.
YEAH, THEY DO THAT WHEN YOU TRY TO CUT 'EM OFF.

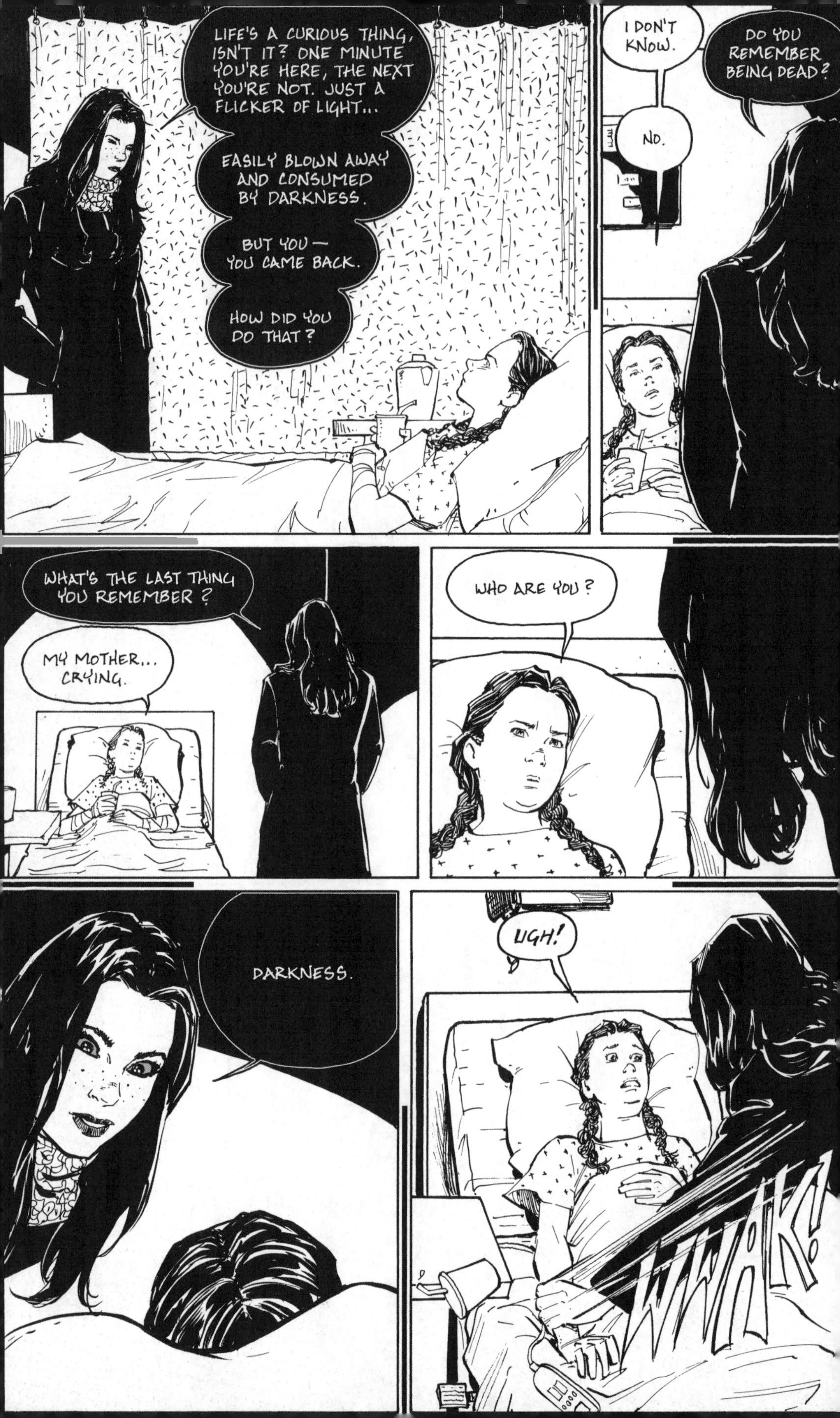
LIFE'S A CURIOUS THING, ISN'T IT? ONE MINUTE YOU'RE HERE, THE NEXT YOU'RE NOT. JUST A FLICKER OF LIGHT...
EASILY BLOWN AWAY AND CONSUMED BY DARKNESS.
BUT YOU— YOU CAME BACK.
HOW DID YOU DO THAT?
I DON'T KNOW.
DO YOU REMEMBER BEING DEAD?
NO.
WHAT'S THE LAST THING YOU REMEMBER?
MY MOTHER... CRYING.
WHO ARE YOU?
DARKNESS.
UGH!
WHAK!

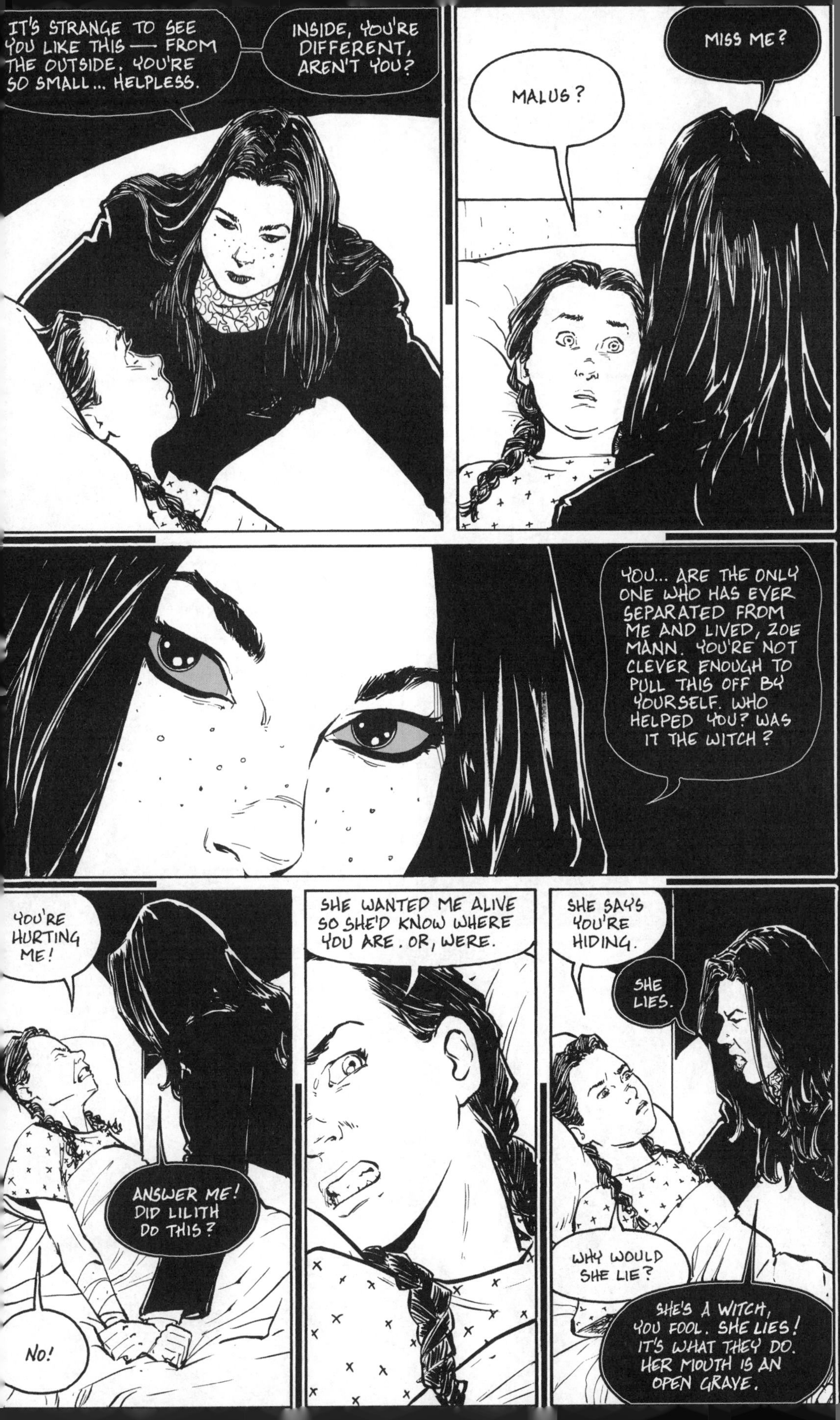
IT'S STRANGE TO SEE YOU LIKE THIS — FROM THE OUTSIDE. YOU'RE SO SMALL... HELPLESS.
INSIDE, YOU'RE DIFFERENT, AREN'T YOU?
MALUS?
MISS ME?
YOU... ARE THE ONLY ONE WHO HAS EVER SEPARATED FROM ME AND LIVED, ZOE MANN. YOU'RE NOT CLEVER ENOUGH TO PULL THIS OFF BY YOURSELF. WHO HELPED YOU? WAS IT THE WITCH?
YOU'RE HURTING ME!
ANSWER ME! DID LILITH DO THIS?
NO!
SHE WANTED ME ALIVE SO SHE'D KNOW WHERE YOU ARE. OR, WERE.
SHE SAYS YOU'RE HIDING.
SHE LIES.
WHY WOULD SHE LIE?
SHE'S A WITCH, YOU FOOL. SHE LIES! IT'S WHAT THEY DO. HER MOUTH IS AN OPEN GRAVE.

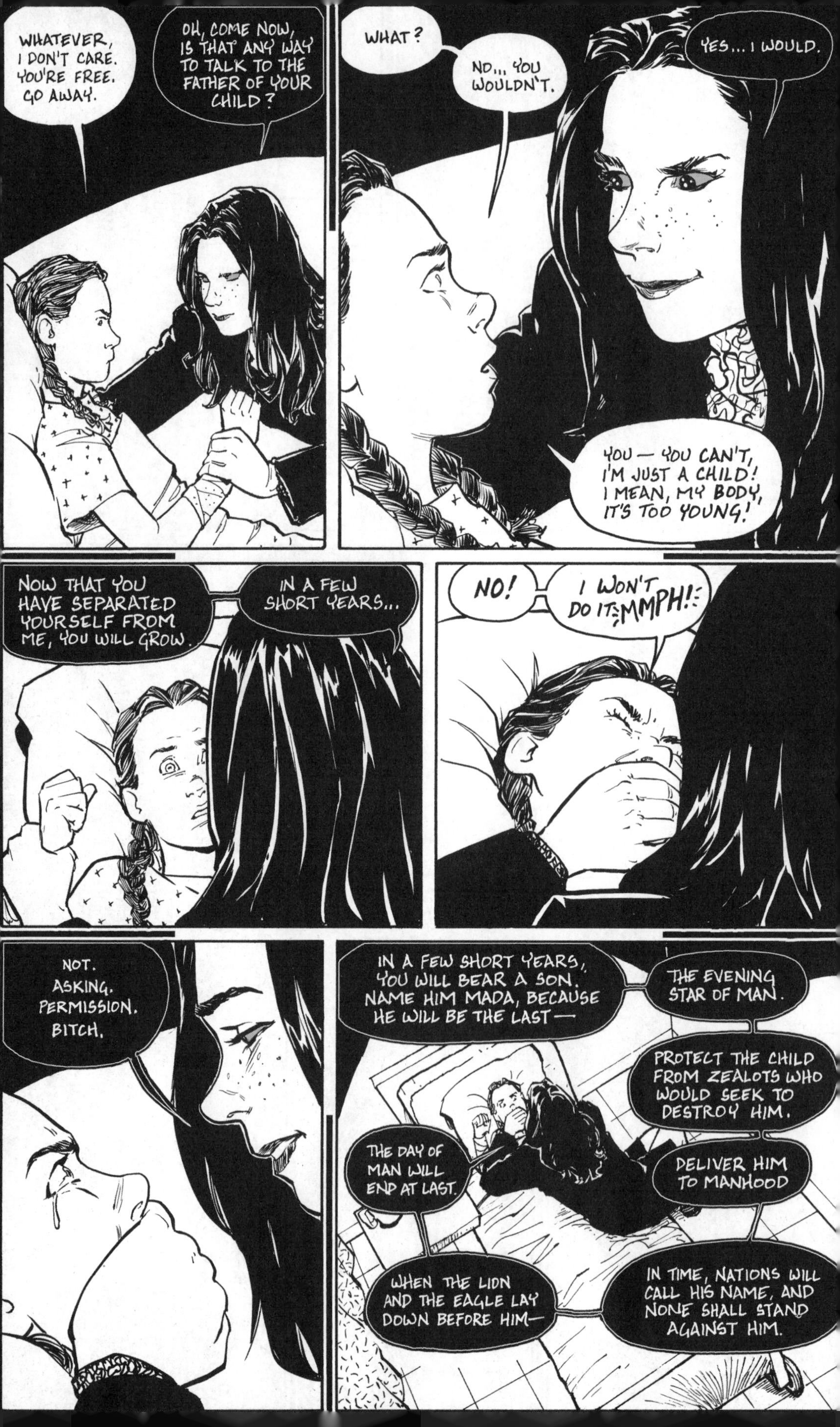
WHATEVER, I DON'T CARE. YOU'RE FREE. GO AWAY.
OH, COME NOW, IS THAT ANY WAY TO TALK TO THE FATHER OF YOUR CHILD?
WHAT?
NO... YOU WOULDN'T.
YES... I WOULD.
YOU — YOU CAN'T, I'M JUST A CHILD! I MEAN, MY BODY, IT'S TOO YOUNG!
NOW THAT YOU HAVE SEPARATED YOURSELF FROM ME, YOU WILL GROW.
IN A FEW SHORT YEARS...
NO!
I WON'T DO IT; MMPH!
NOT. ASKING. PERMISSION. BITCH.
IN A FEW SHORT YEARS, YOU WILL BEAR A SON. NAME HIM MADA, BECAUSE HE WILL BE THE LAST—
THE EVENING STAR OF MAN.
PROTECT THE CHILD FROM ZEALOTS WHO WOULD SEEK TO DESTROY HIM.
DELIVER HIM TO MANHOOD
IN TIME, NATIONS WILL CALL HIS NAME, AND NONE SHALL STAND AGAINST HIM.
WHEN THE LION AND THE EAGLE LAY DOWN BEFORE HIM—
THE DAY OF MAN WILL END AT LAST.

PPHHT! HA! HA! HA!

I'M NOT DELIVERING THE ANTI-CHRIST, YOU IDIOT!

GOD, HOW STUPID DO YOU THINK I AM?

YOU LAUGH AT ME?!

LET ME GUESS, YOU'VE TRIED THIS BEFORE AND NOBODY WOULD DO IT.

YOU FILTHY PIG— YOU ARE DEAD WITHOUT ME! DO YOU UNDER-STAND? DEAD!

OH, BITE ME. LIKE I CARE. THE SOONER I CHECK OUT, THE SOONER I'LL LEAVE ASSHOLES LIKE YOU BEHIND.

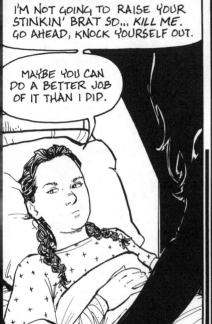

I'M NOT GOING TO RAISE YOUR STINKIN' BRAT SO... KILL ME. GO AHEAD, KNOCK YOURSELF OUT.

MAYBE YOU CAN DO A BETTER JOB OF IT THAN I DID.

>HMPH<
OH ZOE, YOU REALLY ARE JUST TOO PERFECT.

GO BACK TO SLEEP, CHILD. THERE'S NOTHING TO WORRY ABOUT... IT'S JUST A DREAM. THAT'S ALL,

JUST A DREAM.

A DREAM.

Life is but a dream.

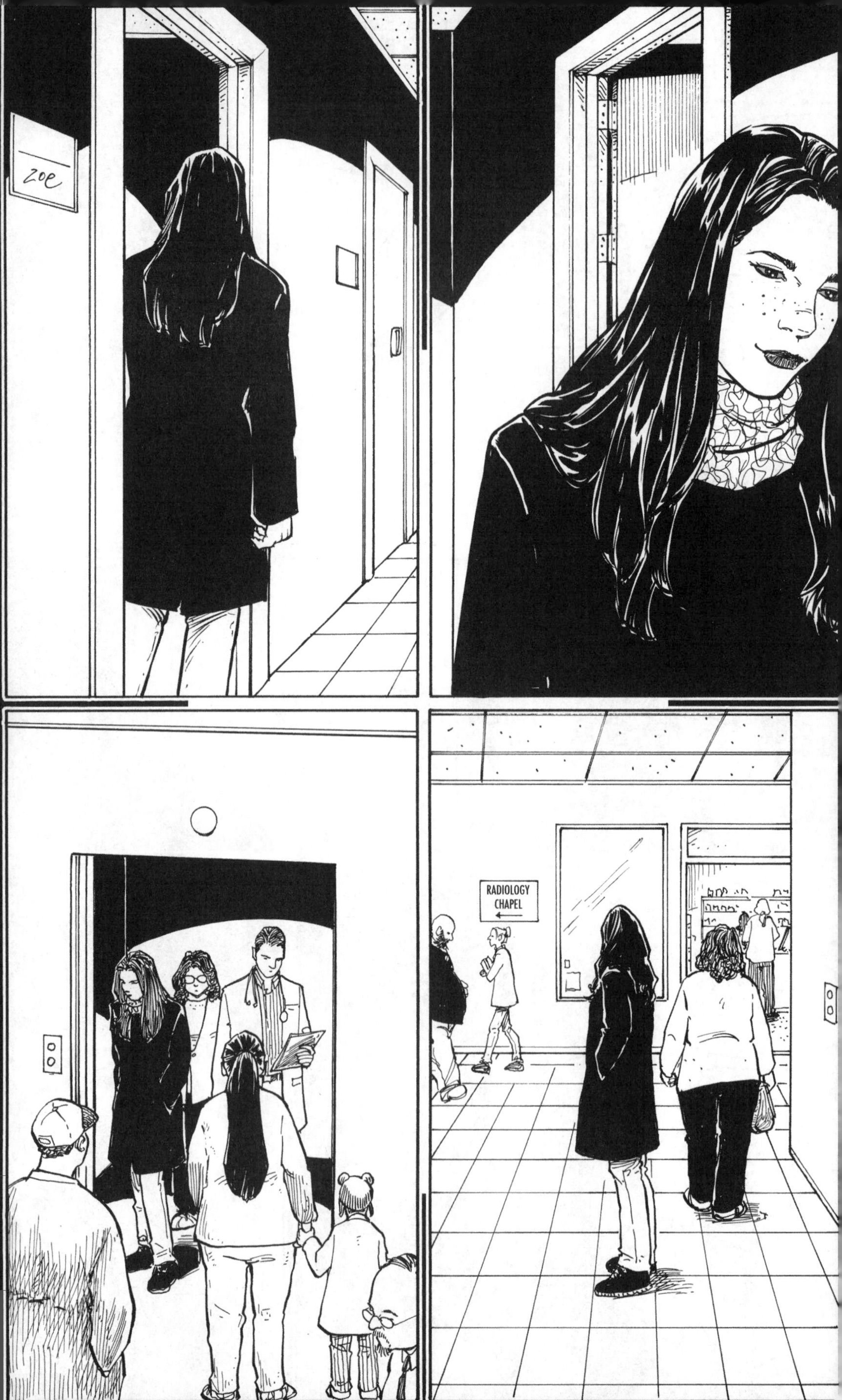
zoe
RADIOLOGY
CHAPEL

EXCUSE ME, FATHER?

PLEASE, CAN I TALK TO YOU?

IN PRIVATE?

HAVE A SE...

SMACK!

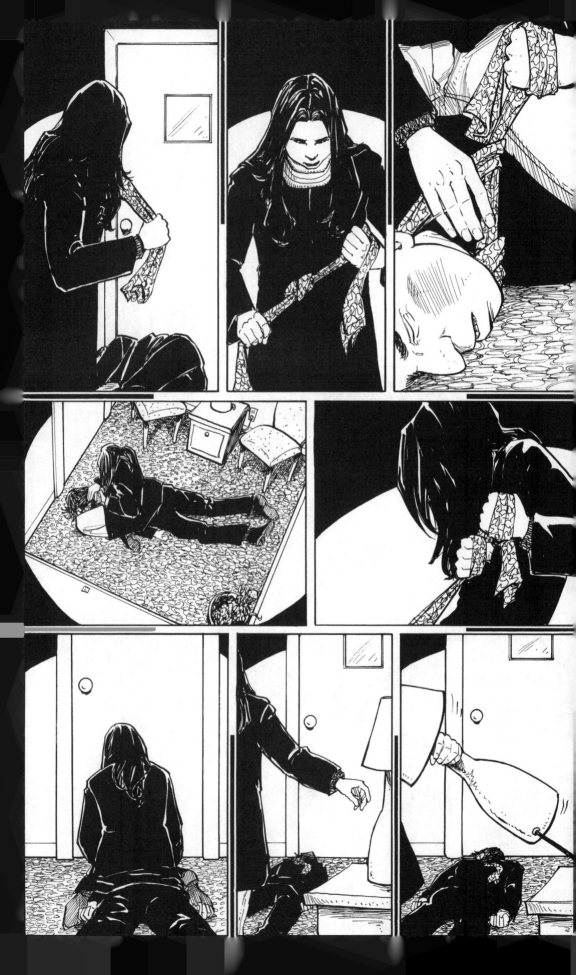

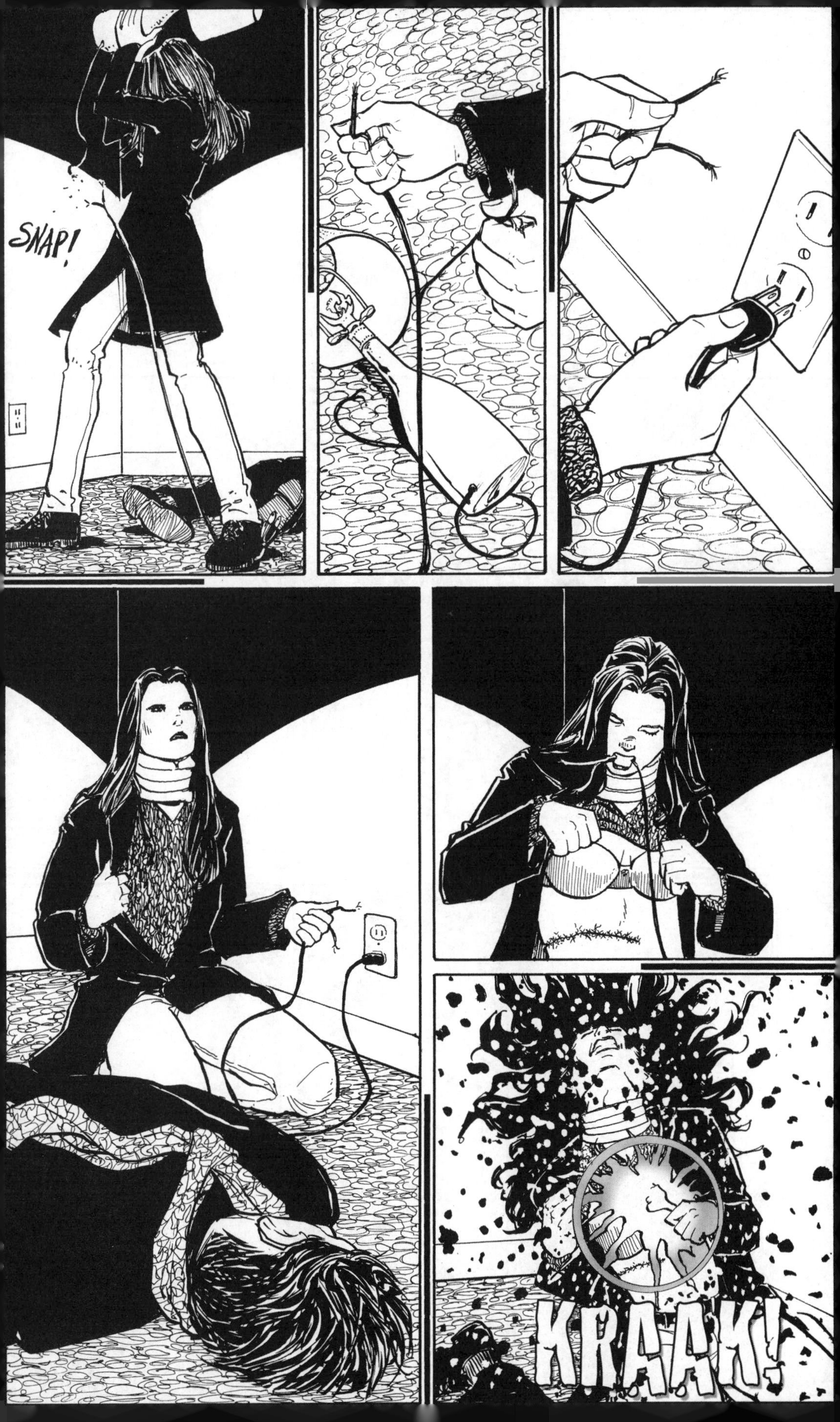
SNAP!
KRAAK!

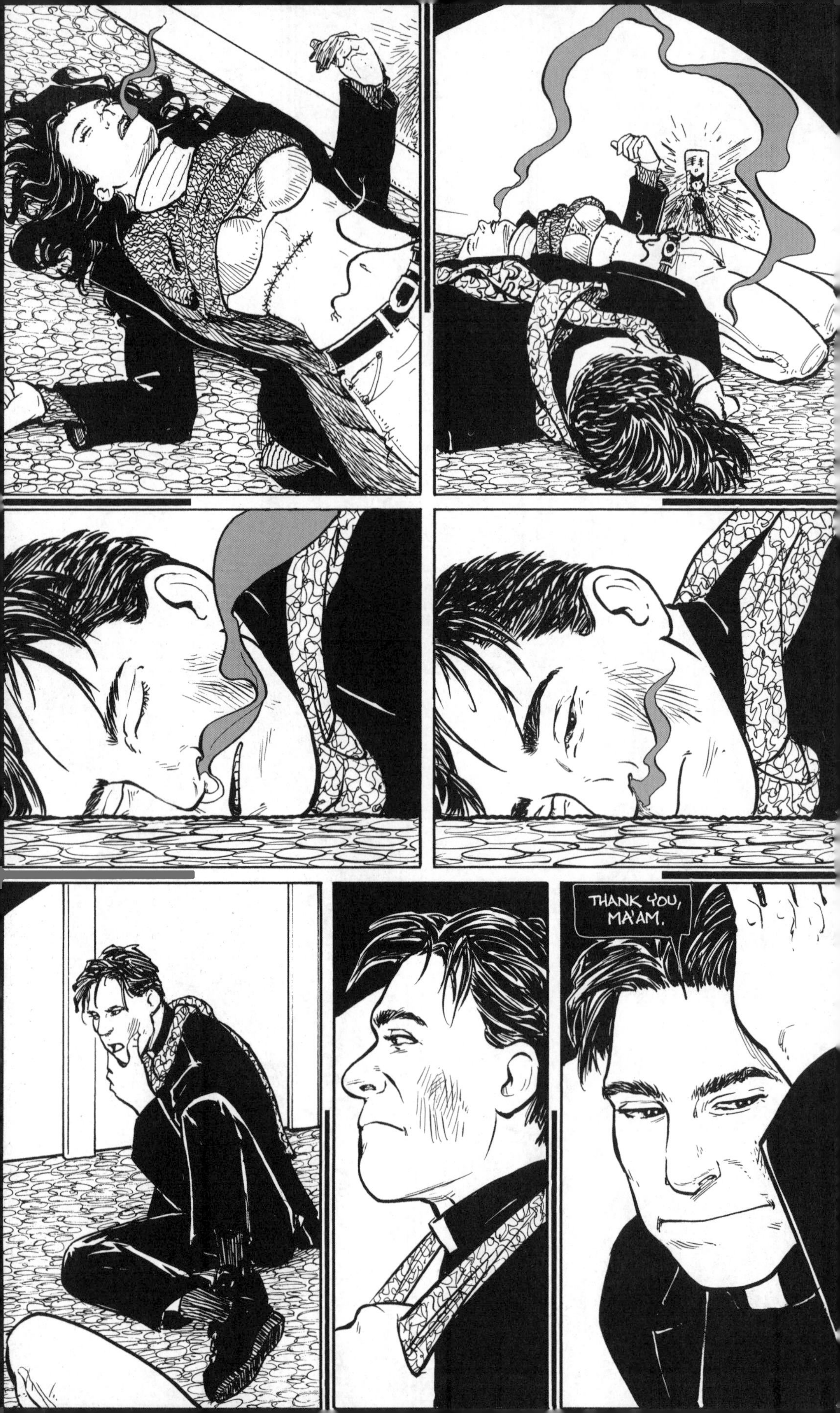
THANK YOU, MA'AM.

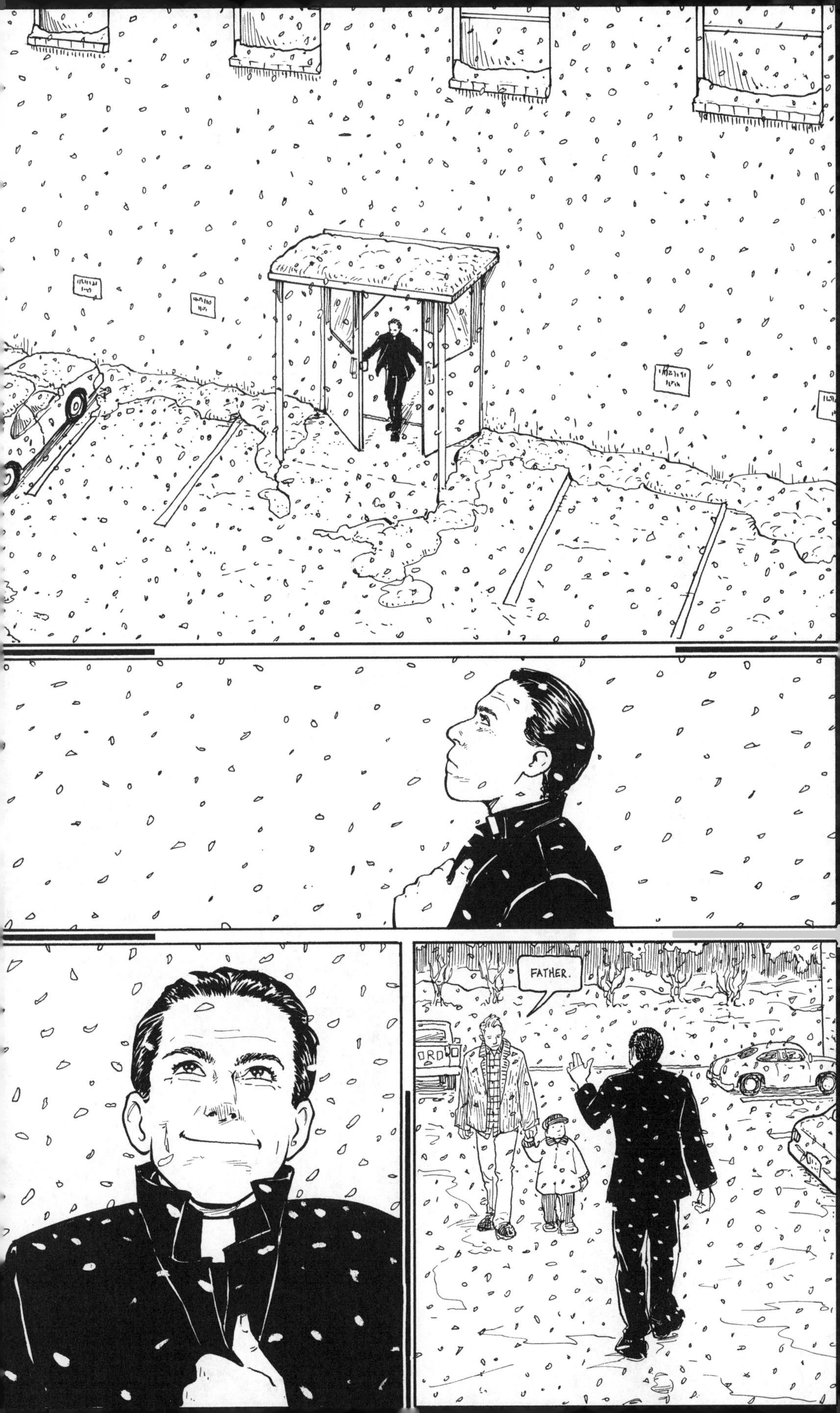
FATHER.

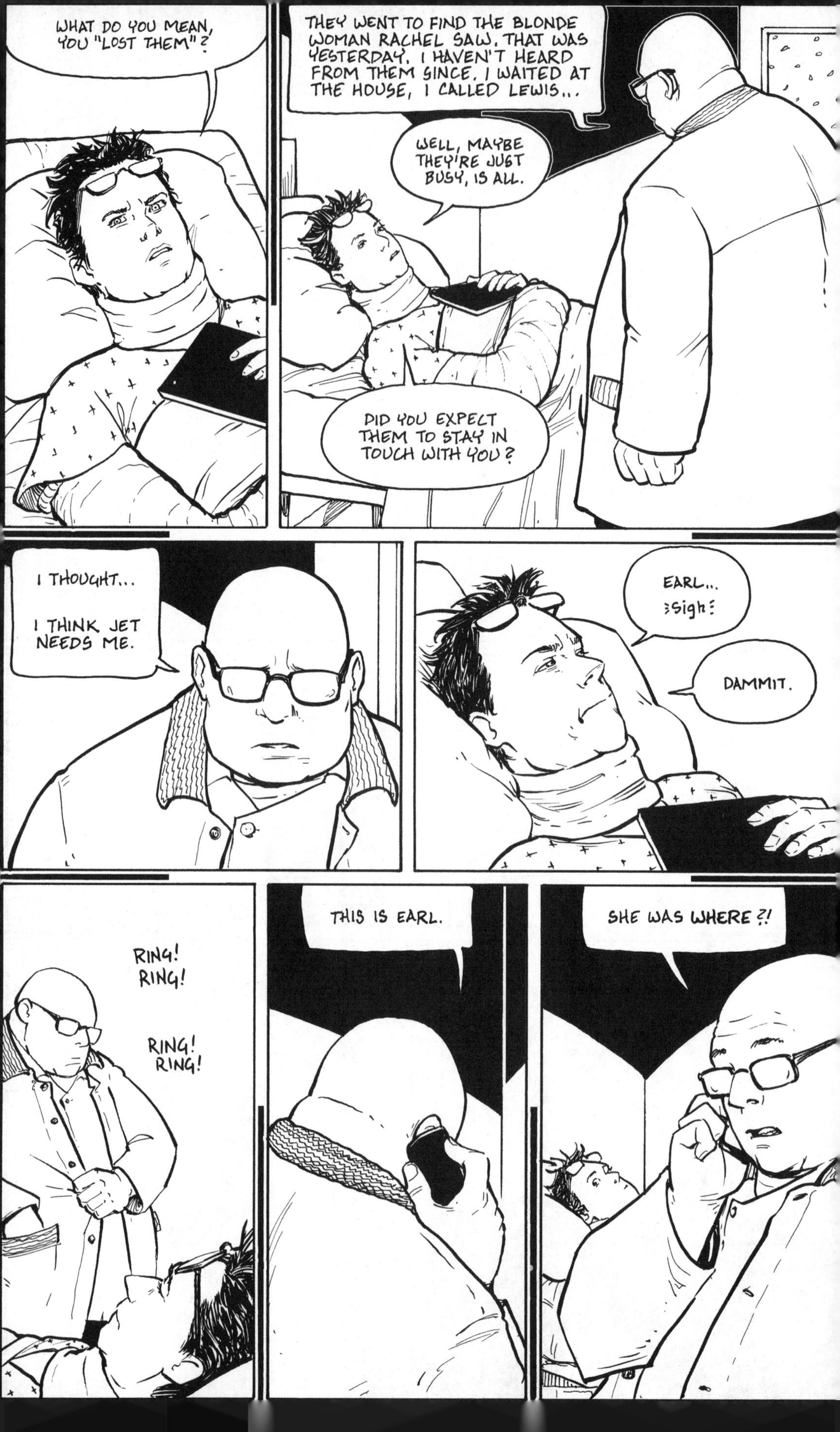
WHAT DO YOU MEAN, YOU "LOST THEM"?
THEY WENT TO FIND THE BLONDE WOMAN RACHEL SAW. THAT WAS YESTERDAY. I HAVEN'T HEARD FROM THEM SINCE. I WAITED AT THE HOUSE, I CALLED LEWIS...
WELL, MAYBE THEY'RE JUST BUSY, IS ALL.
DID YOU EXPECT THEM TO STAY IN TOUCH WITH YOU?
I THOUGHT...
I THINK JET NEEDS ME.
EARL...
:sigh:
DAMMIT.
RING! RING!
RING! RING!
THIS IS EARL.
SHE WAS WHERE?!

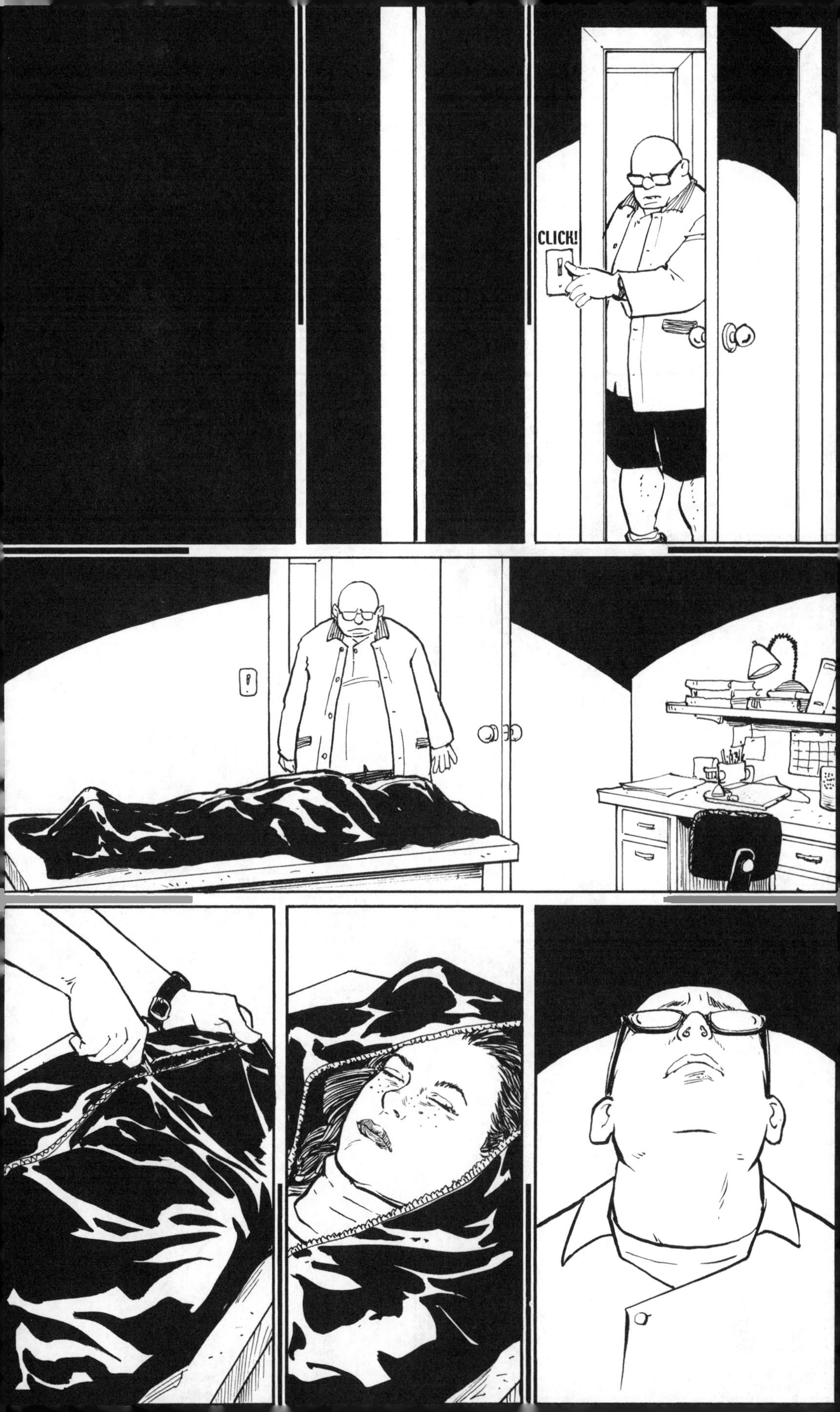
CLICK!

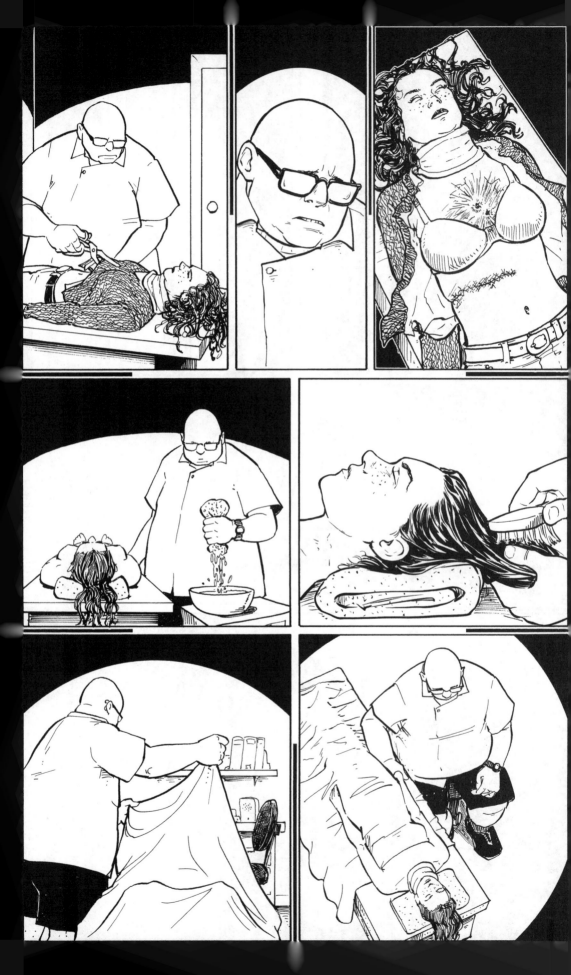

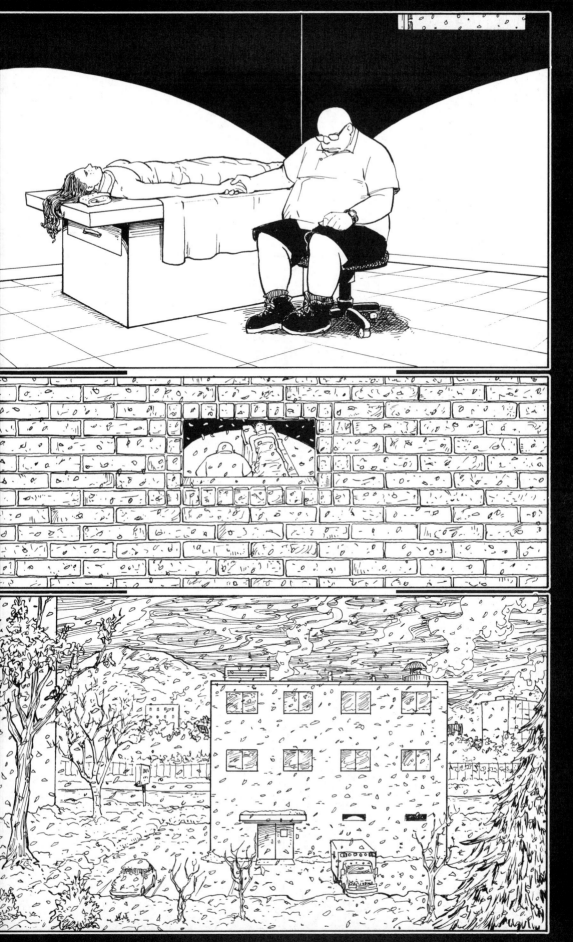

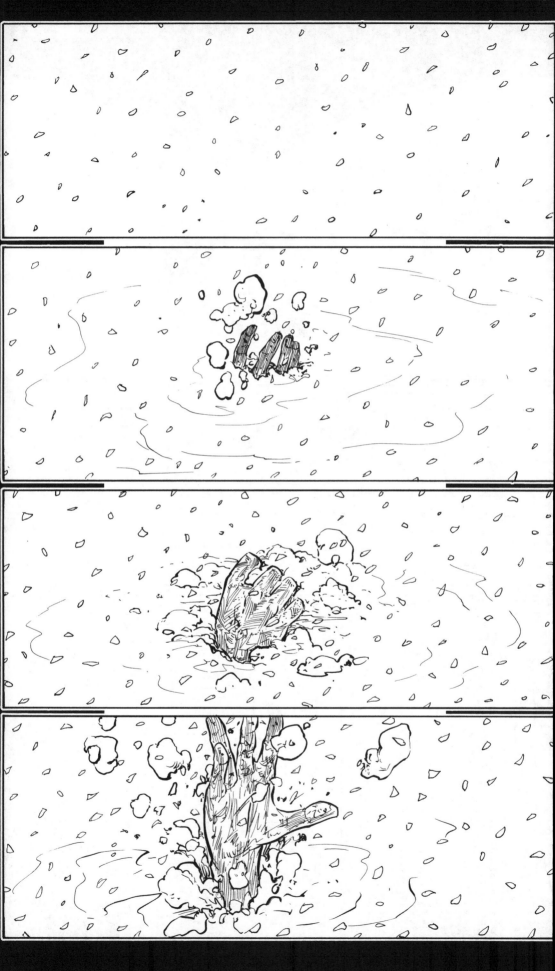

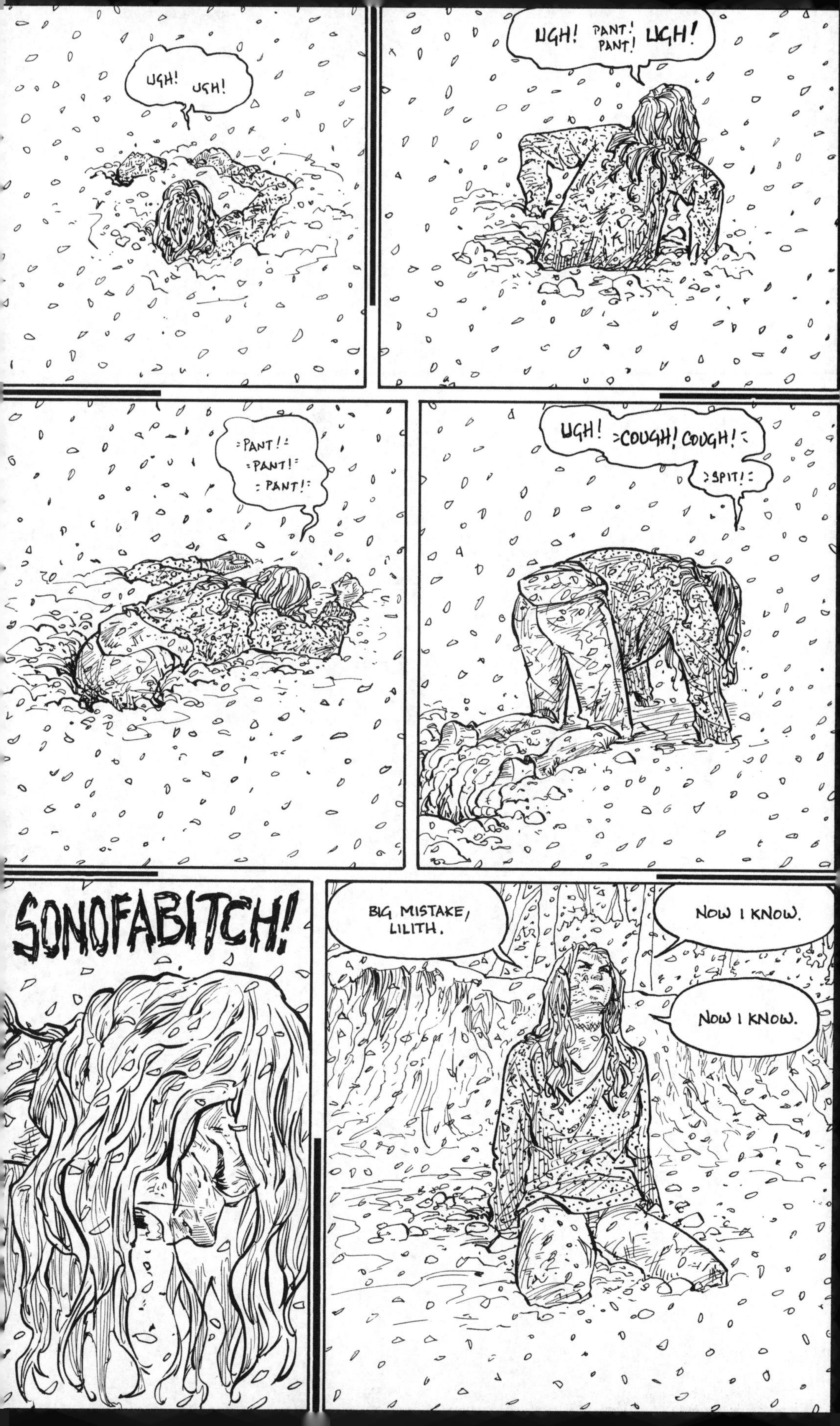
UGH! UGH!
UGH! PANT! PANT! UGH!
PANT! PANT! PANT!
UGH! COUGH! COUGH!
SPIT!
SONOFABITCH!
BIG MISTAKE, LILITH.
NOW I KNOW.
NOW I KNOW.

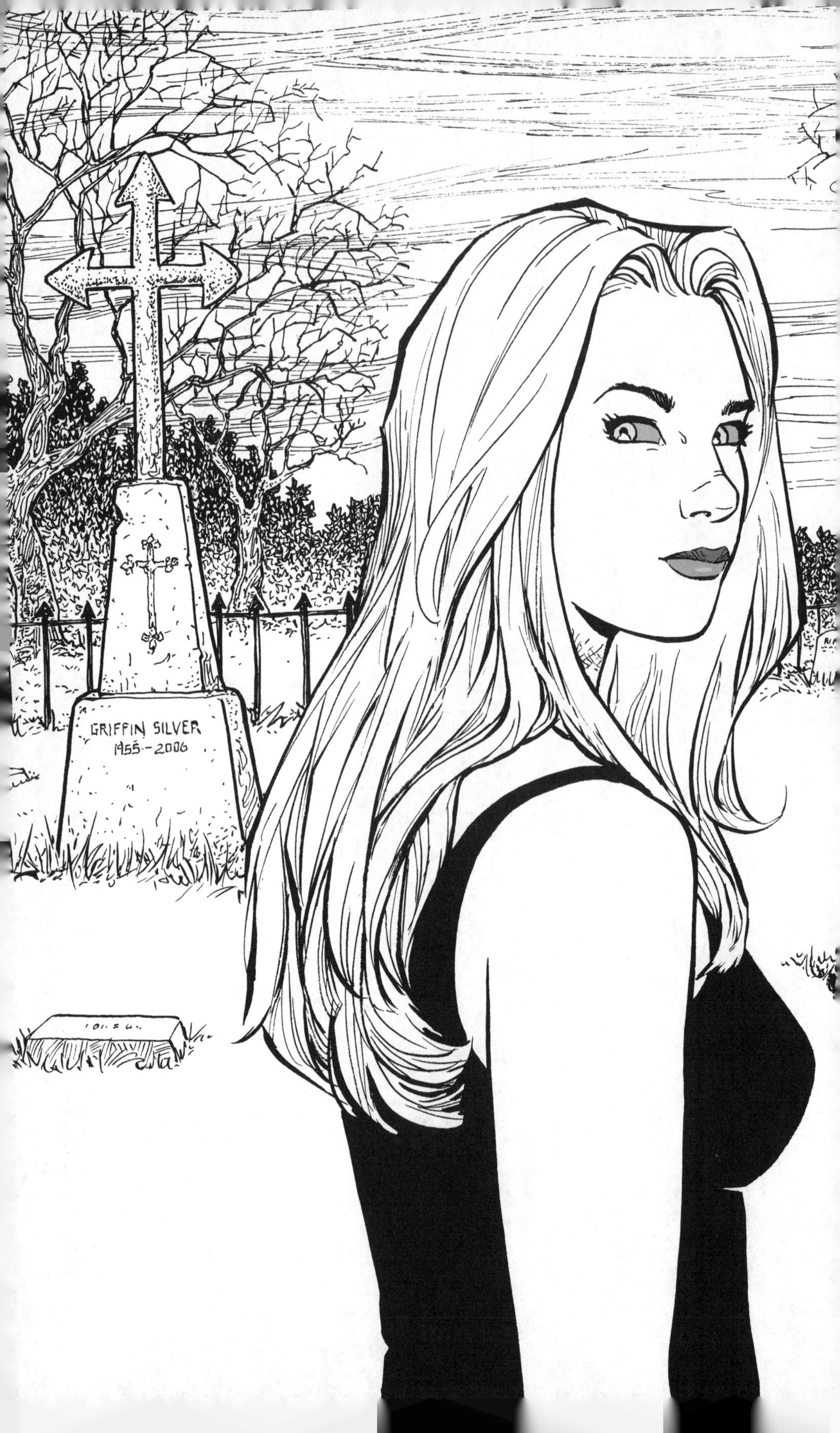
GRIFFIN SILVER
1955 - 2006

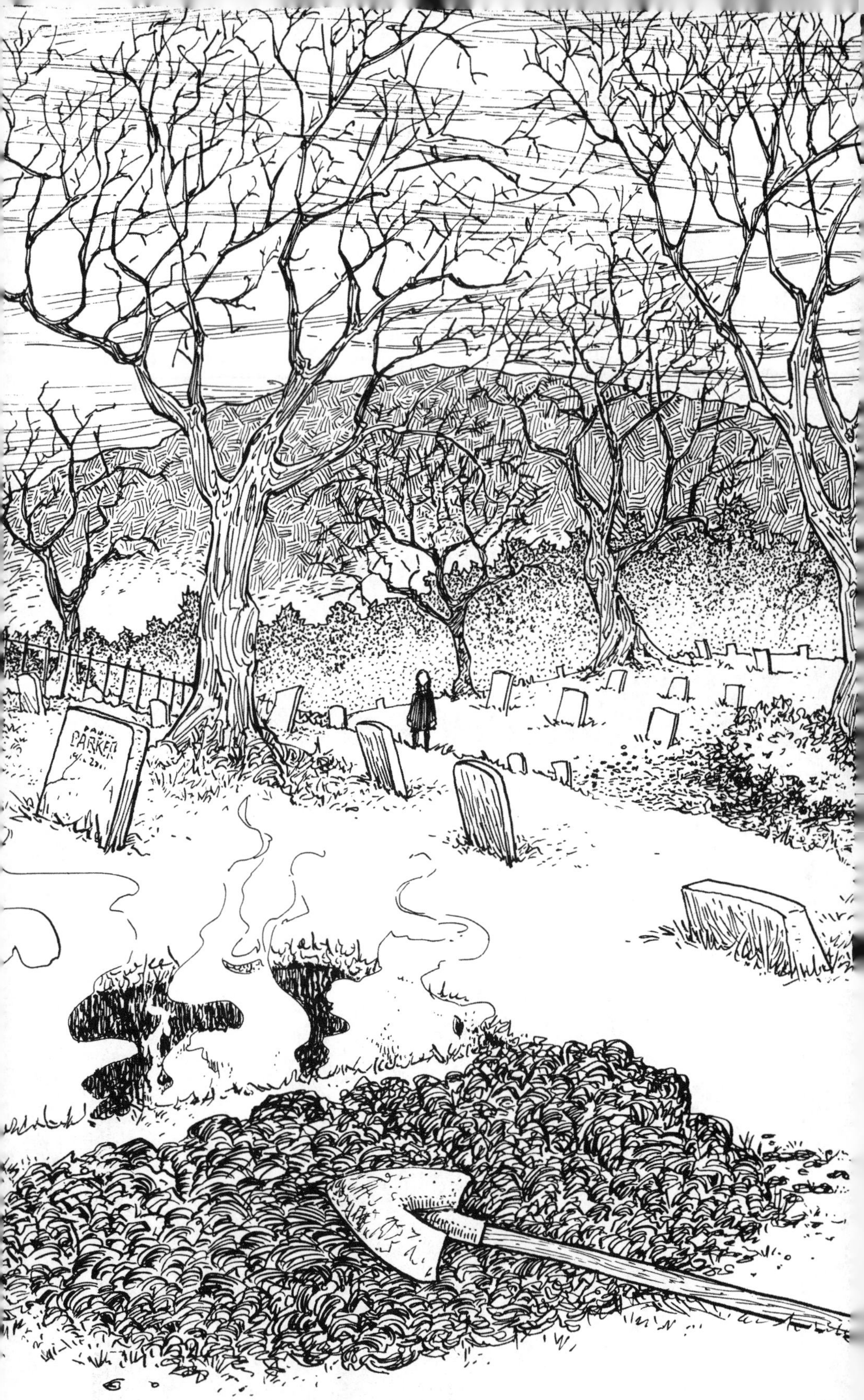
PARKER

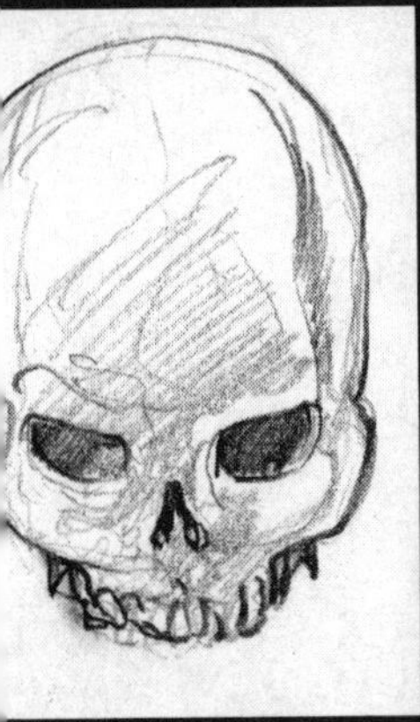

idea for Rachel came
e several years ago
e I was still working
trangers In Paradise.
d all my friends I
thinking about this
d girl" story. They
ested therapy. I
e this book instead.

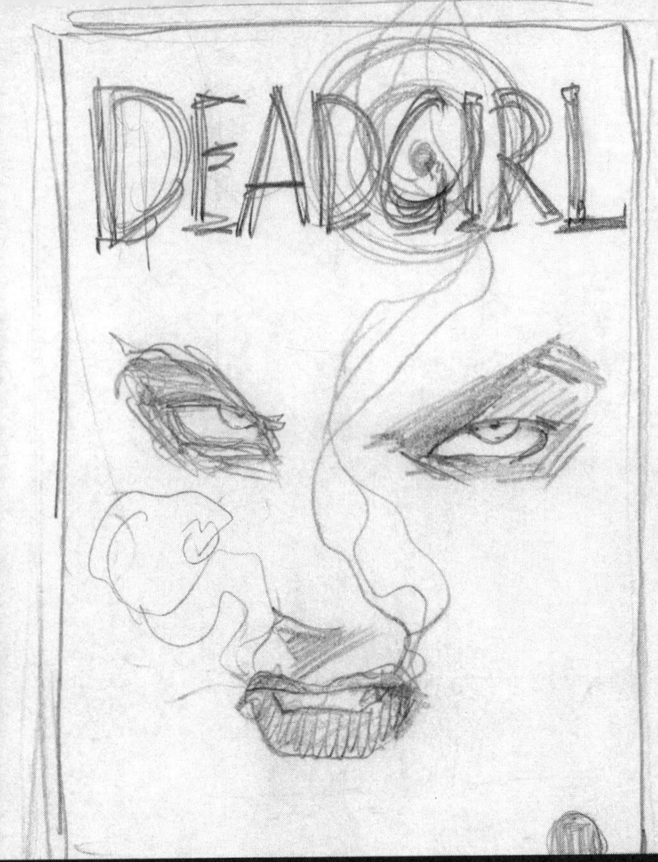
DEADGIRL

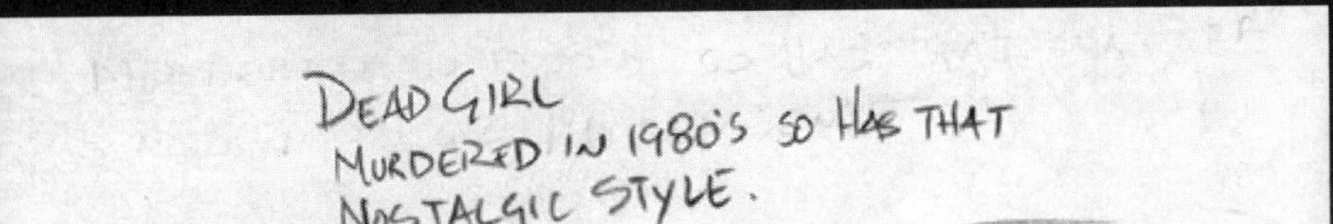
DEAD GIRL
MURDERED IN 1980'S SO HAS THAT
NOSTALGIC STYLE.
WHAT CAN I TELL YOU — I'M DEAD!

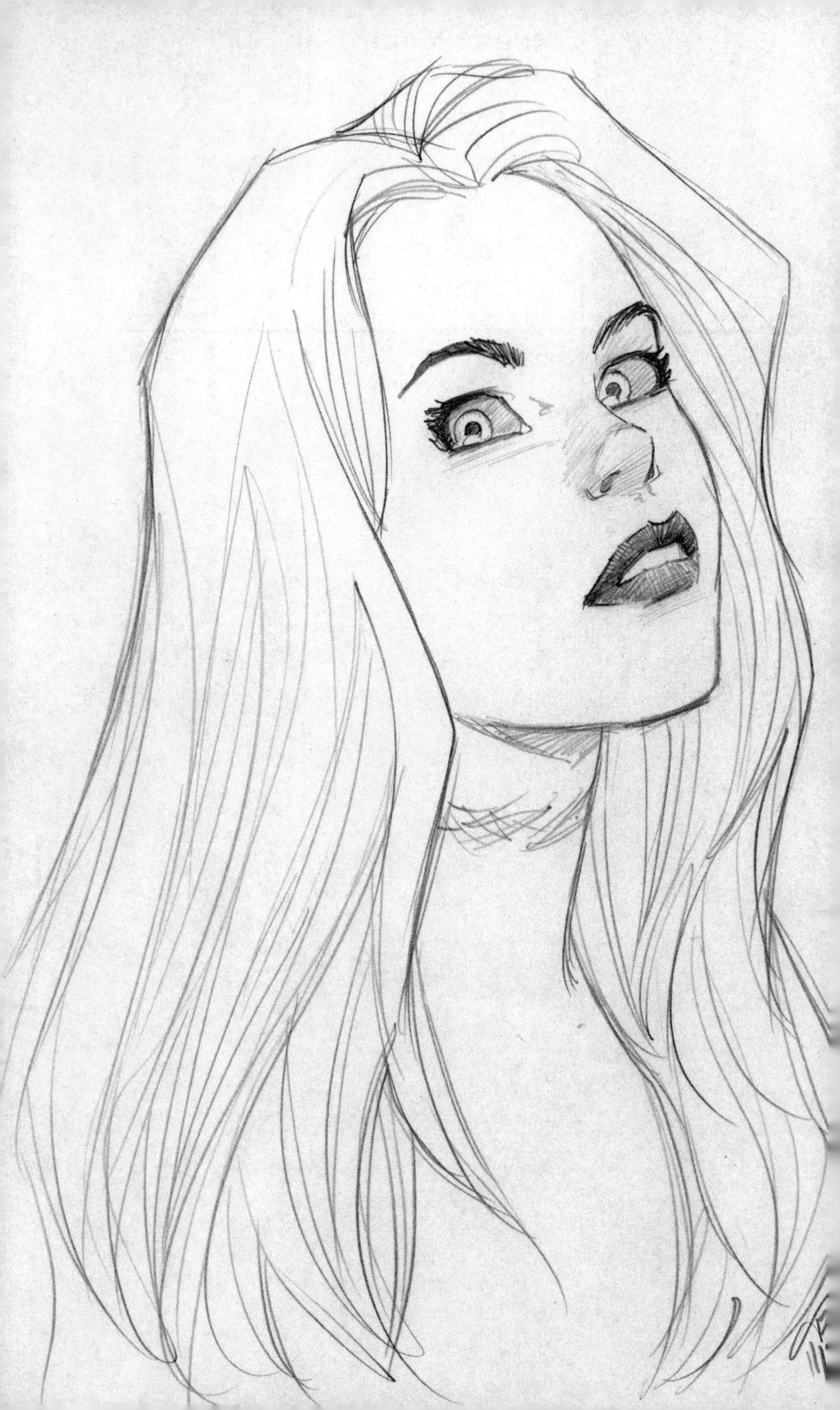

STORY & ART
TERRY MOORE

TERRYMOOREART.COM

ROBYN MOORE
PUBLISHER

PUBLISHED BY
ABSTRACT STUDIO
P. O. BOX 271487, HOUSTON, TEXAS 77277

EMAIL: SIPNET@STRANGERSINPARADISE.COM